Your
Dream
Interpreter

Your Dream Interpreter

Over 1,200 Symbols and Themes Revealed to Bring Clarity and Insight to Your Life

TONY CRISP

Reader's Digest

THE READER'S DIGEST ASSOCIATION, INC.

Pleasantville, New York/Montreal

Address any comments about
Your Dream Interpreter to:
  The Reader's Digest Association, Inc.
  Adult Trade Publishing
  Reader's Digest Road
  Pleasantville, NY 10570-7000

For more Reader's Digest products and
information, visit our website:
  www.rd.com (in the United States)
  www.rd.ca (in Canada)

A READER'S DIGEST BOOK
This edition published by The Reader's Digest Association
by arrangement with CICO Books

FOR CICO BOOKS
Editors: Mary Lambert, Liz Dean
Illustrations: Jacqui Mair
Design: Ian Midson

FOR READER'S DIGEST
U.S. Project Editor: Lisa Pierce
Canadian Project Editor: Pamela Johnson
Project Designer: George McKeon
Executive Editor, Trade Publishing: Dolores York
Director, Trade Publishing: Christopher T. Reggio
Vice President & Publisher, Trade Publishing: Harold Clarke

Library of Congress Cataloging in Publication Data is
available upon request

0-7621-0606-9 (Hardcover)
978-0-7621-0612-7 (Paperback)

Printed in China

10 9 8 7 6 5 4   (Hardcover)
10 9 8 7 6 5 4 3 2 (Paperback)

Contents

Introduction

Dreaming is one of the most extraordinary experiences any of us can have, which is why dreams have fascinated men and women in every culture throughout the ages. In our own times, a great amount of experimentation into the nature and meaning of dreams and sleep has been conducted. This has occurred both in the laboratory and in the testing bed of everyday experience of tens of thousands of men, women, and children, along with the professionals dealing with human problems. A vast amount has been learned, showing that dreams are more profoundly revealing of transforming insights and self-understanding than even ancient cultures realized. This flood of new understanding has shown that dreams are not mysterious jumbles of random images but arise from the innate mental and physical processes of life within us. They express the unconscious wisdom that sustains the growth and health of our minds and bodies. This vast research has also defined techniques that each of us can use to understand the dramatic and graphic language of our dreams.

WHAT ARE DREAMS?

As with any area of thought, there are a wide variety of views as to what dreams are and what function they play in life. But if we attempt to find a synthesis of these ancient and modern views, it is that dreams are an expression of the most fundamental processes of life in us reaching toward awareness. Creatures have dreamed for millions of years, and in dreaming we see the biological life of our planet arriving at its own kind of consciousness, but achieving it in a very different way than we know in our waking life. It is like a huge pool of collective awareness that never knows itself as any one thing but is the experience of all living creatures. The psychiatrist Carl Jung called this shared awareness the Collective Unconscious. The Aborigines called it The Dreamtime. They recognized that all creatures emerge from it and pass back into it in sleep and dreams.

THE AMAZING EXPERIENCE OF DREAMING

Research into dreaming has shown that each of us dreams about four or five times each night. While we dream, our voluntary muscles no longer respond to our attempts to move, and our eyes move rapidly under closed eyelids. Our muscles are paralyzed in this way because if they were not, we would actually run around or act out what we are dreaming. Animals in which the brain area that blocks such impulses has been damaged do live out their dream in movement, practicing hunting or survival tactics. So we see that dreaming extends your range of experience to the point where you double or treble your experiential life span; while dreaming it is as if you are living what is being dreamt. This ability of the mind to play with experience or information, to rearrange it and try it in different guises, as one does in dreaming, is fundamental to the creativity and functioning of human life. Dreams reveal to you what you fail to see about yourself while awake. They show the directions you are taking in life and unveil things that lie beyond the boundaries of your five senses. But their information is sometimes obscured in apparently strange drama or feelings. Using the techniques presented within the following pages will enable you to gain insights that can transform the way you live, allowing you to release old tensions and hurts.

The Dreamers' Workbook

Dream symbols are the language that our inner self uses to talk to us. This book is a dictionary of that language. In this section you will learn how to recall your dreams and interpret the themes and symbols that appear in your dreams.

RECORDING YOUR DREAMS

Every night, most of us have at least two sessions of sleep that produce several dreams, each of them unique. When you remember and record your dreams in detail, you consciously access your innate creativity. You become the creator and producer of your own drama, just as many artists, musicians, and writers have used their dreams as inspiration for their work.

Each dream provides its own message, and it is only by making a record that you will become aware of these messages. This book will help you record, examine, and interpret your dreams. Dreams often melt away as you wake, so write or recite your dreams every morning (see Dream Recall, p. 10) using a notebook or recorder. Record everything you remember. In addition to recording the details of your dreams, it is essential that you consider how the themes in your dreams relate to your daily life.

Ross Campbell and Robert Hoffman at Carleton University, Ottawa, Canada, carried out a research project on dream recall. They used three groups of students: Group One simply made a note of any dream remembered; Group Two wrote down the dream in as much detail as possible; and Group Three wrote the dream in detail, but in addition they also kept a personal journal of daily events. In other words, they reviewed and considered their day. Group Three remembered more dreams than Groups One or Two.

As you get used to recording your dreams, you will notice how rewarding the results are. Your recall will improve the more you practice so that no matter how random the images may seem, you will soon note the recurring characters, themes, and objects in your dreams; these make up the key symbols your unconscious is using to carry the vital messages to you.

EXERCISE 1

DREAM RECALL

1. Place a notebook or journal by your bed. Before you fall asleep, try to spend a few moments imagining yourself waking up, remembering a dream, and then writing it down.

2. As you wake, move as little as possible. The process of forgetting our dreams as we wake each morning is stimulated by physical movement, so try to stay still for a few moments.

3. Gently hold in mind the question of what you dreamed. Imagine sinking back into the dimness of sleep, feeling your way back to your dreams. Your question is a fishing line that you drop into your unconscious. If you are quiet, a dream will take the hook.

4. Once you have remembered some images, and perhaps some fragments of the narrative, try to piece together the whole dream story. Record it, with the date, in your journal. Write as full a description as possible. Give each dream entry a name.

5. Later in the day, read through your dream again. Do not attempt to interpret it at this stage. Simply consider whether the theme, characters, or images remind you of a previous dream. Make a note of any common elements in your journal.

6. If you are still not remembering many dreams, set your alarm clock to wake you about 45 minutes earlier than your usual time. Mentally associate the sound of the alarm with the question, "What am I dreaming?"

How will remembering my dreams help me?
Dreams express the unconscious wisdom that enables and sustains the growth and health of your body and mind. Research in sleep laboratories has indicated that we dream every night, sometimes as often as five times a night.

You may be one of those lucky people who easily remember their dreams almost every morning. If you feel that you never dream or barely remember your dreams, work through the recall exercise every day for about a month and you will be rewarded with a series of images and stories. Interpret the key images using the Directory (see pp. 38–219). Recurring dreams (see p. 25) are often sent to heal a major life issue; reliable dream recall can be the key to revealing what these issues are and how to confront them.

WHERE DO DREAMS COME FROM?

Science has revealed that all mammals dream and babies dream in the womb, so we know that humans were dreaming long before they could speak. We can therefore be certain that dreams arise from what lies beneath language and our thinking selves. They arise from feelings, from instinctive or passionate responses to events. Dreams flow from the formless energies and dynamics of life's processes. Images communicate these energies and processes to our waking selves. In most cases, they reach the level of myths, symbols, and dramatic expression. We respond to this, otherwise we would not be moved by theater, movies, or dance. Recognizing this process in your dreams is the first step to discovering a rewarding interpretation.

Now that you have written down your dream, examine it using the following questions:

What is the primary action of my dream?

What are you doing in your dream? Are you running away, showing affection, climbing a hill or a tree? You may experience one or more themes: solving a problem, searching for something, or going somewhere new.

For the moment, isolate your primary action from the context of that action in the dream. For instance, if you were climbing a hill, simply record it as "climbing.". If you were searching a house, write it as "searching." Write these down in your journal as an annotation to the dream, and ask yourself how they apply to your waking life. For example, if you were searching in the dream, ask yourself if you are aware of searching for something in waking life, and if so, what? Take a few minutes to consider, and leave it to work in the back of your mind. If you gain an insight, write it in your journal.

Possible themes include: being trapped, starting something, building or renovating, relationships, being with others, being alone, leaving things behind, death, birth, and growth.

What am I feeling in the dream?

Your feelings are often the main element of a dream, around which everything else is developed. Strip away the images and action of the dream and see if you can recognize what feelings are involved. If possible, feel something of what was felt in the dream and ask yourself what that feeling connects with in your waking life, when you first felt like that, and if that feeling occurred recently. In your journal, write down the feelings and any connections you make.

Am I active or passive?

This is a vital question, because your relationship with others in your dream may indicate your habitual response while awake. If you are the driving force in your dream, for example, this often reflects your active behavior in daily life. Passivity may be shown by:
★ Not being the main character in your dream
★ Others taking what is yours or blocking you
★ People dominating you

Note signs of passivity and add this to your remarks about the dream in your journal. You can learn to transform passivity in your dreams by using visualization techniques, such as talking to your dream characters (see p. 14).

Am I afraid of anything?

Some dreams reveal an anxiety, or something about yourself that you are avoiding. Fear is a natural and necessary part of life. It helps you avoid, or deal with, dangers. But in dreams it has a different role. Fear of your own feelings or urges can hinder your potential and isolate you from the full range of your abilities and feeling responses. For example, fear may lead you to turn away from an opportunity or a relationship that would have satisfied you. Such turning away means you are not experiencing your potential.

When a fear appears in a dream, even in the format of a nightmare, it usually means that you are ready to meet it. In your journal, note what the fear is, and through what theme or situation it is depicted. Read through the sections on dealing with nightmares (p. 23) and controlling recurring dreams (p. 25), for more detailed information on how to deal with fear more fully.

What is the drama of my dream?

The questions that you have looked at so far have clarified some aspects of your dream's meaning. Now you need to bring what you know into an overview of the dream. To do this, think of your dream not as something connected with you personally, but as a piece of drama that you might see on television. What is it saying to you? To some extent, this will have been defined through asking yourself what themes your dream contains, and what feelings were felt. But now you need to integrate these separate pieces of information. Bring them together in an overall view, and write them out as if you were describing to somebody else what your dream reveals about you and how it connects with your everyday life.

true dream story
EINSTEIN'S DREAM

As a teenager, Einstein had a dream in which he was riding downhill on a sled. The sled went faster and faster until it reached the speed of light. At that point, the stars began to change into amazing patterns and colors, dazzling and beautiful. His meditation on that dream throughout the years led to the Theory of Relativity.

TO IMAGINE IS TO CREATE

Being able to visualize and work with your dream imagery and feelings has enormous benefits. Visualizing can enable you to gain greater insights into your dreams than you can experience by using the questions alone (see p. 14). This is because many dreams leave questions unanswered. For example, fear dreams may not lead to a resolution of anxiety. Visualization allows you to work with, and transform, this situation. Visualization also enables you to have a fuller connection and involvement with your dream. You can enter into any character or environment your dream presents, then—almost magically—you can explore its qualities, weaknesses, and strengths, and see how these may add to, or detract from, your waking life.

You can alter your dream to find satisfaction

Remember that there are no bad parts in dreams, but often a dream leaves you feeling unsatisfied, incomplete, or even scared. This was Eve's experience.

Eve dreamed that she was in a small community. It was evening, and people had shut themselves in their homes because there was a strange dog loose on the streets. The dog wasn't "normal." It was ferocious, and if it got near you it would eat you. So Eve was looking for somewhere to hide, but she had no home.

After she woke up, Eve visualized herself back in the dream, facing the crazy dog. No matter what she did, the dog was still chasing her. Once she realized that the dog was the most important part of the dream, she imagined herself becoming the dog to see what it felt like. She immediately sensed its anger and frustration. As she allowed herself to feel this, she understood that the dog was both afraid of, and angry with, people. Eve then recognized these feelings as her own. As a child, she had often been made to feel unwanted and rejected because she was of mixed racial parentage. As an adult, Eve was still cautious about allowing people into her life. She still felt some anger

EXERCISE 2

STEPPING INTO YOUR DREAM

When learning to visualize, it is helpful to be in a quiet, undemanding environment. As you gain mastery over the skill, you can use it in almost any situation.

1. Choose a "practice" dream that has fairly clear images, and is not too long or complicated. Sit quietly and allow any unnecessary tension in your body to melt away. Slow your breathing slightly, and think of your body as a television screen that you are going to watch. Now remember your dream, and imagine walking into it, moving into your dreamscape. You do not need to have very clear images of this, just the sense, however vague, of what is in the dream. What does it feel like? Watch the screen of your body to see if there are any slight shifts in feelings, or if certain memories or ideas suddenly come to mind.

2. When you have done this for a satisfying time, imagine that you are now one of the characters, animals, or objects in your dream. Try to see what it feels like to be them. It doesn't matter if they are somebody you know, such as a member of your family, or they are an animal, or even a tree. Take time to explore how you feel, and notice if any memories or ideas arise.

3. To end the exercise, move from one of the people or objects to another reasonably quickly to see if you can sense any difference in the way you feel. This is important, because sometimes you will not become aware of what you are feeling until you shift perspectives.

EXERCISE 3

SPEAKING YOUR DREAM

After you have practiced Exercise 2 a few times, you can use a similar technique to explore other dreams more deeply, but this time you will add your voice.

1. Choose a dream that has a fairly clear theme, and imagine yourself in the dream environment, walking around and noticing what you feel and observe. This time, try to stand up and move with your eyes closed. Do not hurry.

2. Next, take time to be each of the characters, animals, or objects in your dream, just as you did for the first exercise. Now, describe yourself as the person you are being or the object you are experiencing (see the example of Justin's dream, p. 15). Do this by speaking aloud, describing what you feel about yourself. In this way, build up a description of each part of the dream. It can help to take up the physical posture of what you are exploring.

3. When you have finished, see if you can summarize the dream by saying aloud what it has helped you understand about yourself or your life situation. Record it in your journal or onto a tape recorder.

about how people had treated her. As this became clear, Eve understood her dream. She had been trying to hide from her own anger. People were shutting themselves indoors, suggesting that others sensed her hidden anger and were cautious. Eve then imagined knocking on doors apologizing, saying that the dog was hers, that it had been hurt as a puppy, and that she was now loving it.

Eve reentered her dream while awake, and explored it by playing with its imagery and noticing what she felt. She then used these insights to direct the dream to a satisfying conclusion. In this way, she changed the fear that led her to run away from the dog into a feeling of caring and social connection. But she also did something else in this imagined scene: She embraced the idea that she could alter her behavior in daily life. She did this by becoming consciously aware of the feelings created in the dream, and by experimenting with a new approach to people and to herself.

A great deal of research has been conducted on the effects of visualization. When used to improve performance, in sports, business, or relationships, visualization has been found to be 75 percent as effective as physical practice. Using visualization to explore your dreams helps you arrive at the sorts of insights and change that Eve discovered. It builds new blocks of experience and understanding that transform the way you respond to everyday events. It allows you to experiment, speeding up your personal growth. Exercises 2 and 3 will get you started. The first is visualization practice, and the second shows how to "'talk out" your dream.

This example shows how Justin used his dreams to talk his way out of grief.

I am getting off a train at a station. To get out of the station, I had to walk from the roof of an old castle fortress, down the stairs—which were all newly decorated—and then out the door.

—Justin

Justin said, "I am a castle. In the past I defended myself so strongly. This caused many conflicts. But now I am a station. People come and go. I do not defend myself against the train of events." Of course Justin was describing himself, and the dream assured him of his progress.

true dream story
PAINTING THE FLAG

Artist Jasper Johns was supporting himself as a window dresser in New York City in the mid-1950s when he had a dream about painting an American flag. He acted upon his dream inspiration, and that flag painting became part of a revolution in American art.

EXERCISE 4

DRAWING YOUR DREAM MAP

1. In your dream journal or notebook, draw a large circle. Look back to previous dreams you've recorded, and make a note of common themes, characters, and objects. Draw a shape to represent you, such as the outline of your body, within the circle. Now add your dream content, drawing people, animals, items, or words to describe feelings within the circle. Include recurring images by drawing them as often as they appear (providing you have enough space). If you're assessing many previous dreams, you may want to draw your maps on a large piece of paper rather than your journal.

2. If you have not yet recorded any dreams, close your eyes, and visualize yourself standing within a circle. Who or what else is with you there? Draw what you see, including yourself, within the circle. Don't feel that you need to include lots of content. You may only see one or two things that you feel a connection with, or you may want to include lots of items or characters on the same theme.

3. Give personal names to the different places where your dreams take place so you can make a stronger conscious connection with them. Also, create cross-references to your recurring themes and subjects. Looking at several dreams with the same theme or subject brings much greater insight than a single dream. Where possible, write on your map what you learn from looking at these multiple dreams. It will begin to show you the things you constantly confront, and the life direction that you seek.

MAPPING YOUR DREAM WORLD

In your dreams, a host of beings and objects surrounds you. They appear separate from you, and frequently seem to have a will of their own. If you visualize yourself in the center of a circle, and put all your dream characters, animals, and objects around you, you will have an image of the many things influencing you in the way you think, feel, and respond. If you could transform these objects and beings into the things they depict, such as sexuality, thinking, will, emotions, intuition, and social pressure, you would see how you stand among diverse influences.

In general, dreams visit certain well-known subjects. We can name these: baby, child, teenager, adult, aged person, animal, home, places, nature, and objects. Then there are certain themes that most of us encounter in our dreams. Some of these are archetypal or universal. These themes make up a collection of motifs that reflect human nature, such as the experience of birth and death. When you map your dreams, some of your themes may be archetypal, but what makes your dream map unique is how you as a person relate to the archetypal aspects of your life. You can construct your personal map of dreams by noting the themes, people, animals, and places that feature in your dreams (see Exercise 4, opposite). These point to the important things you are dealing with in your inner and outer life. The following dream gives an example of this.

I am in a room with a woman and a young man. The woman and I were discussing him, and he was sometimes with us, or sometimes hidden in his room. We were discussing his difficulty in relating to females. It seemed that he always withdrew from what at first appeared to be a promising relationship. Then the man became a small boy. In that condition, the cause of his difficulty was easily seen. He was an orphan, and in trying to hide his painful need for love, he had built a wall between himself and women.
—Alex

This theme of being abandoned appeared often in Alex's dreams. It was an important issue in his life, and so was an area of his dream world he visited regularly.

true dream story
RICHARD BACH'S DREAM

Richard Bach, the author of the best-selling book *Jonathan Livingstone Seagull*, had left the manuscript unfinished for eight years. Then a dream gave him fresh inspiration and impetus, enabling him to complete the book.

EXERCISE 5

RESOLVING A CONFLICT

Visualize a dream that involves conflict, then proceed with the following steps:

1. Recognize that an internal conflict wastes vast amounts of energy that could be better directed. What you are dealing with is another aspect of yourself.

2. If you can visualize reasonably well (see p. 13), stand in the role of each of the opponents in turn. Speak the feelings of each to define their opposite needs or irritations. Take time with this until the cause for opposition is clear.

3. If you cannot easily use visualization, clarify the cause of the conflict by examining the theme and action (see p. 11). Define the feelings or attitudes that create the conflict, and what holds the opponents or protagonist in the uncomfortable position.

4. Aim for a win-win situation. Talk out the opposing attitudes as a dialogue. This enables the opposing aspects of yourself to move toward agreement. If you have a sympathetic friend, talk it over with them. The following example shows how this can be done. This dream occurred to a 14-year-old boy.

I am with my father. We have been away from home together, and he is now driving us back home. He asks me if I am pleased to be going home. In fact I don't want to go home and tell him so. —Andrew

Andrew's conflict is not with his father, but with living at home. First, he took the role of himself in the dream, saying, "I don't want to go home. I don't like it, and I want to get away as quickly as possible. I hate school too, and if I leave school at 15, maybe I can get a job and move out." He then took the role of his father, saying, "Andrew, you know yourself better than anyone else. What are you going to do?"

This question placed Andrew in the role of adviser to himself. He said, "You know you are not going to be satisfied with low wages, and that is all you'll get if you leave home and school early. Why not work hard to get the qualifications for a college course? Then you could live away from home."

Andrew then returned to the role of himself. He said, "When I take that in, I can really feel a change." He followed his own advice, leaving home to complete his training, and moved on to a good job.

DREAM HEALING: RESOLVING CONFLICTS AND WOUNDS

Your body and mind are always striving to maintain balance in the face of extremity—from heat and cold to stress and conflict. To do this, your body perspires when hot, and shivers when cold. It recognizes and excretes toxins. Likewise, your psychological health is maintained by similar processes, and especially through dreaming. A nightmare, for example, is the mind's way of expelling negative emotions and fears. This self-regulatory action is one of the major functions of dreams. But it is not perfect, and can be made much more efficient by working consciously with your dreams.

So how can you do this? Your conscious self can observe, analyze, and reason in a way that your instinctive, largely unconscious, processes of body and mind cannot. In fact, these two aspects—the conscious and unconscious—are complementary.

Studies of the left and right lobes of the brain and how they interact illustrate this. The right lobe of the brain represents the "dreaming" unconscious self. It deals with the big picture and with intuition. It senses connections between apparently separate things. The left lobe of the brain can be likened to our conscious self. It deals with rational, analytical thought, language, naming, and definitions. The right and left brains are interdependent. Without the logical left brain, the "dreaming" right brain can't critically analyze a situation. For example, take Alex's dream about fear of relating to women (see p. 17). Although his dream process created a drama in which a young man fails to maintain a relationship with a woman, it didn't say, as his rational analytical mind can, "So, I am experiencing difficulties in my relationships with women due to my childhood fear of abandonment, but what can I do about that?" The dream process shows the problem, but it doesn't by itself ask the question as to what can be done to resolve it. Put another way, when Alex consciously recognized why he avoided women, from then on he could see his behavior in a different light. Asking what could be done about it opened up to him the possibility of creative changes to resolve the situation. Understanding these different actions of dreaming and waking awareness helps us to make the most of our problem-solving and healing functions.

Conflict in dreams

A conflict usually appears in dreams in the form of war, a fight or struggle, rejection, or killing. Opposing elements in a dream may represent opposing aspects or desires within you. Conflict can also be internal—a fight between an internal urge, such as sex, and your conscious will or anxiety. An internal conflict needs to be dealt with quite differently than an external one. An internal conflict is like your left hand fighting with your right. Both get hurt in the struggle, and in the end you are the one who suffers. But conflict is a natural part of life, and meeting it in the right way leads to greater maturity.

When we are in conflict, it is often because something is preventing us from moving into an alternative stance. Exercise 5 (see p. 18) is aimed at uncovering why this stuck position is occurring and helping the stuck aspect of the self to accept change. Often this requires real honesty. Obviously, some situations may take more than one dialogue to change.

HEALING DREAMS

May, a woman who had suffered years of depression due to being alienated from her father and family, dreamed that her son was the size of a small cartoon character. He sprayed her with a magic spray and this made her small, too. Her son led her to her father, who was sitting on a park bench. May said, "I hesitated, feeling I could not go to him. My son told me not to worry. He said, 'If you can't love your father, I will love you both.'" May then saw how silly it all was, and she and her father laughed, and "got the feeling of forgiveness and saw how we had wasted all those years because we didn't have the simple love of a child."

May has now reconciled with most of her family, although she says, "I doubt if they can understand the reasoning behind it. Although life still has its difficulties, I now have this wonderful feeling of well-being."

Through her dream, May tapped into an experience of forgiveness that was not usually a part of her nature. If it had been, she would not have held a grudge and suffered from depression for so many years.

Your feelings and ideas can often stand in the way of allowing healing to take place. If that were not so, we would all be made whole each time we slept and dreamed. Instead, ideas, grudges, old hurts, or even the beliefs that we hold, can block the healing process. For example, the idea that the healing we seek is far off, or that we must be deserving of it, are blocks. If you imagine you are truly opening yourself to be healed, this will start the flow of healing dreams.

SLEEPING ON A PROBLEM

A young woman, a computer programmer, recently told me that she had confronted a problem in her work. She had tried various approaches, but they had not succeeded. Yet the next morning, she awoke from a dream that had shown in detail what could be done to solve the problem. She tried it, and it worked.

Creativity and the ability to solve problems are not restricted to geniuses. We all have the potential to develop and harness the creative impulse. Unfortunately, many of us have had our creative abilities suppressed. We are often told to avoid failure rather than use it as a step toward problem-solving. Trained in the acute recognition of our limitations, we can become blind to the unbounded possibilities of the mind and creativity.

Creative dreaming

Dr. Frank Barron, a research psychologist at the University of California Institute of Personality Assessment, compared 5,000 creative individuals with others in their field with a similar intelligence quotient (IQ). The data showed that creativity and problem-solving do not depend upon having a high IQ.

Other research in problem-solving and creativity shows that the human mind has possibilities that are rarely used. When dreaming, many of the limitations that we place upon ourselves through our learned attitudes fall away. In the dream state, we have access to our total memory (see p. 37). (see p. 37). The subliminal perceptions we gather every day through body language, relationships, and the many things we take in out of the "corner of our eye" are accessible, so our creativity, problem-solving capability, and ability to arrive at insights are magnified.

true dream story
INVENTION

In 1940, David Parkinson, a Bell Laboratory engineer, was developing an automatic leveling recorder to improve the accuracy of measurements in telephone transmission. He dreamed that he was with an anti-aircraft crew in a gun pit. One of the guns brought down an airplane with every shot. A member of the crew beckoned Parkinson to come closer to the gun and pointed to the exposed end. To Parkinson's surprise, he saw that the control potentiometer of his level recorder was mounted there. From research based upon his dream, the first all-electric gun director evolved.

EXERCISE 6

MEETING YOUR MONSTERS

1. Remember that while you are dreaming, things are dramatized and felt very deeply. So do not fear that something will overwhelm you. Dreams and nightmares are a part of your self-balancing process.

2. Imagine yourself back in the dream and meeting the frightening thing or scary situation. Notice how you feel and what changes occur in your body. If you have this attitude of quiet watching, with the intent of understanding and helping the healing process, memories often arise. For instance, a man woke from a nightmare in which a terrifying creature was trying to get at him and a child. He then imagined himself allowing the creature to reach him. Next he remembered the fear he felt as a child from living in a war zone, and recognized that this fear had prevented him from leading a freer and less restricted life.

3. Visualize yourself developing a different relationship with the fearful thing or situation. Take time with this, as it needs to reach into areas of experience that you have probably kept buried.

4. If you find it difficult to visualize or enter the dream, draw or write down the dream and its characters. If you draw it, you can change it to deal with the central fear in a different way. This is helpful for children, too. The "creature" can be put in a cage, or in a less threatening situation. The aim is to play imaginatively with words or images until you feel at ease with the nightmare.

5. Have a dialogue with the fearful thing. Sometimes it helps to have two chairs—you can start the dialogue in one chair, then shift to the other chair to get a response. Ask it why it is appearing in your dreams in this scary way. What does it want from you? What can you do to change things? If you imagine yourself as the "thing" and say whatever arises, this can produce great insight.

Common nightmare symbols

Being trapped or bricked in
Being attacked or chased
Gravestones or a graveyard
Being in a down-and-out environment surrounded by
    threat or malice
Death in its various forms or images
Something that possesses you, or in some way will
    gradually attack you, like a malevolent disease
A black hole or void
An animal that you are frightened of
An intruder in your home or coming up your stairs
The threat of insanity or the irrational
Being tortured
The devil or a demon of some sort
Blood or injury
Indefinable threat
Spiders or maggots
Teeth falling out
Loss of a partner
A death scene that is apparently from a past time
Losing control
Hitting high-voltage electricity
Being bombed by a plane or attacked by a bird
Anything that represents a trauma in your own past

DEALING WITH NIGHTMARES

The trauma experienced by soldiers in the First and Second World Wars shows that there is in the human mind a process that attempts to push to the surface the experience of past shocks, conflicts, and fears. After returning from the field of battle, doctors discovered that soldiers dreamed of past incidents again and again, their bodies often making the same movements they had made at the time of the trauma.

The purpose of nightmares

When explored, nightmares always show themselves as an attempt to heal a past hurt or a present fear. To understand this, it is helpful to form a picture of the two polarities of daily experience. One polarity is your waking state. In this state, you generally feel distinct and separate from others. You see yourself as an object moving about the world, and you know the vulnerabilities of your body and mind. Your particular experiences and thoughts color the way you feel about existence. Tragic events in your life may have left psychological scars. The other polarity is that of sleep. To fall asleep, your ego has to surrender all effort and will. As you enter sleep, you lose awareness of yourself as a separate individual. Experiments that have allowed people to enter this realm of sleep with some awareness say that body awareness disappears. Your sense of self melts as if it were a drop of water merging into an ocean. This merging brings healing, and in dreams this wholeness attempts to flow through to our waking self. But the fears and tensions that we have gathered act as blocks. These blocks are pushed to the surface by the action of dreams when our ego is strong enough for them. This is what we experience as a "nightmare." The block, or traumatic experience, is like a frozen chunk of emotion, or an attitude stuck in one position, which stops you from flowing with the changing current of life. You may have been hurt in love, or had your trust betrayed, and so some of your feelings and attitudes are held tight. Allowing them to become conscious and learning to understand their cause means they can melt away. Some nightmares are about present fear. These nightmares offer the same opportunity for healing. Such fears usually arise from an unbalanced view of who and what we are. When the waking and the sleeping self are balanced, the fear usually disappears.

EXERCISE 7

DEALING WITH RECURRING DREAMS

1. A recurring dream is important, so take time with it. Work through the questions regarding the theme of the dream and your feelings (see pp. 11–12). Write down and consider what you arrive at.

2. In a quiet situation, talk yourself through the dream again as if you were dreaming it. Do this by imagining yourself in the dream and going through the experiences. Speak out loud, describing the dream in the first person and using the present tense. As you do so, take note of any feelings or memories that arise, and allow yourself to feel or explore them.

3. Have a dialogue using the two-chair method with any characters in your dream (see Dealing with Nightmares, p. 23). Alternatively, you can simply "talk" to the dream as a whole, asking it such things as, "What is your message? I am unclear and really am trying to understand." Then to get the response, try to take on the feeling and attitude of listening, and simply allow any spontaneous feelings and ideas to arise. Afterwards, note any insights you experience in your journal.

John's recurring dream

I hated my father. I saw him as a horrible, unfeeling man who wrought a great deal of pain and suffering on me and my mother. I ran away from his home and for 16 years remained estranged from him.

But a few years back, I had recurring dreams of returning to see him. The dreams were always unpleasant. When I explored the dreams, I discovered my father was the most important person in my life. I couldn't quite understand how all this could be. But I traveled to the distant city where he lived.

The instant we met, something happened. A weight of decades was lifted from me. I literally had the feeling I was walking with my feet off the ground. He and I spent many powerful and intimate moments together during the ensuing week. I had found a soul mate. I made plans to return for Christmas. For the first time in 16 years I had a home, I had someone to spend a holiday with. A week after I returned to New York, my brother phoned that my father had suddenly died. My waking mind would never have decided to go back to see him in time—never.

UNDERSTANDING AND CONTROLLING RECURRING DREAMS

Dreams do not usually occur unless there is something you haven't realized or dealt with. They indicate that something needs attention. Recurring dreams are sometimes like chores that haven't been done, and so they keep pushing into your awareness. In some dreams, the theme and action are almost identical. In others, the theme develops over time. The following dream is one that recurs for many people.

I have a disturbing recurring dream. There is a baby, so small it fits into my palm. I know it should be fed but I always forget. I leave it until the last moment to pick it up and give it a bottle. It looks at me with sad eyes as if to say, "Why do you do this to me?" —Lydia

Lydia's dream is about neglect. In some way, she is not nourishing a facet of her own personality. Because it is a baby in the dream, it probably depicts her need for love and support. Most recurring dreams are calling out for our attention. If we give such a dream just a bit of our time they will be transformed, either into a dream with a similar theme, or they will disappear altogether.

Recurring dreams deal with subjects that are as varied as the challenges and opportunities that we face. Try not to have a preconception of what your recurring dream may be saying. It can simply be about an attitude that is not allowing you to experience the sort of freedom you are capable of, or it may be a nudge asking you to be aware of something. We may know in the back of our mind that there is a danger we are not attending to—say, a loose floorboard—and recurring dreams are sometimes the voice urging us to take care.

UNDERSTANDING DREAMS OF FAMILY

Our families provide the environment in which we make the long and often difficult journey toward emotional and physical independence. During those early years of childhood, the most fundamental lessons of our life are learned. As children we experience a desperately felt need to be wanted, to have emotional and physical shelter in which we can survive, and to be given attention. The way our parents and siblings appear in our dreams often relates to these issues. It is also important to remember that whatever responses to love and relationships we have developed from life with our mother and father are now undoubtedly projected onto those around us. So a man's wife often receives the anger he felt as a child toward his mother. A woman's husband may get tortured for the lack of love from her father.

Brothers, sisters, or your children in your dreams represent the many different qualities or difficulties you experience in your daily life. So one sibling or child might represent your vulnerability and caution, whereas another might depict daring curiosity.

In your dreams, your most intimate fears and longings are expressed as exterior people, objects, and places. Therefore your sexual drive may be shown as a person and how you relate to them. Your feeling of ambition may be shown as a business person, your changing emotions as the sea or a river. Therefore, in drawing out the meaning of family dreams, define the character or characteristics of the family members in the dream. Do this by looking at what they are expressing in the dream, and how you see them in general. It is helpful to gradually define each of them in your journal, so that in future dreams you already have a key to their dream meaning.

Mother and father

Your mother and father are the foundations of your development as a person. Like any dream figures, they have many faces. Because of this, your mother can appear as witch or fairy godmother, the destroyer or the ground of your being. Your father may appear as a giant, destructive ogre or a protective eagle. The context, imagery, and tone of the dream will show which face you are dealing with.

Yet however they appear, it is your feelings that you are meeting. Your dream may indeed depict a shrewd insight into your mother or father, but it is best to see the dream as expressing aspects of your own power or fears. In this way, you are in a position to work with and transform what shows itself.

The overall themes you may face in dreams about your mother and father are concerned with meeting the fears, anger, and need you felt toward them in childhood. The aim is to transform the way those things influence current relationships and activities. One dreamer, who lost his mother through being put in an orphanage, and so was constantly seeking her as an adult, wrote in his journal:

The dream showed me that I love M. as a child would love its mother. This caused me to break down emotionally. I realized I was unfair to expect M. to love me as if she was my mother. —K

When we think of our forebears, we use the term "family tree" and this is the other side of parents and grandparents in your dreams. They are the heritage, the past, and the trunk from which your life is a branch. They contain all the traces of history from which your own story develops.

At a more adult level, your brother or sister may be the one who faces death or illness before you do. In such cases, you will probably dream about them in a way that helps you to meet those crises with greater ease.

BABIES AND CHILDREN

As birth and childhood are so formative in your development, most dreams that include a baby or child express some feelings that were formed in your early years. Children have wonderful potential, a great ability to learn, and vast curiosity. When we are children, we feel love and anger with great passion, and usually the first people this emotion flows to are our parents. These feelings can still dominate the way we deal with others as adults; we may still feel soul-crushing pain when the person we love leaves or betrays us. This arises from the child alive in us. We may want to possess, or forever be desperately wanted by, our partner. We rarely see this constant love, yet our inner child takes no notice. So your dream child shows your emotions at an earlier age. Events may have stopped a particular line of growth—for example, you may have stopped loving a parent at a certain age because they deserted you. Out of this, your ability to love would have remained stuck at that age level.

Baby dreams can also link to pregnancy, new beginnings, and reclaiming joy and eagerness.

EXERCISE 8

DEALING WITH THE CHANGING FAMILY

1. Consider what the changes are that are happening in your family.

2. Look at all the dreams about your family and note what themes appear in them and what the dreams suggest regarding those changes.

3. What messages can you extract from the themes of your family dreams? Use a dream map and key words (see Drawing Your Dream Map, p. 16) to expand upon your insights.

4. Now take time to get an overview of what you have gathered, and what it says about your relationship with your family, and the changes in them and within yourself.

5. Ask yourself how you can best use the insights gained, and how you can meet the changing circumstances. Talk this over at an appropriate time with your family.

EXERCISE 9

BRINGING YOUR ROMANCE DREAMS TO LIFE

1. Most of us achieve deep and satisfying love in our dreams before we manage it in waking life. But even in our dreams we often need to practice it.

2. In your actual relationship, stand aside from your usual approach if it does not satisfy. Remember that you are capable of a fuller loving response.

3. Think of yourself as an actor and take on the role of your successful and loving dream self. This might feel strange at first, but persist until you feel at ease.

4. Consider what makes your dream love satisfying. Wherever possible, tell your partner what you need from them, and express or do what you can see makes your dream of love so rich.

UNDERSTANDING DREAMS OF LOVE AND ROMANCE

Although love is often spoken of as a fleeting emotion, it is fundamental to your life. When the sperm penetrates the ovum, they give each other their most vital treasure: their genes. Each of them dies to what they were, and their blending becomes something new and unique. This complete giving is the foundation of human existence and love. If we could allow even a small part of that giving into our everyday life, we would begin to experience the love that underpins the phenomenal universe.

Your dreams of love will show you how you are relating to the stream of love that is flowing through you. The dreams will attempt to expand the way you express love, clearing away any fears and frozen emotions, until you can love without grasping or wanting to possess. Very often we are afraid of love, or find it painful. Do not accept the hesitations and excuses that may arise in your dreams. These are only expressions of your own doubts and uncertainties. Claim your love.

RELATIONSHIP DREAMS

Most dreams about relationship dramatize the dreamer's own feelings, and how they are influencing the relationship. Patterns of relating, and our confidence in love and being loved, arise in our earliest childhood. So dreams of relationship often use a child in the dream to illustrate how early feelings of need, of feeling unloved, disrupt present relationships. To understand a dream in which you are relating to others, ask yourself what situation it is dramatizing.

RELATIONSHIP GROWTH

Perhaps none of us had a perfect childhood. And although the pains of growing often leave hurdles in the way we relate and love as adults, these hurdles are actually the building blocks of strength, deeper understanding, and sympathy. They offer an enormous opportunity to learn and grow. More than anything else, they enable us to develop if we dare to face them and admit them honestly to our partner or loved ones.

Dan's mother had frequently threatened that she would put him in an orphanage. As Dan had already been admitted to a hospital when he was three, this was not an idle threat. The threats became so painful for him that at six he killed all emotional connection with his mother. This meant he grew into an adult not knowing how to love a woman. In fact, he had built what he referred to as "steel doors," which he could close against any emotional contact. A turning point for Dan arose when he dreamed of being in a hospital and seeing some girls with badly malformed bodies. He says:

I went and sat on the end of one of the beds and I felt very warm toward the children. I held one of the girls' legs affectionately. They were so eager for any affection, one of them came over to the bed I was sitting on, and got into my arms. I held her tenderly and there was a great feeling of warmth between us.

The dream shows how Dan's feelings—shown in his dream as the girls—had not developed properly. But his loving contact with those old hurts transformed them.

What do your dreams show that is standing in the way of giving and receiving love? What is holding you back from a fuller participation in other people's lives, and in your own?

DREAMS AND THE BODY

Any part of your body you dream about has two possible associations. One is a link with the actual body organ or part, and the other is its psychological meaning. Usually, it refers to the psyche rather than the body. So your sexual organs reflect all the deep feelings or uncertainties you link with that part of you. Your legs would indicate everything involved in "standing up."

SEXUALITY

Sex is one of life's great creative mysteries. Although principally about reproduction, dreams suggest that it is also about bathing again in the fundamental joy of being, of connectedness. At our core we feel connected with each other and life. But our waking self, through its difficulties, often feels alone and cut off. Sex is a doorway to connecting again. During sex we reach beyond ourselves and include another, if only for fleeting moments. Bodies merge. You and I have extended beyond the narrow boundary of ourselves and dared to want another person, to need, to admit we are not self-contained. Clumsy as it may be, lovers want, offer, take, and give. Without love, there would only be containment, isolating and isolated. There would be no need to take in what a lover offers, there would be no absorbing and growing from the infinite richness of another person's difference.

Sexual dreams offer you the ability to explore any aspect of your desires and needs without implicating anyone else, or running any of the personal, health, or social risks external sex can bring. This exploration means that you can gradually discover what it is you really seek and need in a relationship. Usually this process of discovery and fulfilment is not something that is accomplished in a few dreams. And, in a general sense, the end of it is a total merging with one's partner. The following dream illustrates this:

I was with a woman whom I loved. The love was so intense that we gave ourselves to each other to the point where I absorbed her personality with all its memories, and she absorbed mine. This felt like a very important and wonderful thing to do. —J. S.

This merging depicts the female in the male and the male in the female being integrated. The result of this in love and sex is that the painful need for someone else melts away. What replaces it is an ability to love without needing to possess.

EXERCISE 10

SOLVING A SPECIFIC PROBLEM

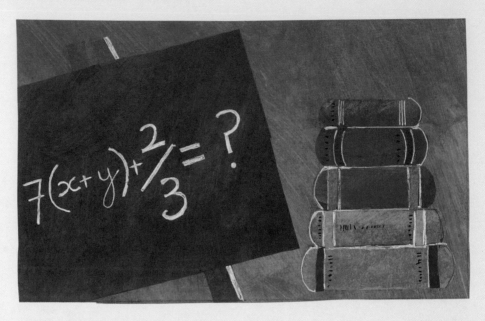

1. What is your problem? Have you already explored all the ways you can think of to solve it? Dreams do not usually respond creatively to waking inertia. They are stimulated by your efforts to learn or wrestle with a real-life problem. So, define your question. This should be done with one single issue in mind, and not be several questions in one. So it might be a question like, "What should I guard against in this issue?", "Which direction should I take?" or "What sort of relationship can I expect from my new lover?" An example of how not to frame a question by asking several questions in one would be, "Will the relationship with my new boyfriend work, or if not, should I go back to my husband, or should I simply concentrate on my job?"

2. Write the question on a piece of paper and stick it somewhere you will see it often during the day. Then, when you go to bed, review the question and ask for a response from your dreams. On waking, record whatever you dreamed. Consider any possible links with your question and what the dream is commenting on.

Remember that dreams are showing you a possibility, and there are infinite perspectives on any situation. So although the dream might be showing you the highest probability for resolving your problem, it is not an ultimate truth.

Math test

During the 1990s a British psychiatrist, Morton Schatzman, researched whether people could solve problems in their dreams. He tried several problems, among them mathematical questions that the subjects were not able to answer while awake. Some dreamers could find the answer to the question while they slept. Here is one of the problems:

The following sequence is the beginning of an infinite progression: "OTTFF." Carry it forward. (See page 220 for the solution).

UNDERSTANDING SCHOOL DREAMS

At school we learn a lot more than spelling and arithmetic: we're confronted by more than exams. School is probably the place where we first experience the stirrings of love, or find our confidence undermined by the demand to perform according to external needs. In fact, many dreams about school include the theme of exams and the tension they may have left regarding what feeling you have about yourself in competition with others. The following dream has something of this in it, but extends to a more inclusive theme:

I dreamed three times that I was to star as all the parts in a school play. The other cast members had dropped out. On the opening night I am pushed onto the stage dressed as a king, but I do not know the plot or any of my lines. I open my mouth, but do not know how to speak. I recently starred in a school production as a king. —D. H.

As this dream suggests, we are the star of our own life drama, and take all the parts we play during our lifetime—baby, child, youth, lover, worker, husband, old man/woman, and corpse. It would be so nice if we knew the plot beforehand and what lines to say—or would it? The dreamer is looking to know what the events of his life will be. But the dream also shows him facing greater independence and public attention. As with any schooling, it is preparing him for adult life, and for standing alone. His life doesn't have a script, so he needs to respond to events. The dream image applies to all of us. The key question is "how would you handle being on the stage without your lines?" Can you play your part and learn what you need to be the actor in your own life? Or will you be a passive victim of events and your relationship with teachers? Your dreams will portray to you a clearer course through the complexities of choices and responses if you take heed.

true dream story
ADOLESCENT AWAKENING

I am walking along a corridor at school. I am wearing no clothes, so I try to cover myself. People don't seem to notice me and I wonder why. Then a group of boys goes past, and they point and laugh at me. A teacher gives me some clothes. They are too big, but I wear them because I have nothing else. —H. M.

Adolescent sexual awareness provides a new level of experience that often makes us feel conspicuous. The clothes image is probably to do with finding an identity or sense of self that "fits." The teacher is a role model, but not the one that feels right yet.

EXERCISE 11

DREAM YOUR WAY OUT OF A DILEMMA

1. Clarify what you want to explore. This can be anything—an urgent work dilemma, a current relationship, a health problem, or a creative idea.

2. Choose a place and time during which you can sit quietly without disturbance. Close your eyes and imagine you are walking alone in a pleasant parklike area. It is beautiful and relaxing, so let your body feel that there is no rush, nothing to cause tension.

3. As you are walking in the park, you come across a high old stone wall enclosing an area you cannot see into. You discover an ivy-covered door leading into this hidden place. You know that the answer to what you are seeking is beyond the wall. So you open the door and walk through.

4. When you walk through, take your time to look around and notice what you see and feel. Let any fantasy arise and take note of it. This is how your unconscious will respond to your question.

EXERCISE 12

PRODUCTIVE DAYDREAMING

1. Close your eyes, and become aware of your body and your feelings. Notice that even without your attention, you carry on breathing, digesting, and creating your awareness. With the slightest of efforts you could direct this amazing vehicle that is your being to move in various ways—from chasing an idea down the avenues of thought to dwelling on a memory that brings laughter or tears. Where do you want to direct your vehicle? If you do not direct it, it will meander along pathways that may be happy or depressed, depending upon your background and habits. Your thoughts, desires, images, and daydreams will make it move.

2. Let go of any tension in your body. Recognize any messages of sickness and despair you are giving yourself by constantly thinking about illness, or how awful you look, or any other negatives. Drop them. Now imagine healing energy, like clean, pure water flowing through you, washing away doubts and fears. Feel grateful to your body for carrying you through so many years, so willingly.

3. The power that lies within dreams is not manifested only while you sleep. Unless you block this power with feelings of doubt or inadequacy, it flows into your daily life. So clarify where you wish to go and what you wish to do today. Have a daydream about yourself doing that, while remaining open to your potential. See yourself living through your day with enthusiasm and creativity.

UNDERSTANDING YOUR WORK DREAMS

Dreams that deal with your work are usually easily recognizable, because in one way or another you are either at work in the dream, in a building or situation associated with work, or in work clothes, as in the following dream.

I take a summation look at my work in cabinet-making and I find the cabinets are all in warehouses being stored and forgotten. I remember riding around the big warehouse, like Citizen Kane, looking at my finest work. I felt lost. I didn't want to do cabinet-making anymore because it felt hopeless. —D. A.

The dream pinpoints the problem D. A. has with his work—hopelessness and feeling lost. Such clarity really does help, even though at first sight it might indicate negative feelings. It helps because in making D. A. aware of the situation it gives him the means to do something abut it. If he enters his dream again in his imagination, he can explore the situation to see if he can find any satisfaction, rather than looking at his work judgmentally. He can also talk over his dilemma with friends, and consider the various options he has.

true dream story
MASTERCLASS

The visionary artist William Blake's waking life and dreaming life were closely intermingled. His most specific acknowledgment of the inspiration he received from his dreams is found in a pencil portrait showing the facial details of *The Man Who Taught Blake Painting in His Dreams*. Blake also had a dream in which his dead brother taught him a new method of printing. He went on to use that method to print his books.

Wyatt Rawson, writing about his work as a teacher and his use of dreams, described a nightmare from which he awoke fighting for breath. Realizing that if he ran away from the difficult feeling he had experienced in the dream it would be in control of him, he imagined himself back in the dream facing the creature that had frightened him. He says that when he did this:

A violent face rose up before me, and I was seized by a new terror. But I continued to look at it, until I suddenly realized that I was looking at my own face when I was angry. I nearly laughed aloud, and at that the face vanished and in its place a river of golden coins appeared, streaming down toward me.

He goes on to say that the experience led him to realize that he frequently bottled up his feelings until they burst out in irrational anger. The dream also helped him to recognize the unconscious conflict he had regarding control and permissiveness in life and in the classroom.

Because they balance the most worldly and personal of our needs and hopes with the most universal, dreams are among the greatest resources we can use to make our lives as good as they can be.

MONEY DREAMS

Dr. Calvin Hall, along with Henry Reed, both respected dream researchers, investigated thousands of dreams from a man in Cleveland. The man had received little education, but he managed to write down his dreams each morning. He would then refer to the daily horse-racing sheets to see if he could find any connections, and place a bet on the horse accordingly.

He kept a note of all bets, and the notes show hundreds of wins, and the amounts won.

However, most money dreams are indicative of how you feel about your relationship with events and opportunity. So dreaming about having money stolen, for instance, would be indicating a sense of loss. For many of us, money is connected with effort. We work a week for a week's pay. So the loss of money can also suggest a feeling of sinking, of effort expended for nothing, or resulting in no sense of security.

Sometimes money can indicate the weight of responsibility, as when we have to earn enough for our keep. But the unconscious has a different view of money, seeing it as a force in nature akin to electricity. It existed before your personal life, and will be there at your death. Like electricity, it works in certain ways, and some people, understanding these ways, build up great batteries of it. Yet in itself money is nothing, just paper notes or metal coins. We create its power.

LOOKING INTO THE FUTURE

Your unconscious has this power of looking ahead to a remarkable degree. This is because it has full access to your memories, and is deeply aware of your innate passions, fears, and potential, and how you are relating to them. It also has the power of synthesizing the experiences of your life and, like drawing a line on a map showing where you have been and what you have done in the past, can project that line forward and predict where you are going.

Predictive dreams are often very clear because they either show themselves as the future, or indicate it in some way. The following dream is an excellent example of this:

I dreamed I was in a hospital ward sitting beside a bed my boyfriend was on. He was being treated for alcoholism. Somehow I was also above myself looking down on the scene and realizing I was seeing my future self, sitting there with two kids waiting for my man to come out of his drunkenness. It was some-thing that had happened already in the past but without the children, and I realized this was my future if I continued the relationship. It helped me take another direction in life. —Jane

Grace Lewis, a potter, was able to transform her work through her dreams, from making traditional, lackluster pots to real art and gaining personal satisfaction. She says that in the dream she is walking along a street and looks in a window. Behind some portraits on easels are a wonderful collection of ornate pots. On going into the shop and lifting one of the pots, she sees that the signature on the base is her own. She says, "I must have had that dream twenty times now, and each time, I've been shown the pots I'm going to make next. It's kind of scary because I feel out of control, and I'm a person who's always liked to be in control of her life." Grace's dreams have also transformed her income. The top price she could arrive at for her traditional pots was $120. Her dream pots get $2,500.

The Dream Directory

ABANDONED

Fear of abandonment is one of the most powerful of childhood feelings, so your dream may be representing this fear because certain events have made it resurface. Look at your everyday experiences to see if you can discover its source or cause. If you are abandoned and left alone, this could mean you are experiencing loneliness, neglect, or insecurity in relationships. Feelings of abandon or giving way to your emotions represent a lowering of your moral standards, finding new freedom or releasing pent-up feelings. If your dream shows you abandoning someone else, this may express hidden anger, or mean that you are not nurturing some part of your personality. Sometimes, dreaming about abandonment may involve feeling dependent, or supporting dependents.

ABDOMEN/ABDOMINAL

In general, the abdomen refers to your ability to respond in an emotional, sensual and intuitive way. It also depicts your ability to digest or reject experience and food. So if you eat poisonous fruits or suffer sad emotions, there is pain. Your dream may be about your physical health or diet needs. If so, it will in some way be connected with food or activities that bring illness or health. If you are shot, stabbed, or punched in the abdomen, it usually indicates being emotionally hurt or physically injured.

For example, losing a loved one may cause actual abdominal pain. Harsh criticism can also produce the same sort of hurt and dream. Speech idioms that are specific to this area include you make me sick; I can't stomach that; I haven't got the guts for that.

ABNORMAL

Depending on whether the abnormal feature in your dream is part of your body, someone else's body, or of the dream objects or surroundings, it suggests two things:

1. You may be harboring fears about your self-image. Or the dream may reflect fears about your physical health. Even if these abnormalities appear on someone else, it may still refer to you, perhaps a part of you that has not developed to its full potential, or has been hurt. Your ability to love, for example, can be damaged, and so may not have flourished.
2. If the abnormality is part of the dream environment, it may suggest you sense that something is not right, either with what is happening around you, or how you are responding to it.

ABORIGINAL

These primal images often refer to your spontaneous feeling or instinctive reactions to the things that happen to you. Often, like unbidden sexual or religious feelings, this side of your nature may be less conscious than your normal or social interactions. It is the part of you that is closest to nature, with the keenest senses. It refers to your instinctive responses to situations and people, the part of you that is older than language and social training.

dream messenger

Where are you in your dream? In the country or the city, alone or with other people; running away from or toward something? Each situation holds a message you can extract by asking the question, "What am I doing here?"

ABOVE

The position suggests a wider view, superiority, or perhaps an advantage. If something or someone is above you in your dream, it can indicate that you feel disadvantaged, or lacking in power, or that you are in awe of something or someone. Perhaps you feel that something or somebody is beyond your reach.

ABROAD

Being abroad, or mention of a country other than your home, is in general a way of expressing your particular feelings or situation. For example, if Italy is abroad for you, you may see it as a warm and romantic place and this will be represented in your dream. But seeing a country at war represents conflict. So in most cases, being abroad suggests a change or a different feeling or life situation than your current one. The dream may refer to exploring new interests, or new areas of yourself, or even of being in an uncomfortable situation. If you have visited that country, the dream most likely refers to the events or emotions that occurred while you were there. If the country is a place your family originated from, it may depict the unconscious influences and cultural attitudes you inherited from them. If you have

lived or worked in that country, you need to define whether you were happy or stressed there, and what you absorbed of the atmosphere, because the dream is referring to this.

ABSORB/ABSORBED/ABSORBING

Two separate qualities that merge into one. In a relationship, whether a feeling relationship or one in which you are learning something, you often absorb things from the other person. You may take in such things unconsciously, as you did from parents and your upbringing. So the process of absorption in a dream may refer to such influences. The dream's meaning depends on the situation of the absorbing. If your body is absorbing something, this may refer to food you are eating, or some influence in your life.

ABUSE/ABUSED/ABUSING

Being abused, or abusing, physically or sexually, may point to your own past experiences. The dream may be an attempt to work out feelings you have about these events. Of course, we often abuse our own body and mind by the things we do, such as drinking alcohol and eating junk food, so the dream may be indicating this.

ABYSS

Seeing an abyss usually represents the unknown, or perhaps the depth of your own mind or consciousness. The fear of falling into the abyss, represents your attempt to control your feelings and what is inside yourself. It can refer to feelings about, or fear of, death. Seen in a positive light, it links your conscious mind with the immense potential you hold within. Part of this potential is an experience of going beyond opposites, of resolving paradoxes, of moving beyond the limitations of the rational mind and emotional responses. In these ways it is similar to dream images of the sea. (*see* Sea)

ACCELERATOR

If you are using an accelerator, it depicts your ability to boost or restrict the amount of enthusiasm you put into anything. It is linked with control, or feeling in control, but not as much as a brake. If you are pressing down on the accelerator, it shows a strong drive to reach your goal or desire quickly. If nothing happens when you depress the accelerator, it suggests a lack of response from your feelings for what you are trying to do. (*see* Car)

ACCEPT/ACCEPTED/ACCEPTING

If you are being offered something, be willing to admit or receive what is symbolized. If somebody else if accepting something from you, then it is about feeling acceptable, or having something to give.

ACCIDENT/ACCIDENTAL/ ACCIDENTALLY

In your dreams there are no accidents or chance events—you create the whole dream, so to dream of an accident may mean you sense that attitudes or events are leading you toward whatever the dream depicts. This is not a prophecy, but it may occasionally depict a self-fulfiling incident, so be aware of any events suggesting what is portrayed in your dream. This enables you to avoid the final moves creating the accident. The dream may also show stress or tension that can lead to events best avoided. The event may be a breakup, work crisis, or whatever the dream suggests. Sometimes this shows the feelings it gives rise to, such as shock or fear. Perhaps something has upset or hurt you. An accident in a dream can indicate feeling out of control or extremely stressed.

ACCOUNTANT

This represents either your ability to deal with money, or issues relating to finance, depending on the context in the dream.

ACCUSE/ACCUSED/ ACCUSATION/ACCUSER

This indicates feelings of guilt, or social or relationship difficulty. If you are the accuser, it may show feelings of being victimized or wronged, possibly in the distant past.

ACE (of cards)

This indicates a controlling factor in your life, or some vital point. It also shows ambiguity, as the ace can be high or low.

ACHE

An ache is a warning that all is not well. Perhaps some part of your body is damaged, or your dream could be using your body symbolically. So a heartache may suggest some emotional hurt, or a problem with your legs can represent a lack of confidence. (*see* Arm, Leg and Head)

ACNE

Seeing acne may suggest you feel unclean, or that you feel others do not like you or find you unattractive. You may feel shy about social contacts and expressing yourself, or feel others think you have unpleasant characteristics.

ACORN

With its power of growth, the acorn, or any seed in a dream, can depict a hidden but wonderful potential. It can also represent change, starting something new, or growing stronger.

ACROBAT/ACROBATICS

Depending on the context in your dream, this suggests dealing with challenging events skillfully. It may also suggest psychological agility, or the opposite if the acrobat falls. (*see* Roles)

ACTOR/ACTRESS/ACTING

If you are the actor/actress in your dream, you may be playing a role. This dream may also express a desire for public acclaim or notice. But if you have strong feelings or ideas about the person's character, your dream image may be using them to represent those feelings or ideas. Just as someone's life may be "acted out" on stage or in a film, so actors may represent different parts of your own life. (*see* Stage, Roles)

ACUPUNCTURE/ACUPUNCTURIST

This can indicate giving or receiving some form of healing, or it can be a re-direction of energies. Seeing needles may also represent the barbs that people inflict through their words or deeds. (*see* Stage, Roles)

AD *see* Advertisement.

ADAM AND EVE

Adam depicts the male potential, the dynamic energy leading us toward personal growth. For a man Adam depicts the person they are beneath their social conditioning, scheming, ambition, and fears. Eve stands for the soul or personality, feelings, femininity, or your receptiveness to sensations and temptations. She can also represent a man's wife, or his emotional and sexual relationship with her, and his ability or inability to love. (*see* Eve)

ADDER *see* Snake.

ADDICT/ADDICTED/ADDICTION

Something or someone may be influencing you in a way that undermines your ability to make choices. There may also be a connection with powerful emotional or economic dependence. These activities or influences are not arising from your will or responsibility, but from the emotions and fears that are symbolized by the addiction in your dream. You can be addicted to a relationship, or to work, and your dream may be commenting on that situation. If so, it is wise to consider moving toward greater independence. If someone else is addicted, the other person may represent a part of your character.

ADDRESS

Your home address is your condition or status in life, or your life situation. If it is another person's address, it suggests you identify with that person. You will need to look for clues as to what your dream is telling you about this. It may indicate contact. A past address means you are dealing with things you learned or felt while you lived at the previous place—a past way of life, perhaps. A new address can signify changes you are making in some way, and forgetting your address shows confused feelings about what your life situation is. Ask yourself if you have lost sight of your goals or standards. (*see* House)

ADHESIVE *see* Glue.

ADMIRAL

This represents the ability to direct the many facets of yourself across the sea of life experience, or, in other words, having the ability to meet the difficulties of life decisively. It may also indicate a father or authority figure. The admiral may represent the best or superior parts of you. (*see* Roles)

ADMIRATION/ADMIRED/ ADMIRING

If you are admiring someone else, this may be directing you to become aware of qualities that you either need to develop, or need to recognize. Being admired suggests you either need some appreciation, or you are noticing qualities in yourself. If the dream stresses that you are greatly admired, it may suggest an that you have an inflated opinion of yourself, or perhaps you have a strong need for approval and special acclaim from others.

ADMIT/ADMITTED/ ADMITTING

This may refer to something that was difficult to acknowledge about yourself, perhaps in a relationship or situation.

ADOLESCENCE/ADOLESCENT

In most cases this refers to you at the age shown. It therefore portrays the values you had then, and desires and problems experienced. It may also depict sexual and social experiment or uncertainty. (*see* Teenager) If you are younger than adolescence, it suggests the impressions, fears and dreams you have about becoming an adolescent. (*see* Girl, Boy)

ADRIFT

You may be feeling you are without any determining direction or anchor in life. Ask yourself if any changes have occurred in your family or work that have left you feeling cut off from old ties.

ADULTERY

Everyone has sexual desires about people other than their partner. Or sometimes they relate to people with whom it can be difficult to have a sexual relationship. If you are having sex with another person, the dream may refer to sexual release. This is a harmless way of exploring sex with another person. If you dream your partner is having sex with someone else, you may be feeling uncertain of your own value and wondering whether you are lovable. These feelings may hide painful dependence on your loved one. Making love to someone you dislike can mean you are getting involved with distasteful things.

ADVENTURE/ADVENTUROUS/ADVENTURER

The dream is probably a comment on changes you are making within yourself, or in your external life, or perhaps both. It shows you taking risks, exploring something new. The context in the dream will state whether the risk is worth taking, or whether fears or other factors hold you back.

ADVERSARY *see* Enemy.

ADVERTISE/ADVERTISEMENT/ADVERTISER

The dream may be bringing something to your attention or suggesting that you bring other people's attention to what is advertised. There may also be questions of desire, needs, or choices connected with this. Looking at what the rest of the dream portrays, and any feelings involved, will define this.

ADVICE/ADVISE/ADVISER

Whether the advice is given or received, this often suggests information you need to think about, and perhaps act upon.

AERIAL/ANTENNA

This is intuition or contact with others through more subtle means.

AEROPLANE/AIRCRAFT/AIRPLANE

Being in a plane indicates that you are making changes, or altering your situation in some way. It may also connect with a desire to get away from your present lifestyle, or suggest a business opportunity, or a desire for love. In dreams where you watch an aircraft take off, or fly, it can point to a project you have launched, or an undertaking you are trying to "get off the ground." There are many analogies you can use in your dreams connected with a plane. For example, a crash landing may indicate problems ahead causing a difficult end to plans, projects, or hopes. Taking off shows the beginning, the launch, the rising excitement of what you are doing, or where you are going in life. Being attacked or bombed by aircraft can indicate anxiety attacks, or feeling threatened. A grounded plane represents difficulties in getting your plan, relationship or hopes off the ground. Doing or seeing aerobatics or stunts suggests you are, or will be, daring in your life or undertakings, but often links to relationships, work, or personal growth. The success or failure of the flying will show how fearful or confident you are in expressing your daring. This is largely a matter of nerve, and feelings of anxiety can bring you down.

AEROSOL

This is something that may influence you in a subtle, or perhaps invisible way. It can indicate feelings of being under pressure that may escape at the press of a button.

---

dream fact

Psychologist James McClelland says that dreaming "is the opposite of forgetting." He explains that daily experiences are stored in the brain's hippocampus, which then replays the stored memories during dreaming sleep, helping them to be translated into long-term memories recorded in the brain's cortex.

AFFAIR *see* Adultery.

AFFECTATION

If some sign of affectation appears in your dream, you need to ask yourself what you are doing that is not in accord with your deepest feelings or character.

AFFLICTION *see* Illness.

AFRAID *see* Fear.

AFRICA/AFRICAN

If you are not black and dream about a black African it may represent your spontaneous and natural feelings and responses to life. If you have strong ideas associated with Africa and Africans, then your dream is using the image to depict these, so the African in your dream may represent feelings about racial prejudice. If you are black, then treat it either as contact with your own cultural heritage, or as a dream about yourself. (*see* Aboriginal, Abroad)

AGE/AGED/AGING/AGELESS

The age of characters, family, animals, or objects or your own age in a dream often carries very definite associations or information. What these associations are depends a great deal on your age. If the person is ageless, it depicts the part of you, your fundamental core, which does not change. A baby or child refers to your feelings of dependence or vulnerability, perhaps even helplessness or powerlessness. But often it suggests a need for love, support, and care; it may even represent memories of being a baby or childhood. Extreme old age suggests feelings about death, an old way of life,

or an influence in yourself or surroundings that pre-dates your birth. Influences from family, such as attitudes or fears, may be generations old, so they may be depicted as incredibly ancient. This in turn represents something with a lot of wisdom or experience. You may therefore feel the person is holy or revered in such dreams.

A middle-aged person represents achievement, maturity or the aging process. An older person may depict feelings about your parents or a parent/authority figure, the wisdom gathered from many years of living; your declining power or creativity; or feelings about aging, decline, and loss within you. So an older person in your dream may refer to feelings you have about a parent or grandparent, such as dependency, love, or anger. A teenager can represent whatever difficulties you faced, or are facing, in the process of meeting sexual drives, adult relationships, and the need to become a motivated part of society. So there may be uncertain feelings, shyness, inexperience, or idealism suggested in the dream teenager. (*see* Teenager) The young adult points to yourself at that age or period of life, at your physical peak—a period of worldly opportunity.

AGGRESSION

If you or someone else in your dream expresses anger or aggression, it still relates to your own feelings. It must be remembered that aggression or fear—fight or flight—is a fundamental response to threat. Animals constantly practice aggressive acts, or acts of flight, to be ready for actual threat. The more threatening your environment becomes or appears to be, the more fantasies or dreams of aggression you will experience. Alternatively, you may become passive and withdrawn or cower, which is another form of response to external stress, or fear of it. Therefore some aggressive dreams, whether practiced against someone else, or yourself, may have their origins in external threat or fear of it. Such dreams or fantasies may be a form of preparation, as with animals, to defend yourself or find an escape from the threat or an appropriate response to it. Hostility toward society or authority sometimes becomes directed inward and is self-destructive. This hostility can make you unable to express yourself, causing illness and a lack of self-belief. Meeting anger, aggression and hostility in your dreams is healthy, and does not make you suppress it or express it socially. Therefore, consider what the anger is about, when it dates from, and in what way you can safely release it now. (*see* Anger)

AGONY

Think about what feeling or decision, what responsibility or concern is tormenting you. Or is the dream suggesting that this is a physical pain? If so, *see* Illness.

AGORAPHOBIA

As with fear of falling, this may represent an actual fear. But as a symbol it means a fear of being exposed, being seen, possible attack, and of having nothing to hide behind or under. In general, it is about anxiety and vulnerability.

AGREEMENT

This represents a coming together of previously unreconciled opinions, emotions, beliefs, etc. that are still held in your psyche.

AIM

You may be directing attention or energy to what is depicted by the target or goal. If you are the target, you may be feeling as if you are being criticized or attacked. When a gun or weapon is aimed, it suggests directing anger, sexuality, or attention at the target.

AIR

Dreams use air in two ways. The first way depicts the sort of feelings you have if you have ever struggled to breathe through illness or danger. So the lack of air can show a struggle to survive in the present situation. Air also is often used as the medium through which you fly in dreams. In these dreams, the air probably represents the invisible social atmosphere in which we unconsciously exist and strive. Therefore, occasionally a dream shows the dreamer losing the air or wind out of their sails that sustains their flight, suggesting a loss of support usually gained from public acceptance or approval, or even their own confidence. When we talk about "clearing the atmosphere" or say that there is "something in the air," this is precisely what dreams of air can describe.

AIRCRAFT/AIRPLANE *see* Aeroplane.

AIRPORT

This symbol concerns making changes, an urge to get somewhere other than where you are, or to achieve goals. It depicts the things that drive you to undertake journeys, to make changes, such as a need for love, a need to escape or leave things behind. Sometimes, it shows you reaching for independence, depending upon the details of the dream. So the airport can show a turning point in your life. Occasionally, it relates to the departure of a loved one or the end of a relationship.

AIR RAID

You are probably feeling extremely anxious about something, such as imagined fears or an attack on you. The raid may also depict a threat from new ideas or opinions, or something that "descends out of the blue."

AIR-SEA RESCUE

To be rescued at sea indicates that you are at the mercy of powerful natural forces that you are not dealing with well. This may refer to a difficulty in dealing with life's demands generally, and a dangerous attraction to giving up and losing your identity as you withdraw inward. Taking part in an air-sea rescue suggests you are actively trying to deal with threatening feelings. (*see* Sea)

AISLE

An aisle usually indicates a way you can move through obstacles or a lot of people. So it suggests a method or attitude you are using to get to where you want. But it may also confront you with other people seeking their own ends, and put you in the limelight. In other words, your attempts to gain your own ends can make you stand out. (*see* Corridor)

ALCOHOL

Drinking can represent a transforming process. It portrays an influence that can change the way you act for better or worse. You need to consider your dream to see which of these it is. It can also represent stimulation, relaxation, and a way to face inner anxieties, even if only temporarily. Occasionally, it refers to a power you possess that can transform you. (*see* Coffee)

ALCOHOLISM *see* Addicted.

ALIEN

This can be something you do not understand about yourself. It usually refers to a misunderstood part of you that is foreign to the rest of your character. If you feel isolated in the dream, it may suggest you feel alienated from others. Or it can link with your timeless side. This is because aliens have come to represent an influence from the stars, something from beyond what we understand. It can therefore depict the deep unconscious or spiritual core of oneself. (*see* Flying Saucer)

ALLERGIC/ALLERGY

This may show an allergy you have. Or it may be used symbolically. If so, consider what is represented by your allergy. Look it up in this dictionary.

ALLEY

This represents limited possibilities. An alley with a dead end suggests concern about a tight situation or direction that appears to have no way out. (*see* Highway, Cul-de-sac)

ALLIGATOR

The alligator or crocodile is similar to the serpent and depicts the power of unconscious emotions and fears. If you do not relate to your unconscious urges constructively, conflict can occur. This can make you feel scared of these forces inside you, making you fearful of being swallowed, dragged down into dark feelings, or becoming irrational. The Egyptians worshipped a crocodile as a guide to the dead in the underworld. It represents not only a threat, but a wealth of wisdom about the unconscious.

ALPHABET
Seeing this symbol may refer to childhood, or to basic lessons in life.

ALTAR
This symbolizes the sense of awe in face of life, nature, or God. It is also a willingness to sacrifice some personal desires for a universal or social good. The philosopher Albert Schweitzer once said, "A man who picks a worm out of a puddle is acting for life as a whole, not just personal self." The altar may also depict a meeting place between your personality and "life as a whole."

AMBULANCE
Generally, an ambulance expresses your feelings that something is wrong, or shows an anxiety about health, or the health of someone close. Such dreams often depict life-threatening situations, and so deal with anxieties.

AMBUSH
This may signify an intuitive feeling about something being planned by others. But some-

times it is paranoia about being victimized. If you are creating the ambush, then you may be feeling angry about what someone is doing, or you may be using underhand methods for your own ends.

AMPUTATION
This dream can be a symbol of losing the power that is represented by the limb depicted. (see Leg, Arm, Left, Right)

AMUSEMENT PARK/ARCADE
This indicates something about being childlike and playing at life. It may be suggesting escapism, or perhaps you are testing yourself to define your overall self-image. (see Fairground)

ANALYST/THERAPIST
If someone who is helping you analyze your dreams appears in one, they usually represent your unconscious wisdom, or the difficulties you face in dealing with yourself. An analyst or psychologist can represent self-assessment, or self-insight, or the things or urges that have led you to seek such understanding. The symbol can also represent your personal feelings about, or your actual relationship with the analyst. (see Psychoanalyst)

ANCESTORS
These can show your deeply ingrained characteristics or the talents and weaknesses you have absorbed from family influence and culture, but which may be largely unconscious or unacknowledged.

ANCHOR

This is part of your makeup that holds you firm to a task or code, such as determination, love, etc. But it has a deeper meaning; for the anchor reaches the seabed, or deepest part of your unconscious self. So it suggests a power of resolve or security coming from deep within. Or it may suggest being tied down. If the anchor is not holding, it shows influences that are weakening your confidence, or difficulties in meeting the influences affecting you.

ANCIENT

Something ancient can point to life experiences that are deeply buried, or even forgotten, such as childhood experiences, or to the person you were in a past relationship or job. It can also represent the deeply unconscious wisdom in your body, or in your racial memories or family traditions. Therefore, it can sometimes indicate inherited knowledge and your instincts that are older than your personality. But in general, it is knowledge or wisdom gained through long experience.

ANESTHETIC

This is an attitude or experience that is making you unconscious of what is happening. Something is deadening your feelings and sensitivity. Because anesthesia puts you to sleep, this dream image sometimes links with death, or an encounter with something that creates a wider awareness than offered by your senses.

ANGEL

When we are very small, someone who loves us appears to us to be an angel. So the angel can represent the positive side of a relationship with someone you love, such as your mother or grandmother. It can also depict religious concepts, feelings or intuitions about death, a need for a parent figure to guide or instruct you in decision making, or it can be innate wisdom. Angels are often associated with death or dying, or the communication of an important message.

ANGER/ANGRY

Like fear, anger is one of the fundamental and instinctive responses to a situation or pain, a danger, or an attack. It involves a lot of physical and emotional energy, and if blocked or repressed may cause psychosomatic illness or hurt. Therefore, it is important to acknowledge anger in your dreams, and find ways of expressing it without directing it at other people. Remember that an angry response is one of the ways you cover up hidden pain or upset. Accepting that it is okay to express your anger in your dreams encourages better physical and emotional health. (*see* Aggressiveness)

ANIMAL

Dream animals are images of your most basic instinctive feelings and responses. The "flight or fight" response, for example, is part of our animal or inherited behavior. The underlying natural feelings we have about wanting a partner to love and possibly have children with, are also expressions of the animal in us, as is the caring and love we can give to our children and each other. We can observe these things in animals as they mate and care for their young. But our social training from infancy may have put us at odds with parts of our natural heritage. This is shown in our dreams when we run terrified from an animal or when we meet a wounded creature.

But we also develop personal association from our relationships with our pets and the animals around us. Therefore, some animal dreams may display such diverse associations as a personal need for affection, a desire to be touched, or the need to care for another creature and feel needed. It can even be pregnancy and parental caring. Pets, for example, have given each of us very different experiences. We therefore have personal associations and responses to pets that we may dream about. Sometimes in dreams you meet a shining animal, or one that is deeply loving or wise. It may speak to you and tell you things that on waking you realize are profoundly perceptive. This is because such a dream character is an image of your unconscious connection with your insight.

ANTIQUE *see* Ancient.

ANUS
This symbol reflects the things you reject or excrete after you digest experience. The anus may also represent your will, as you can control this area and hold back natural urges to go to the toilet. So it may refer to holding yourself back or being in control. For many people, dreams about anal sex or a finger in the anus may represent an introverted sexual drive, fears about sex, or sex that has been restrained so it has turned inward. (*see* Feces)

APARTMENT *see* House.

APE
An ape can depict the physical, instinctive, wild, animal person that is within you. But it can also represent your inner wisdom. In this case, it refers to the instinctive knowledge of social relations, sex, and parenting. (*see* Animal)

APPLE
This denotes sexual or material temptation. When it is a golden apple, it also represents wholeness, knowledge of the world or yourself. It can also mean the fruits of your actions, or the consequences of action, the fruits of your labors, pleasure, food or sustenance.

APPOINTMENT
To dream of an appointment may mean that you need to remember something important about a relationship. Or it can suggest you unconsciously feel you are about to meet someone or something.

ARAB
This represents masculinity, passionate manhood, or possessiveness. (*see* Abroad)

ARCHER *see* Aim.

ARENA
This may mean you are feeling tested, or are in some area of conflict. It can also point to important issues being brought to your awareness.

ARGUE/ARGUED/ARGUING
This can refer to a conflict or indecision. It may also indicate unexpressed feelings.

ARM
Arms represent your power to express emotions, desires and ideas, to construct or destroy. They may also be referring to your ability to love, give, take, create, defend, or reach

out. Injury to an arm suggests loss of power to act or to support action, an inability to reach out or create. The left arm indicates your supportive feelings if you are right-handed; the right arm is your extroverted actions. (*see* Left, Right, Body)

ARMOR

This represents the rigid emotional or intellectual barrier you may use to protect yourself from being hurt, frightened or influenced by others.

ARMS (weapons)

Guns, spears, etc. usually depict aggression and destructive urges and wishes or sometimes male sexuality. If you are being attacked, they indicate your own fear of being hurt or dominated, either by your own emotions or someone else's. (*see* Arm for body limb)

ARRESTED/ARRESTING

This literally means to be stopped. If it is by a policeman, then you are probably restraining yourself morally with self-imposed rules or social restraints. You may feel some of your urges are "unlawful" or wrong. If you suffer anxiety dreams because of a previous fearful relationship with authority or police—for example, if you have survived a harsh political regime and are terrified of being arrested—then you need to seek help to heal the damage from these experiences.

ART/ARTIST

This is the display of an inner idea, feeling or direction, or the expression of inner thoughts that can be a source of self-realization. The artist may represent the urge toward fruition or self-realization. The art object, however, can depict some meaningful understanding within yourself that is not yet clear enough to put into words. (*see* Painting, Role)

ASCENDING/ASCENT

There are several possibilities for this symbol in your dream. One is that passion, excitement, energy, or enthusiasm is rising. Getting higher is also often linked to your ability to see further, or your ability to become aware of a wider experience or a more inclusive viewpoint. It can involve change—leaving one place to arrive at another. So there may be the leaving behind of what was in the lower place. Occasionally, it involves ascent, especially if there is an irrational element in the dream, such as going out through the roof of a house in an elevator. This can suggest some excessive, possibly manic excitement. Lastly, we can climb

true dream story

Brenda dreamed that her friend Sandra's newborn baby was ill and needed help. The baby, Billy, did not seem to be ill apart from not feeding well. But Sandra took Billy to the doctor, who felt that further tests were needed. The tests showed that Billy lacked a digestive enzyme, and therefore could not absorb calcium. Without it he would die. But a simple drug righted the condition.

up stairs, a tree, or to another high place, to escape any perceived danger or to deal with our fears. If this symbolism appears in your dream, ask yourself what you are trying to escape.

ASCETIC

This may indicate avoidance of sex and the restraint of normal appetites. Such restraint may be caused by anxiety, previous pain, or religious ideas. The ascetic can also indicate leaving worldly activity and ambitions behind, and the discovery of greater freedom. (*see* Role)

ASH/ASHES

These show the purified aspect of whatever has been burned. Ashes express the past, what is left from something that was formed or alive previously. If difficult feelings are attached to the ashes, they may be associated with cremation of a loved one, or with a feeling of being "burnt out."

ASS *see* Donkey.

ASTHMA

This illness is associated with struggling to survive, or being smothered in a relationship, environment or situation, or it can represent anxiety. (*see* Air)

ASTROLOGER, ASTROLOGY

The dream astrologer often represents your intuition or unconscious insights into yourself and others. There may also be a link with destiny. If you do not believe in astrology, your dream may be suggesting you are being misled.

ASTRONAUT

Seeing an astronaut points to attitudes, feelings, or ideas that can take you beyond the ordinary view you have of life and yourself. There is also a suggestion that you have the courage to grow and explore something that you cannot yet define. (*see* Space)

ATOM BOMB

This symbol often shows you that enormous changes are taking place within yourself, or are about to take place. This is because the old way of life can be destroyed or lost by some sudden change. But the bomb may also depict anxieties about your future, or the way of life surrounding you. Whichever feelings are most appropriate, the bomb usually shows enormous potential energy.

ATTACK/ATTACKED/ATTACKER

If you are being attacked, the dream usually arises because in some way you are repressing, in conflict with, or are frightened of your own emotions, sexuality, or anger. Occasionally, the fear is about your own potential or expanded awareness. If you are attacked by an animal, the repression or fear relates to your own natural primal urges. Sometimes, your dreams show an animal as depicting someone who you feel is expressing anger toward you. If you are attacked by a shadowy or frightening figure, it usually points to old childhood fears and hurts. If you are the attacker, this is more positive, as you are not being passive and hurt in your dreams. But you are still experiencing a conflict with whatever it is you are attacking. The object of your attack is probably a part of your own personality, so it may be better to meet it in some other way.

ATTIC

This may refer to your mind, or if the attic has things stored in it, then perhaps it indicates past memories or things you have not accessed for a while. Being trapped in an attic suggests that you are limiting yourself to a purely intellectual way of looking at life, or that you are caught up in the past. Alternatively, it may show that you are isolating yourself from ordinary life.

AUDIENCE

Standing in front of an audience may depict that you are trying to express something important, or deciding how you will "play out" your life or some situation. You may also be trying to get people's attention or be applauded for what you are doing. If you are in an audience, your unconscious may be showing you something important on the stage in front of you. This is because it may be difficult for you to become aware of it in any other way. (*see* Arena)

AUNT

The meaning of this symbol will probably depend upon whether you are male or female. If you are female, then the aunt may be a suggestion of who you may become—either negatively or positively. But the most likely connection is through what you feel about your aunt. Work on defining these feelings, and find out what your dream is depicting. (*see* Family)

AURA

This type of symbol shows an awareness of the usually unconscious processes of your life and your mind.

AUTHOR

This depicts a creative part of yourself. It can indicate a desire to tell the story of your real self or your inner passions and dreams. (*see* Roles)

AUTOGRAPH

This refers to something on which you have put your name. It indicates what you will do or say, and represents an agreement. It is a mark of your determination or existence. (*see* Name)

AUTOMOBILE *see* Car or parts of a car, such as Engine.

AUTOPSY

This reflects a deep, and probably painful, self-examination. Usually this indicates a search for something, perhaps a cause of pain or the death of love.

AVALANCHE

Anything that relates to snow can point to long-frozen emotions and urges. Therefore, the avalanche may show that something is disturbing inner feelings that have lain cold and apparently dead for a long time.

AWAKE/AWAKENED/AWAKENING

This shows you "waking up" and becoming aware of something.

AXE

This represents material power or authority. It can indicate a desire to hurt or destroy, or it can be a fear of these emotions. (*see* Arms)

B

BABY

This represents your infant self. Or some part of you that is still in the early stages of development and needs nurturing in case it dies. This is your inner potential. As such it may represent a new phase of your life, a new project or a new way of life. Depending upon what is happening to the baby, it may also represent the infant part of you that needs love and help to release traumatic emotions. Or perhaps some aspects of infant feelings were not grown out of, such as an intense need for bonding. It can also show a great dependence on a partner's emotions.

BACHELOR

If you are a bachelor it can represent your situation. The dream will describe what is important to you, but it may be an unknown situation. If you are an unmarried woman or are looking for a partner, it probably depicts feelings you have about a possible partner. In a man's dream, it represents feelings about single life, or comparing it with the present, if you are married. In a woman's dream, it can show feelings or realizations about a single male friend, or desires for a sexual relationship. (*see* Man)

BACK

In general, the back of someone or something usually refers to being unconscious, or to unknown things, things that are out of sight. If it is the back of a house it means being more private, less formal, or a hidden social situation. If this is your physical back, it is your strength or moral uprightness, or what is past.

BACKGROUND

The background or environment in a dream is very informative. It usually illustrates the situation you are in, and what you may be taking for granted. In many ways we cannot do without background support. When we were children, for example, this "background" or lack of it, that our parents gave us was extremely important. So work out your message.

BACKPACK *see* Knapsack.

BACTERIA *see* Germs.

BADGE

This symbol depends on what sort of badge it is. It may be the focal point of your inner resources, or represent your inner possibilities. It may also depict your feelings of identification with a group or organization if the badge is connected with it. A police badge or a cross may also connect to authority or confidence.

BAG

This represents female sexuality. But if it is a handbag, it often stands for your sense of identity and ability to get your social needs fulfilled or identified. So it can show what you feel about yourself as a social force, or what you carry with you. You may be feeling a loss of self-esteem, for instance. A bag may hold something valuable and represent protection or the ability to hide something. (*see* Luggage)

BAKER

This is a power within you that can transform everyday life into something enjoyable. Because we use the word "dough" to suggest money, there can be a financial link. (*see* Roles)

BALANCE

This shows your ability to judge and discriminate, to measure one thing against another. It may also suggest a conscience that judges outer acts.

BALD *see* Hair.

BALL

If it is a ball game, the ball may depict something about a relationship and what is going on. Or, it may represent competition and ways to win or play the game of life, love, or business. The ball can also stand for wholeness. (*see* Games)

BALL GAME *see* Games.

BALLOON

This indicates light-hearted party feelings to do with celebration, or something insubstantial that can easily be destroyed or suddenly lost.

BAND

If it is a particular band or group, it may link with what you feel about them. Otherwise, it can depict feelings you have at the moment

about working in harmony with others, or expressing your own creativity. Sometimes, this refers to teenage feelings and emerging sexuality.

BANDAGE

This represents feeling hurt, or a fear of injury. The bandage also connects with healing and sometimes death.

BANDIT

This is male sexuality in its adolescent, aggressive stage.

BANK

Linking with money, this symbol can connect with your feelings about it. So it can relate to security, worry, or getting or not getting the things you want. Money and banks also associate with emotional and personal resources, the potential you have used or spent. (*see* Money)

BAPTISM

You are probably undergoing a mental and emotional cleansing, and letting go of feelings, opinions, and prejudices. You are becoming ready for new ideas or intuitions. In the Bible, water is spoken of in a particular way. For example, "Their hearts melted and became as water" (Josh. 7:5). Water is also used to wash with and to quench your thirst. So baptism in water cleanses you, changes you inside, and indicates achieving desires. (*see* Water, Desert)

BARBER

There may be a question in your mind of how you can change the way people see you. It may also link with attention to the way you think, or how you appear. (*see* Hair, Roles)

BARE

This can indicate an anxiety about having your motives, feelings, secret hopes and fears, revealed. Sometimes being bare represents a desire to reveal yourself to others, to have them see you as you are underneath, depending on the dream's content. (*see* Naked, Clothes)

BAROMETER

This shows the state of your inner feelings or emotions. It can also depict what you sense about coming events or situations.

BARRICADE

This represents the defense you use against others, or defensive events used against you. It may be an excuse, such as "I'm too ill to go to work," or "I'll never get anywhere, so what's the use of trying." (*see* Armor, Fence)

BARROOM

What happens in the bar may indicate how you relate to social relationships. A public bar can represent a sense of pleasure, love of company and entertainment, or sometimes the place where you experience changes in yourself (shown by the influence of alcohol or spirits). It can also represent retreating—perhaps from home or a relationship. (*see* Alcohol)

BARTENDER *see* Barroom.

BASEMENT

This area represents hidden motives, unconscious, unknown feelings, memories or past experiences. It can also be your biological past, or the place where your conscious mind contacts hidden powers, universal wisdom, and even other minds. Sometimes, it can mean base deeds, low morals, or underlying dislikes. It is from the basement, below, or within, that libido, or life energy, arises. Fears and terrors sometimes come from this space, because it is in the unconscious that we hide old memories and hurts. But it also contains the understanding of your essence. (*see* House)

BATH/BATHING

The bath or bathing may remind you of feeling relaxed, of being more presentable and acceptable. It may also indicate healing and change. If you are bathing in a river, it suggests being open to flowing feelings and urges within about growth or expansion of awareness. Bathing in the sea is being open to a more universal, or less self-centered, awareness of your relationship with life. (*see* Baptism, Water)

BATTERY

This is energy—your life force. If the battery is low or damaged, it may indicate health problems.

BATTLE/BATTLEFIELD

This is usually connected with conflict, the sort of battles you fight within yourself over love or anger, over feeling betrayed or being ignored. Another possibility is that of being attacked, or feeling attacked by others. You can also be fighting against the effect of fears, doubts, and memories, This can be especially true if you have been in a battle scene in waking life.

BAY

Depending on the weather in your dream, this suggests a place of receiving, of being in contact with the natural state or your body and mind. A crescent-shaped bay may show female sexuality. (*see* Beach)

BAYONET *see* Arms.

BEACH

This symbol indicates the borderline between your unconscious and conscious self. To find something on the beach is to find something that has come from deep within. It is the point of connection between your conscious self and all that exists in the background of your body and mind. It can also link to happy times or romance, if these happened on a beach. (*see* Sea)

BEAD/BEADS

A single bead suggests isolation; a string shows connection with people. (*see* Ball)

BEAR

This can represent a possessive mother, and the feelings this has aroused. But often, the bear indicates a meeting with dangerous emotions such as anger. There may be associations with independence or strength. (*see* Animal)

BEARD

This represents male feelings. It is also often used to show great wisdom, authority, or even saintliness, such as when the person has a white beard. If the beard is very long, it can symbolize great age, eternal life, or wisdom of the ages. Some people use a beard to hide their youth or bad skin, so it can be some sort of mask, or desire to be hidden. (*see* Hair)

BEAST

An animal of extraordinary power or a creature causing great terror is a feature of many dreams or nightmares. The figure may be partly human, or an animal that has strange characteristics. Or perhaps a figure that never quite declares itself, remaining unseen but causing or projecting great fear. In some dreams, the beast takes the form of a prehistoric creature. Overall, it represents our natural primal responses, from which we gradually mould our social and intellectual self. Unless we make friends with our beast, there may always be conflict between the rational and non-rational. We existed as a beast for millions of years before developing personal awareness. Self-

true dream story

A woman radio researcher was offered the job of presenter. She was thrilled but fearful, and dreamed that, as she was walking, planes were flying overhead, dropping bombs. She dived into a ditch to avoid being killed. She realized from the dream that she was afraid of facing the public directly, and that this fear would have caused her to refuse the job. She faced the fear and accepted the job.

awareness is still new and vulnerable. It needs the wisdom of the beast to survive (*see* Animal).

The theme of the beast is important in women's dreams, but is different from men's. This is illustrated in the story of Beauty and the Beast, where a young girl meets and lives with a powerful beast. The story emphasizes the girl's relationship with her father as a counterpoint to that with the beast. It suggests that a young woman meets a different kind of love when she leaves her father's affections. To become fully a woman and mother, she must discover her deep animal urges that underlie her personality and social traits. These urges are certainly primal and open her up to experience deep sexual longing, and the power to give herself passionately to her children and to her partner. So she allows something forbidden in her relationship with her father to develop within herself—an erotic and procreative love.

BED

There are many associations you may have with a bed. It can represent rest, sleep, unconsciousness, sexual pleasure, relationship, dreams, or blissful sleep. Try to define what feelings you associate with the bed, and ask yourself where they apply in your waking life. You may also link a bed with sickness, or insomnia and worries. Speech idioms for bed are: a bed of nails; a bed of roses; make one's bed and lie on it.

BEER *see* Alcohol.

BEES

This symbol means work, social life or order. Dreaming of bees can also represent mass power, individual weakness or unity of effort.

BEETLE

This insect is sometimes used as a symbol of eternal life, of fate, or cause and effect. (*see* Insect)

BEGGAR

This is the side of yourself with which you do not identify. The symbol represents parts of you that you do not allow into everyday affairs because of shame. Or, it can indicate inadequacy or feeling like an outcast. It can also represent a wise man who can tell you that the secrets of your destiny lie beneath the rough exterior. (*see* Roles)

BEHIND

If you are left behind, it links with feelings of inadequacy. You may feel burdened with things that prevent you from being accepted by others, or feel you can't keep up with what is needed. If the dream is about things behind you or behind something, *see* Back.

BELL

With this symbol, ask yourself what you are being told to be aware of, or warned about.

BELLY

This symbol normally relates to vulnerability, but it is also sensual feelings, passions, hungers, the physical side of you. Or, in a body dream, it may refer to an internal organ. (*see* Abdomen)

BELOW

If something or someone is below you, you may be feeling superior, or you are looking back on something, like your past. If you have climbed up to somewhere, then what you are looking back on is a more inclusive viewpoint.

BELT

If it is a clothing belt, it can suggest something that restrains you, gives support, or contributes to your image in some way. Occasionally, a belt refers to protection. If a belt used on a car or machine it may depict that your energy is lost.

BERRIES

The meaning of these depends on what the dream portrays. If the berries are poisonous, for example, it suggests possible contact with something that may poison your mind or disturbing thoughts. If the fruit is healthy, it may be contact with a nourishing experience. (*see* Food, Fruit)

BIBLE

This represents moral feelings or collective social wisdom, or perhaps your feelings or ideas about institutional religion.

BICEPS

These muscles show your confidence and ability to do things, or it can be your strength in relationship with another person. (*see* Body)

BICYCLE

This suggests personal effort or motivation. A bicycle may represent your first way of gaining independence. It also links with the acquiring of a difficult skill in regard to confidence and balance. For bicycle race, *see* Race.

BILL

To receive a bill often symbolizes a bill of reckoning. In other words, something you have done or thought is now producing consequences that require payment. (*see* Money)

BILLIARDS

Most games, with their winning and losing, their tactics, skill, and luck represent the game of life, with its difficulties, triumphs, and despairs. Billiards may also represent sexual intercourse. (*see* Games)

BINOCULARS

This shows the clarification of something obscure in your life, or the bringing closer of something or someone in the distance or future.

BIRDS

Many countries use the word bird to refer to a girl or woman. In Italy it means the male organ. But to dream of a bird may also suggest a sense of freedom from material ties. In ancient myths birds denoted the soul or freedom of a mind released from its constraints. Usually, however, the bird represents the mind and flights of fancy. It can also refer to how our minds can travel far away—in our imagination and dreams. (*see* Air)

Because the lifecycle of birds so clearly illustrates some of the most powerful transitions we face as humans, we use this symbol often in our dreams. So being in the nest and hatching depicts pregnancy, birth, and becoming independent. The first flight is an extraordinary thing, and is deeply felt as we struggle to exist unaided by parents—some of us never make it.

BIRTH

This represents a new beginning, a fresh start or beginning life under the influence of a new power. In Christianity, the new birth indicates opening to the transcendent power of change. Birth dreams can also be expressions of actual infant memories of birth, with all its difficulties, terrors, and events. In this way the unconscious emotions and fears may be made conscious in order to allow us to deal with them. Remember that birth of one part of us brings death to another. The womb experience dies when the baby is born to outer life, and as the baby dies the youth emerges, and so on.

BIRTHDAY

This sign shows good feelings, recognition and warmth regarding friends, or a change occurring. Maybe it is a special time when good things or favors can come to you. Dreaming of your birthday may suggest that you are in need of attention and love. If it is someone else's birthday, it can be designed to remind you of a social obligation or a need to show affection.

BIRTHRIGHT

This shows the innate qualities you are born with but may never utilize in life.

BLACK

This is the unknown, what you are unconscious of, feelings of evil, death, absence of knowledge, or the ability to see or understand. Because we cannot see in the dark, black can refer to activities that we are unaware of, or find difficult to navigate. This may cause anxiety. But black, like earth, is rich in possibilities,

and has the elements of growth. (*see* Colors)

If a black person appears in your dream, the meaning depends on what skin color you have. If you are white, it often means your most honest feelings, the person you are if you are not putting on your social front. It may also depict your instinctive urges. If you have black skin, then it is an ordinary dream about yourself. (*see* Man or Woman)

BLACKBIRD

This bird shows something, perhaps intuition, emerging from your unconscious. It can also be bad news as blackbirds are sometimes thought of as messengers of the dead. (*see* Bird)

BLACKSMITH

This symbol may be connecting you with your deep creative powers and masculine strength in shaping the metals of your life or your innate possibilities. It also depicts forcefulness or material creativeness. (*see* Iron)

BLAMED/BLAMING

This is most likely the feelings you have about being blamed or blaming someone else. Therefore the things to watch for in the dream in connection with blaming are: What are you blaming someone or something else for? Define what it is. Ask yourself if you are doing this in your waking life, and how deeply you feel about the issue. How valid is the blaming? Is the blaming a way of avoiding responsibility or efforts to change? While we are blaming someone or something, we do not direct our own life. This is because blaming is like saying, "What has happened to me is all due to 'so-and-so' or 'such-and-such.' Each time this happens it does this to me." If we stop the blaming and wonder whether we can take charge of the situation, then we gain more power to change. If you are blamed: Do you feel rightly accused? If so, perhaps you are taking on unnecessary feelings of failure. You may be overly self-critical or perhaps you are not letting yourself learn something important.

BLANKET

This usually links with protection from the cold, or being alone and wrapped up in your own feelings. It can also stand for what a "security blanket" represents for a child—a feeling of security when alone. Sometimes the blanket has associations with illness, sex, or caring.

BLASPHEMY

A denial or curse regarding your inner self, or latent possibilities. It can show free will turning away from possible direction within.

BLEACH

This can show a healing process, or the cleansing of old hurts or feelings. This can be an attempt to "clean up" your emotions or attitudes, especially if applied to clothes or pain.

BLEEDING *see* Blood.

BLINDNESS

You may be failing to see or understand something obvious. This may reflect an inability to see something about yourself, or to listen to what your intuition is telling you.

BLISTER

This represents an irritating or painful experience. It is something that has gradually hurt you over a period of time, or it can be protective attitudes.

BLIZZARD

If you see a blizzard, there are usually blocked or frozen emotions connected with this dream. It also suggests powerful and stormy feelings. (*see* Weather, Snow)

BLOCKAGE/BLOCKED

This is something that is stopping you from expressing yourself easily. Tensions resulting from withheld emotions can exist in the body for years, especially in the chest, neck, and back. Try using some visualization techniques regularly to get things flowing properly in your body again.

BLOOD

Because we usually associate blood with injury, blood in your dream mostly indicates hurt or pain of some sort; perhaps emotional pain. Blood may also signify a family connection or inherited traits. It also carries disease, so the dream may be using it to signify some danger or illness in some way. A heavy loss of blood can lead to death, so seeing bleeding can show a great loss of energy or motivation in your life. In a woman's dream it can link with monthly menstruation, but the dream will probably make this clear in some way. The speech idioms for blood include bad blood; blood from a stone; blood is thicker than water; blood money; draw first blood; in cold blood; in the blood; written in blood.

BLOSSOM

This represents the unfolding and expression of what was latent within yourself right from the beginning.

BLOWOUT/BLOW

This shows physical problems or injury, being let down by something unexpected, or a sudden delay in some area of your life that may be causing frustration or irritation.

BLUE

This color relates to the mind, religious feelings or intuition. It deals with expansion, such as when we sense new ideas and views. Dark blues, however, can link with anxiety or depression. The speech idioms for blue are many, and suggest the ways your dreams can use the color: the air was blue; baby blues; between the devil and the deep blue sea; blue in the face; blue moon; out of the blue. (*see* Color)

BOAT/SHIP

This often depicts how you are dealing with the ups and downs of life, with its tides, currents, and changing weather. Or perhaps the ship or boat is showing how life is dealing with you, rather than you with it. In many boat dreams the drama is actually about a relationship, what you face, what your involvement is with one or more other people. It can represent the storms or calms you meet. Therefore, in some dreams it can represent sexual adventures. Sometimes, the boat portrays the journey of your self-discovery as you investigate your unconscious. The voyage you take on it stands for your adventure into the unknown, and how you cope with what is experienced. In some myths, the boat carries the soul to the underworld or land of the dead, and here denotes contact with the changeless part of you.

BODY

The condition of your dream body often represents what you fear or feel about yourself, maybe unconsciously. For example, you may be frightened of illness, so dream of a sick body. You may lack confidence, and so dream you are lame or your face is twisted. In brief:

1. Your body, or another person's body, can represent: physical existence, the process of life in your body, as represented by maturing and aging, and the potential from which your growth occurs.

2. It can also represent an aspect of your personality, your experience, or memories.

3. A body of the opposite sex can depict your non-dominant side, the parts of you that are not given much expression.

4. Your body is an expression of your total history, not only of your own personal life, but also the countless generations and stages of history and evolution of which it is the latest version.

5. Your body in a dream can be a graphic illustration of your hidden feelings or worries, or your pains and strengths.

6. Dreaming of a body that has been killed or buried usually refers to events of your own past, especially deeply felt emotions or struggles. (*see* Abdomen, Arm, Face, Head, Leg) Speech idioms for the body include: over my dead body; body language; play dead; on my last legs; fresh legs; it costs an arm and a leg; shake a leg; don't let it go to your head; loggerheads; lose your head; make headway; make your head spin; hold that over my head; off the top of my head; like the back of my hand; out of hand; wash your hands of; offhanded; an old hand; stick your neck out; feet of clay; cold feet; jump in with both feet; itchy feet; swept off your feet; arms full; good arm; shot in the arm; twist my arm; rubberneck, etc.

BOIL
This represents a buildup of painful emotions.

BOMB
This shows explosive emotions or fears that terrify you. Your anger may explode and do you and others damage. The bomb may also suggest anxiety about unexpected events, or dangerous emotions about to explode.

BONE
This may indicate a deep hurt—you feel cut to the bone. It can also suggest inner strength. But

dream messenger

Many dreams bring us messages from the depths of our body processes. It is not uncommon to dream about foods to eat or avoid, vitamins or minerals that the body needs, or situations to be avoided for the sake of health.

often the bones we find in our dreams are old and indicate things from the past that we still carry with us. Another association is with death. There is often a sense of implication with the death of the people whose bones are found. This is because we have at some time denied or killed a part of our own emerging self or talents.

BOOK
This is a symbol of memories, ideas, a record or expression of yourself or others. It also links with learning or vicarious life experiences, or may be a way of escaping from the world.

BOOT *see* Shoes.

BORDER
You are probably meeting some barrier or hesitation. It can be a point in your growth where you may have to prove yourself or make changes. Crossing the border can bring a different life or life experience. Hesitations may stop you crossing. (*see* Frontier)

BOSS
This shows the prevailing major driving force in your life, such as ambition, desire, or love.

BOTTLE

This is often associated in dreams with the vagina. It may also connect with having resources, or whatever you associate with what is in the bottle, such as alcohol. It can also denote courage.

BOWEL *see* Anus.

BOX

This shows the things you store or hide inside you, such as memories or emotions. A closed box can represent the womb or emotions you repress. Depending on the size of the box, it can represent memories or treasured experiences. (*see* Chest)

BOY

If you know the boy, your dream is probably using his image to depict the qualities you see in him. You may see him as: clever, shrewd, weak, sensitive, a thinker, or a crook. In whatever way you see him, this represents the trait in yourself. If you are a male, the boy may also indicate yourself at that age, and what you felt and what issues you faced. If you are female, the boy can depict your growing ability to express yourself creatively, or what you feel about having a boyfriend. If you are a mother then it can relate to feelings about your son.

BOYFRIEND

This symbol shows what feelings or fears you are facing about your boyfriend. In dreams you explore not only your anxious feelings, but all your longings too. So difficult dreams about your boyfriend are usually about what you fear, not what the boyfriend will do. Dreaming about an ex-lover often shows that you have carried feelings with you from the relationship, and your dreams about him or her are trying to work out some way of feeling at ease within yourself about the breakup. This is especially true if the breakup was painful. Unless these emotions are freed from your past, they are not available for the present.

BRAIN

This relates to your thoughts, and intellectual faculty, your potential and creative ideas.

BRAKES

This shows your ability to control or let go of such things as anger and sexuality, but also your motivations or desires. If the brakes will not work, it is about feeling out of control. (*see* Car)

BREAD

This represents the physical needs or sustenance of your body. As it was often used in rituals to represent sharing of life and experience, it can also depict your link with others in a subtle way—the collective life. Occasionally, a loaf of bread is an unborn baby. (*see* Food)

BREAK/BREAKING/BROKEN

Breaking something in your dream suggests broken promises, a break in a relationship, or a shattered hope or ideal. There may be feelings of loss or hurt attached to this. So see if you can identify these in your everyday life.

BREASTS

In general, the breast represents a giving of yourself, or your own sexual pleasure. It is an expression of female love and nurture and sexuality. To go to a woman's breast in a dream may represent an expression of the baby's desire to be fed, loved and made to feel secure, that is, a regression or reliving of infant desires. A woman expresses male sexuality through her breasts, in that she fulfills the body of the infant. It may also represent emotional security.

BREATH

Breathing equates to being alive. The condition or speed of your breathing in the dream may depict your pace of life. If you are holding your breath, this shows you holding on, staying in control. It may also suggest fear or stress. Fast breathing shows excitement or stimulation. Being under water and not breathing indicates the womb, where we existed without breathing. It is also connected with a different awareness, where there are no sexual or biological drives, and no opposites. It is usually deeply peaceful but may be an escape from reality. (*see* Air)

BRIDE

This symbol is usually connected with marriage. The dream may be exploring your hopes and desires, or your anxieties or presentiments. A bride in your dream can also suggest love, receptivity, and fertility, perhaps a desire for physical love, marriage, and children. If you are an unmarried female, then it can point to the urge to leave home and experience marital pleasures and responsibilities. In a man's dream the bride often indicates his feelings and emotional nature. (*see* Marriage)

BRIDEGROOM

In a woman's dream seeing a bridegroom may express the desire to be married, or to find a loving partner. It may depict feelings about the man you want to marry, or show a move toward merging with your inner and outer capabilities. In a man's dream, the bridegroom mostly shows feelings about marriage, or an attempt to integrate both the conscious and unconscious.

BRIDGE

This is a link between opposing or different emotions, desires, or directions. It can relate to coping with difficulties. Sometimes, the bridge signifies changing from one phase of life to another. It can mean leaving something behind, like youth. It can be a link between people, such as someone you love. Or it can represent work, a link between you, and an opportunity.

BROOCH

This is often a statement about you in some way. Is it expressing a beautiful or ugly side of you? Or perhaps it has associations with family as an heirloom, or a person who gave it to you or remarked on it? (*see* Badge)

BROTHER

This symbol probably represents your feelings about a brother. These may include rivalry, anger, feelings of persecution, love and admiration, authority, or an outgoing ability to deal with the world. If you don't have a brother, it most likely depicts either a personality trait illustrated by the dream character, or your male side.

BUBBLE

This is often used in art, literature and dreams to represent the transience of the world, worldly ambition and our physical life. It can depict the soul and its relationship with the eternal.

The bubble may burst, but the consciousness that experienced being a body and a person remains.

BUD

This is your undeveloped side. It can also represent the sexual organs, full of sensual sensitivity.

BUDDHA

This represents the part of you that is eternal. (*see* Christ)

BUILDING *see* House.

BULL

The bull connects with your powerful sexual, protective, and family feelings. If you are frightened of the bull, it suggests you are anxious about your sexual drive or aggressiveness. The bull also denotes bodily or mental strength and inherited qualities or possessions.

BULLET

This can signify a desire to, or feelings of, hurt. It can be force, sexual impregnation, or the penis in its aggressive form.

BURGLAR

In women's dreams, the burglar is often a fear of sexual intercourse or being entered unwillingly. In male dreams, it may be guilt about stolen love, or goods. It can be a cry from your unconscious to contact your repressed side.

BURIAL

Connected with death, burial can represent fear of personal death, or that of loved ones. It can also be an unconscious desire to see others dead or removed. But it is often used in dreams when we feel buried away from society, or by life. Sometimes, we repress a memory, emotion, desire, or talent. Our past is buried within us. Your dream may indicate letting go of the past, of something dead, or allowed to die. The earth can also represent your mother or the past. Burial may therefore symbolize being dominated by an over-possessive mother, or the inability to break away from her. If you are being buried alive, it may be birth memories and fears.

BUS

This is something you are doing or undertaking with other people or in public. Sometimes this relates to feeling overweight. A bus stop suggests waiting for something to get you involved, or take you to where you want to go.

BUTCHER

This may denote a fear of someone's anger; or being a butcher may symbolize aggressiveness, worldly attitudes, or a lack of love.

BUTTERFLY

This is the beautiful creature that emerges from an unpromising start. It relates to vulnerable beauty or the changeless state that emerges from physical experience. It is also transformation.

BUY/BUYING

This is your desire for things, or searching for something you want. It is about making or being able to make choices. (*see* Shop)

CAB *see* Taxi.

CACTUS

This refers to something where you are likely to be hurt, or being "prickly" in a relationship.

CAFÉ

This is about feelings of relaxation, a connection with others, or loneliness if you are alone. (*see* Food, Barroom)

CAGE/CELL

This points to your feelings of frustration and perhaps anger, or even a sense of defeat or emptiness. The prison in your dreams is of your own making, created out of your attitudes and fears. So it is important to define just what you feel in the cage, and what the associated feelings are with the cage/cell itself, and all the other people involved. (*see* Prison)

CAKE

This indicates pleasure and sensual satisfaction. It may even relate to childhood pleasure and rewards, or marriage or birth if it is a celebratory cake. (*see* Bread, Food)

CALENDAR

The calendar represents the passage of time or a schedule you need to remember. It can also be memories or intuitive thoughts of events times, or looking forward to the future.

CALF

This is the vulnerability of your babyhood, or perhaps one of your children. If you are a farmer, it may have associations to do with farming. (*see* Animal)

CALL BOX *see* Telephone.

CAMEL

This may relate to a sterile or dry situation you are in, and your ability to deal with it. Occasionally, the camel is also associated with being pregnant, because of its hump.

CAMERA

This symbol suggests something to do with memory, the recording of impressions, or the attempt to capture a fleeting idea or experience. It can relate to noticing events or people and recording fleeting impressions. (*see* Photo)

CAN *see* Tin.

CANAL

The dream is probably a comment on the way you direct your emotions and energy, and what this control or decision making means in connection with your relationships and goals. There may be a link with relaxation or pleasure if you have vacationed on a canal, or it can relate to other associations if you live near one. (*see* River, Water)

CANCER

Any dream including the subject of cancer may connect with fear of the illness, and in some rare dreams, a warning. But usually it links with a part of your nature or emotions that do not harmonize well with the rest of you. Therefore, they create conflict or even a threat to your well-being. If another person figures strongly in your dream, it may suggest that their influence is undermining your own well-being.

CANDLE

This often associates with the penis. It is also a symbol of wisdom, understanding, and the passage of time—your own life passing away. If you light a candle in darkness, it shows confidence and awareness of dealing with the anxieties and ignorance that can emerge in the dark. It may also indicate a birth or prayer. (see Fire, Light)

CANDY

This is a return to a childlike way of gaining pleasure or reward. It may link with dieting or your feelings about it, if you struggle with a sugar hangover.

CANE

This suggests the use of authority or aggression, either by you or toward you. Sometimes it links with memories and feelings about school or parents. If it is used for walking, it may suggest some infirmity or maturity.

CANNIBAL

This is the part of you that may be living off the lives or efforts of others, instead of producing them for yourself. If you are threatened by cannibals in the dream, then it is others possibly trying to live off your efforts.

CANNON

This represents the male sexual organ, and aggressiveness or destructive desires.

CANOE see Boat.

CANYON see Valley.

CAP see Hat.

CAPITAL

If it is a city such as London, New York, or Rome, the capital represents the center of your material interests, your physical life and opportunities. But obviously, if you are a Roman Catholic, Rome probably represents your religious beliefs.

CAPTAIN

This reflects your daring, active, positive side. It may show how you relate to father figures or dominant authoritative men. It may therefore depict the side of your nature that is capable, the part that is in touch with the wider issues in your life and makes informed decisions. (see Admiral)

CAPTIVE

This shows a fear of being bound or subject to other people, or of being trapped by circumstances in your life, marriage, or work. It can also be guilt about deeds or desires. You may be a prisoner of your own moral beliefs, ideas, opinions, or emotions, depending on the dream's context. (see Prison)

CASSETTE *see* CD.

CAR

Many car dreams dramatically represent control, or lack of it, as you encounter the opportunities or obstacles in your life. This control is sometimes illustrated by who is driving the car, indicating whether you are taking the lead or allowing someone else to direct the relationship. But there are many other associations with your dream car, such as your energy and drive represented by the engine; your sexuality showing whether you can attract a partner by the type of car you have; your relationship by seeing who is in the car with you; your family life from an outing, and whether you are included; your body by the malfunctioning of some part of the car. The dream of crashing or being involved in a crash can sometimes be about your anxiety about driving, but it is often about the sort of difficult collisions you sometimes have in relationships or life situations, such as when you are at work.

CARD/GREETING CARD

This may relate to thoughts or feelings about other people. It may be about someone that you want to hear from.

CARDS

These denote fate, luck, or the unexpected or unplanned events in life. They represent the skill of managing a social life and coping with what life "deals" you. Cards are sometimes associated with the devil or bad luck.

CARNIVAL

This indicates dropping social or moral restraints by letting go. It can also depict creativity, your social connections, or, alternatively, sexual opportunity.

CARPENTER

This is your ability to shape desires or ideas, and how you build something in your life from raw materials. It illustrates your power of reasoning, and how you control and shape your emotions. (*see* Wood, Tree, Roles)

CARPET

Luxury, richness or splendor is depicted by a carpet. It sometimes represents insulation against worldly influence or physical desires, or flights of soul or imagination. A richly colored, deep carpet may indicate the richness of your mind and feelings, a threadbare carpet may suggest feelings of impoverishment. Speech idioms show other meanings—sweep it under the carpet; on the carpet; roll out the red carpet; a rug pulled out from under one's feet.

CARRY/CARRYING

This usually suggests you possess, or are carrying something within yourself. What it is depends very much on what you are carrying. If it is a positive living thing, can you acknowledge that you have this energy or feeling and can use it to your own benefit? If it is a dead thing ask yourself where in your body or feelings you are carrying this deadness. Why do you need to hold on to something that is not living and growing? Can you now let go of it? If it is an object, is this a useful object? Does it suggest a burden or a possibility? In what way can it be useful? Perhaps it is a waste of energy, such as old memories that are not productive. If so, can you let go of them? If it is a useful thing, what talent or skill do you have that you may not be using?

CART *see* Chariot.

CARTRIDGE *see* Bomb.

CARVE

This symbol suggests that you are working on yourself and carving out qualities. Maybe events are leaving indelible marks, memories, fears, or regrets on your feelings or thoughts. You are working hard at difficult situations and carving out a niche for yourself.

CASE *see* Bag.

CASH *see* Bank, Money.

CASKET

This suggests secret or hidden memories, or maybe wonders or special things hidden in yourself. (*see* Coffin for burial casket)

CASTLE

This depicts the techniques you have developed, possibly in childhood, to defend yourself against attacks from other people. This type of defense is a way of surviving in what is often a harsh world, but in adulthood such defenses need to be reevaluated to see if they are still valid or relevant for you.

CASTRATE/CASTRATION

This represents a fear of not coping sexually or losing sexual confidence or desire. It is to do with cutting off deeper feelings, sympathies, ambitions, and energies. To cut off the penis or testicles illustrates the action of repressing the feelings, emotions, and urges represented by them. You may deny or repress your urges through fear, because you feel guilty about your sexuality, or due to convictions that you are inferior or repulsive. The denial may also be through a dread of pain, the sort of emotional agony that arises from bad times experienced in a past relationship.

CAT

You may have felt a lot of affection for a cat, and so associate it with sensual or even sexual pleasure. It can also represent your physical need to be cared for or to care for someone. In a woman's dream, the cat may depict her need to care for a child. Idioms include: let the cat out of the bag; cool cat; fat cat. (*see* Kitten, Animal)

CATACLYSM

As dream images represent your own life and feelings in some way, fearing the end of the world depicts the powerful and threatening inner and outer changes that accompany major transitions. The transition from childhood to adolescence, for example, is the end of the world that existed for the individual up to that point. Such points of transition occur several times in the life of anyone who dares to grow and adapt. The end of fertility in menopause for women, the leaving home for children, the loss of a job, retirement, divorce can all be represented by the end of the world, or a world. (*see* Atom Bomb)

CATACOMB

This reflects an exploration of your inner contents or past experiences and their effect on your present life. If the dream has an air of mystery, it indicates a descent into the unconscious, to meet feelings about death and rebirth, deception and wisdom. Sometimes this symbol can represent a search for your inner roots, lasting values, and underlying abilities, or it can be showing your unconscious link with your forebears.

CATERPILLAR

This symbol shows the sort of changes we make from infancy to maturity. It is sometimes used as an image of the penis. As a chrysalis it shows the power of transformation that is present in all of us through the power of life, or it shows the need to withdraw as the process of change occurs.

CAVE

This is associated with a woman's sexual organs. It can indicate the womb or the experience of life in the womb, prior to birth. It can also mean contact with the past, with your inner life, or sometimes the treasures of past levels of consciousness. If there is a spring in the cave, it is a link with your core self. Apart from a spring, there may be early man or a snake in the cave. The ancient man is your earliest level of awareness. But the spring and snake can bring you some healing and peace, for you may have tapped into very deep sources of healing.

CD

There can be several associations to choose from with this symbol, so you need to consider the rest of your dream to decide which is appropriate. It can show the feelings that music arouse, or be an indication of stored memories or work. If you make CDs, then it can relate to your ambitions or connect with some aspect of your creativity.

CEILING

This relates to something out of your reach or above you, or something that defines the limits or extent of your mind or ambitions. This means it has a connection with your self-image and what you unconsciously feel about who you are. It can also suggest the influence of others, such as when people live above you.

CELEBRITY

Meeting or being a celebrity may show that you desire attention and acclaim. Or the famous person may be your own potential, often unacknowledged and projected onto the dream character. If you are deferring to the character or feel they have power over you, it may be showing how you relate to a parent or how you deal with feelings about your own

instant interpreter

A sea journey cuts us off from usual activity. In inescapable contact with fellow travelers, it also offers the possibility of missing the boat, which may be irreversible. This all points to being always amid natural forces, times, and tides of activity. Your sea dreams will indicate your relationship with this.

status. If you have difficulty relating to the famous person, you may be struggling with respecting yourself or your desires, ambitions, and efforts to become successful at work. Sometimes, the person may, because of their life or role, represent a particular quality, such as courage or love, or "ruling" drives in life, such as authority, etc.

CELLAR *see* Basement, Cave.

CEMETERY

You are probably dealing with thoughts and feelings about death, your family heritage of attitudes or traditions. In a few cases, the dream may be a form of contact with someone you know who is dead. The cemetery may also refer to things in your life you have "buried." It can also be about any melancholy in your life or feeling "different" from other people. Another possibility is a relationship that you think is "dead and buried."

CENTAUR

This has a similar meaning to the Horse, but indicates a greater harmony between your animal instincts, or spontaneous urges, and your social, rational self.

CENTER

If it is a person or thing in the middle of something, your dream is emphasizing the importance of the thing or person. If the middle is between opposites, it suggests either conflict or balance, depending upon your feelings in the dream.

CEREMONY

Your dream is probably reiterating something that is taking place in your life. For example, at puberty your body carries you from youth to manhood or womanhood. This is an incredibly important event, yet society seldom acknowledges you as a changed person. Your dream may do this, and even reveal some of the mysterious new qualities you have as you move from one stage of life to another.

CHAIN

This relates to attitudes, beliefs, and fears that create some form of bond, bondage, or limitation. It also depicts strength or the feelings or links that bind or connect you to others, to work, a religion, or a set of ideas. A link in the chain represents the strength or weakness of one person, or of a particular attitude or aspect of your strength or linking power.

soul solution

While involved in difficult divorce negotiations, Marianne dreamed of a dinosaur eating everything in its path. She quickly saw that this was exactly how she had been taught to see herself when a child—someone who grabbed to get her needs. Seeing that this was a false self-image, she was able to bargain realistically for a fair share of jointly owned property.

CHAIR

A symbol of passivity, rest, or a relaxed attitude. It can also suggest inactivity, receptivity, or openness, possibly even escapism. A wheelchair often indicates that you have been "in-valid" in some way, or you see the person in the chair as being in some way an invalid.

CHAMELEON

This indicates changing emotions, instability, or a sense of duty. Changing values are occurring to suit outer events or adaptability.

CHAMPAGNE

This denotes luxury, being rich, worldly success, a celebration or a prelude to a sexual relationship. (*see* Alcohol)

CHAPEL *see* Church.

CHARIOT

The difference between this symbol and the car lies in it being drawn by horses. It therefore shows how your internal, spontaneous feelings, or your natural processes, such as growth and aging, are carrying you along. (*see* Horse, Car)

CHARITY/SECONDHAND STORE

This relates to the usefulness of useless items, or a searching for your needs or things you want in what is usually seen as worthless. Perhaps it points to the recycling of past experiences, or things such as ideas, skills, or attitudes, you have got from other people. Maybe these are your discarded or forgotten experiences. (*see* Shop)

CHASED/CHASING

Anything that moves toward you in a dream usually signifies that you are becoming more aware of it and feeling it more intensely. So being chased in a dream usually connotes that you are fearing something strongly and are trying to avoid confronting it. This is not usually a good policy as you can never get away from yourself. If you are chasing something, it shows that you are making an effort to gain something. Try to define in your mind what is holding you back.

CHASM *see* Valley, Abyss.

CHEAT/CHEATED/CHEATING

In some way you are not living up to your real feelings abut your life. Or perhaps you are feeling betrayed, or have had your trust abused.

CHECK

This indicates a valuable promise received or given to someone. It can be something owed to you, or perhaps an outcome of your labors or talent. (*see* Bill, Money)

CHESS

This shows the skills and strategies you use in meeting the circumstances of your life. It may also point to careful scheming or planning to win, or to defeat an opponent. (*see* Games)

CHEST

Sometimes, this points to a connection with your physical chest. But most often it shows what emotions, memories and passions you are storing within you—literally in your chest. You may hide precious and loving feelings too, keeping them locked up, or shut away inside you.

CHEW

This indicates you are carefully considering or experiencing something. It also links with analyzing a problem or possibly absorbing something. (*see* Eating)

CHICKEN

In many cases this depicts nourishment or doing well in life. It may also refer to the female side of a male or being "chicken" or scared. The hen depicts a mothering influence. (*see* Bird)

CHICKS

This is a reference either to your own babyhood or events linked with it. It can also relate to your baby or babies. (*see* Bird)

CHILD

This symbol usually refers to youthful memories or attitudes that still live on inside you. If you become a child in a dream, you may be feeling immature in some way. The child also points to what is growing and eager in you, or what is vulnerable and perhaps easily influenced in its growth. The dream events will give you insight into what is happening to your "child" self. If this is one of your own children, look up son or daughter. (*see* Boy, Girl, Son, Daughter)

CHILDBIRTH

This indicates the emergence of a new part of you that is perhaps difficult to coax into life. It may show you bringing to consciousness a new developing part of you which has previously remained dormant or unexpressed. This may also refer to the desire to have children,

your own pregnancy, or memories of your own birth. Sometimes, giving birth to a child links to new beginnings and it can mean that one way of life is just ending while another, new one is beginning. (*see* Birth)

CHIMNEY

This relates to the female sex organs. It is the channel of female energies or libido. It can also refer to smoking, the birth canal, or be a sign of inner warmth. If it is belching black smoke, it suggests the grim mechanized side of our culture, centered on commercial production instead of humanity.

CHIN

A chin represents resolve, sternness, obstinacy, or character. It is your ability to take the blows of life on the chin.

CHOKE/CHOKED/CHOKING

This is not being able to swallow or accept something. It is also an emerging emotion or memory.

CHRIST

There can be several associations with Christ or Jesus. The first may be whatever you feel about organized religion. In this sense Christ can depict the forces in and around you that create moral pressure from the normal standards lived by society. So He can show the pressure to conform to what is considered normal. Christ is also an internal sense of how your life measures up to the universal life you constantly sense around you. This can be a feeling of what your highest potential is, and how well or badly you have manifested it. Sometimes, this is experienced as a meeting with truth, the truth about yourself. In some people's lives, Christ or Jesus can be an active compensatory force. For example, a baby who does not receive love and contact may later in life create a powerful love of Jesus or some other holy figure. From this figure they internally receive love, which compensates for the earlier lack of affection, enabling emotional growth to occur.

CHRISTEN/CHRISTENING

This can depict a change, a decision that you have made to open up to the influence of the best in you. A christening also points to a greater connection with the goodwill in the community and a feeling of fellowship or sisterhood. Like baptism, it is also about washing away the influence and habits of the past, and making a start without that burden. (*see* Baptism)

CHRYSALIS

This shows an outer inactivity, while you are inwardly going through great change. It can relate to a new aspect of yourself that is getting ready to emerge, or it can sometimes be a desire to retreat from the world. (*see* Butterfly, Caterpillar)

CHURCH

This may show your religious beliefs or feelings about organized religion. It sometimes shows the sense you have of your link with all the life around you, or the lack of that awareness. It also represents orthodox beliefs or the dogma of religious organizations.

CIGAR/CIGARETTE

In some ways this may be similar to alcohol, as it depicts something that can change the way you feel. But as with alcohol, it does so at a cost. It is also habit-forming. So smoking can depict the sort of short-term stimulus and good feeling that comes from something that is potentially harmful. It can also link with dependence, anxiety, and the ways you deal with it. It relates to social contact, how positively or negatively people respond to you, or even worries about cancer. It sometimes depicts male sexuality.

CINEMA

This can be a mirroring of the dramas and passions taking place in you, perhaps unconsciously. It may be a way of exploring issues in your life. If cinemas link with romantic memories, then it can show you how to use the feelings you experienced.

CIRCLE

This connotes completeness, wholeness, and all the parts of your being: mind, body, and spirit. It also represents the universe as a whole or harmony and perfect symmetry. It sometimes symbolizes an enclosure or restraining influence or protection, or it can be the womb or female sexual organs. It may also depict emptiness, receptiveness, or a fertile condition. In some dreams you may walk in a circle, or be spontaneously moved in a circle. This means that you are enclosing, protecting, or bringing the enclosed under the power that caused you to move in a circle. Some speech idioms show other meanings: going round in circles; circle of friends; magic circle.

CIRCUMCISION

Dreaming of circumcision may be connected either with feelings of losing some sexual power, or of cleaning the penis. In some cases, it can indicate the memory of being circumcised. Of course it may also be associated with being Jewish.

CIRCUS

This shows the training or discipline that has been put upon your own instincts and natural feelings. The circus indicates the hoops that you have to jump through in order to survive in life or earn a decent living.

CITY OR TOWN

This shows your relationship with strangers, with life on the street, and your interaction with society and the many choices it confronts you with about direction, relationships, or activities. It also relates to your sense of community, along with the mental and emotional environment in which you live. It can represent a work opportunity, or just opportunity. The town of your birth depicts a familiar way of life, how you usually go about things, or the life you lived while you were young. If it is a strange town, then you may be exploring something new in your activities, possibly relationships with strangers. Or perhaps you are facing new or changing attitudes or a different way of life, new choices or opportunities.

CLAM

This indicates emotional withdrawal. Some part of your feelings may be closed. The clam suggests there is some sort of outer hardness to protect a sensitivity or hurt. This can often be the defensive shell we use to avoid pain or sexual or emotional involvement. It can also relate to the female sexual organs.

CLASSROOM

As so many impressions are formed at school, the dream image of a classroom usually expresses something of these past experiences. It may relate to study, to your relationship with authority, or it can be about issues of performance. Think back, and try to remember what particular experiences were etched into your psyche during all those years at school.

CLIFF

The cliff represents a fear of, or the possibility of, falling in the eyes of others or yourself. It can be a fall from power or achievement, or a fear of not being able to achieve. Other meanings of this symbol can be that you are faced with the feeling of being on edge, facing danger, making a difficult decision, taking a risk, encountering a barrier or the unknown, depending on the dream's content. If you are on top of the cliff it can give you a wider view of life, one that includes death.

CLIMB/CLIMBED/CLIMBING

This indicates that you are trying to overcome, or rise above, difficulties. You may be trying to achieve a new viewpoint, or to learn or develop a new understanding. Sometimes, we climb in a dream to get away from something or to get out of a current difficulty. We also climb to reach something, and in doing so may take a risk. If you are approaching middle age, climbing a hill can represent the first half of your life, and going downhill for the years ahead.

CLOCK

This may refer to your sense of connection with other people, duties, or the disciplines you place upon yourself. The clock can sometimes represent your span of life, and the ticking, your heart. It may be saying, how much time do you have left? What time of your life is it? Speech idioms show the many ways we use time in phrases: good times; bad times; no time like the present; haven't got time; now is the time; time stood still.

CLOSE

This can represent shutting something out, some divide, or not wishing to know, feel, or experience a situation. It may depict fear of being entered, or a fear of sex. But it can also suggest protection and privacy, or even decision making if you close a door against someone or something.

CLOSET

This can depict different social skills or attitudes you use in meeting people or gaining confidence. The closet may also depict feelings about a past relationship, if it is one that was in a house you shared. To be trapped in a closet suggests that past feelings or attitudes are restricting you in some way.

CLOTHES

These can often show ideas and feelings about how others see you, or how you like to be seen. Clothes also allow you to change how people relate to you so they can represent the different ways you express yourself. They may disguise what you really feel, or cover up something. Occasionally, clothes represent the attitudes you use to protect yourself or fend off other people. Underclothes, such as an undershirt or petticoat, refer to your less obvious feelings and attitudes. Armor and protective clothing refer to the attitudes you use to protect yourself against what you feel may be an attack or painful. Changing clothes shows how you can express yourself in different ways or different moods. Children's or teenage clothes in an adult's dream suggest youthful attitudes or behavior. The wrong sort of clothing is probably saying that your social behavior is not appropriate. (*see* particular items of clothing—Coat, Hat, Pants, Panties)

CLOUDS

Very often clouds appear in dreams where there are spiritual or religious feelings. If the clouds are dull, then it suggests worry or depression of some kind that is obscuring your best feelings.

CLOWN

This symbol depicts feelings of being a fool or the readiness to be a fool for the sake of love or your beliefs. It can suggest feeling foolish in your present situation, or even hiding pain under clowning behavior. The clown can also represent the irrational side of you. He can show different aspects of your personality that burst out without any apparent reason, leading you to do certain things that are not to your advantage.

COAL

This is something that has been dormant for ages that you have brought to consciousness so that it can benefit you.

COAT

We all have different modes of behavior, and the coat, unless it is very special, represents your everyday self and the responses and attitudes you use when meeting different people. (*see* Clothes)

COCKEREL

This bird brings a warning, or indicates aggression, masculinity, or the male sex organ. (*see* Birds)

COFFEE

Drinks such as coffee represent a stimulus similar to alcohol, which can change how you feel and act. They release energy and emotions, change feelings, and can shift and alter moods and the way you express your feelings. Coffee may also represent sociability, friendship, or the giving of affection. (*see* Alcohol)

COFFIN

Thoughts and feelings about death are often in the background of your mind, and dreaming of a coffin suggests you may be exploring how you will relate to your own demise. If your coffin dream includes another person you may be subconsciously worrying about their health, or fear that you may lose them in the near future. The process inside you that produces dreams always links death with rebirth, unless you paint its face with deep anxiety or worry. (*see* Death)

COIN

Sometimes a coin has similar symbolism to a circle. It can also link with feelings of worth or things you love. (*see* Bank, Money)

COLD/COLDNESS

This suggests repressed or withheld emotions, desires, and probably your sexuality. Sometimes, it means you are feeling neglected or "left out in the cold." Occasionally, cold and coldness can be connected with feelings about death.

COLLISION

You are obviously feeling confronted by something difficult to avoid. Perhaps conflict is involved, or it may indicate an unexpected event or carelessness. (*see* Car)

COLORS

In dreams, colors usually show shades of feeling, or attitudes of mind. Many people seldom dream in color, so when it appears, it is often to do with strong emotions in the dream. This is particularly true where red appears. It is therefore worthwhile defining what feelings accompany the color in your dream. (*see* Blue, Green, Orange, Red, Yellow)

COMB

This may be describing something you do to straighten out your thinking or to change how you appear to others. (*see* Hair)

COMET

This can show influences touching your life that are subtle but pervasive. It can perhaps signify change or new experiences.

COMIC

This represents a sense of humor, or something that is not serious.

COMPASS

This indicates your sense of direction or decision making. It may relate to expressing what is your best way forward in life, and the ability to continue when facing opposition and other confusing events.

COMPLEXION

This relates to your feelings about how you appear, or how you look to other people.

COMPOST

This is linked to something in your experience that has been thought of as outworn or useless that can be transformed into some available energy or into a new function.

COMPUTER

This can link with thoughts, but also with different aspects of the computer, such as the way we use it to enhance creativity and communication. So it can represent mental abilities or personal potential. The hard disk is mostly to do with memory, but particularly your extended memory and unconscious. (*see* E-mail, Internet, Modem, CD)

COMRADE *see* Friend.

CONDOM *see* Contraceptive.

CONFESS/CONFESSING/ CONFESSION

Sometimes a confession in a dream comes from a very deep place. It may involve a great deal of truth or passionate feelings. So it is worthwhile trying to make contact with the feelings and insights. Where the confession is the Catholic rite, it will probably link with beliefs connected with Catholicism.

CONFORM/CONFORM-ING/CONFORMITY

This is one of the most deeply engraved of human behaviors, so when you have conformity or nonconformity in your dream you need to understand why. Try to define what is leading to one or the other, and what is really involved.

CONJURER

This symbol may be referring to self-deceptions, or the deception of others. But it may also point to the magical abilities your unconscious has. The mind too can shift and change amazingly. It can create apparent realities out of thin air, as it does in your imagination or in your dreams. (*see* Roles)

CONSTIPATION

This represents inner tension, withholding feelings, or lack of self-expression or self-esteem. It may also be referring to a physical problem that you have.

CONTORTION/CONTORTIONIST

This indicates mental and emotional fluidity or a wide range of feelings. If the dream has some darker feelings in it, however, the contortionist may be saying that you are getting yourself twisted up in knots to solve a difficult problem. So ask yourself, are you succeeding?

CONTRACEPTIVE

There are a number of possible associated feelings with this symbol. In recent times the condom has been seen as a means of preventing AIDS, so if the contraceptive is a condom it can reflect worries about sexual contacts. It may also represent feelings or attitudes regarding responsibility. Certainly it connects in some way with sexual decisions and feelings, and also pregnancy. With the pill, there may be a connection with your decisions about motherhood. (*see* Condom)

CONTROL/CONTROLLED/ CONTROLLING

The balance between control and letting go are enormously important in life. Many skills, such as driving, require a lot of learned patterns of control. But if control is too rigid we may not be able to access latent potential or creativity as there needs to be an openness for these to arise. Use visualization techniques to explore a dream dealing with control, to find out from your inner wisdom what is the most fruitful way forward in the present circumstances.

CONVENT

This might suggest introspection, or some measure of retirement from external activities. It is important to see if such withdrawal arises from anxiety or decisiveness. The convent may of course relate to your past experience and feelings connected with it, or your religious beliefs. (*see* Church)

CONVICT

The convict may be depicting your sense of meeting with a part of you that has been treated as anti-social or which has not been allowed freedom of expression. In a few cases it may also represent a play on words to do with conviction. (*see* Prison)

COOK/COOKING

The cook may be illustrating practical life skills that make your life experience more palatable. Cooking may also link to motherhood or responsibility, perhaps of feeding your own family. It can also portray reproduction. If you are cooking food for someone in your dream, it can indicate you are giving yourself to someone. (*see* Food, Oven)

COOKIE

This denotes childhood pleasure, or the giving of pleasure.

COPPER (Metal)

This represents warmth; firmness with warmth or something durable yet soft and impressionable. It is sometimes linked with love through its astrological connection with Venus. Because it is so often used as an alternative aid for arthritis as a bracelet, there may also be some link with this.

CORAL

This can show beautiful inner experiences, ideas, inspirations, or intuitions. Or it can be something that develops naturally out of sight, or in the unconscious.

CORD

This sometimes suggests the weaving together of many smaller interests to one purpose, for strength. There is also a link with restriction, being tied, or even internal knots through tension or ties that are painful. Therefore, there may be some indication of a relationship being involved in the dream, along with the things that bind or tie us to other people. Breaking or cutting the cord suggests breaking with relationships that bind you, or cutting ties that have held you.

CORK

If the cork in your dream is floating it shows confidence, perseverance, high spiritedness, the ability to rise above circumstances or to win through troubles. If the cork is in a bottle, it may refer to feeling compressed, or perhaps being in a bottleneck situation where your progress is impeded. Alternatively, it can indicate keeping something preserved or unavailable.

CORN

This represents fertility or the rewards of your life or labor. It also can mean nourishment and your ability to survive without going hungry.

CORNER

If you are in a corner, depending on the dream, it may show you with little room to maneuver in your life, or in a relationship. You may be feeling trapped or see no way out of the situation. It can also suggest a complete change of direction, a meeting, a turning point in your attitudes, or approach to something. If you are turning a corner, it can literally mean that you are undertaking a new phase in your life, or making some changes. Perhaps you are doing something that opens up a new opportunity or view of things, whether helpful or difficult, depending on the dream.

CORPSE

These are feelings or actions you have denied. For example, you may kill your love for someone if they hurt you. This can be shown as a dead body in your dreams. It can also be a feeling, such as sympathy or forgiveness, that you have deadened. You may say, "Why should I forgive them? They do not deserve it," and this attitude can prevent parts of your inner feelings from being expressed consciously. It can also represent a fear of death or a desire to see someone dead or out of the way. In a few dreams, the corpse represents feelings about disease, human vulnerability, and mortality. (*see* Death)

CORRIDOR

This suggests you are feeling in some sort of "in-between state," as can happen when you are moving from one situation to another. Occasionally, the corridor even suggests the experience of birth. If the corridor provokes difficult feelings, it may be depicting your emotions of being unable to get out of a bad situation. It may also suggest a direction produced by circumstances, or even the female genitals. (*see* White)

COSMETIC

This indicates femininity or the mask we wear in hiding our true feelings or thoughts from others. It can be our attempts not to see ourselves as we are, or not to face facts. Sometimes, it is skin problems, or trying to improve yourself.

COUGH/COUGHING

This represents something, such as a feeling, a painful memory, or something you have not expressed that is felt as an irritant.

COUNTRYSIDE

This shows your feelings of relaxation, and what you are without trying. So it portrays your natural or spontaneous state, or the natural life forces alive in you. If the countryside is wild and rugged or stormy, it can suggest you are encountering a difficult time in your growth. The countryside often depicts moods. So a rainy day can suggest a quiet or slightly withdrawn mood. A sunny environment links to higher feelings of pleasure and hope. In country lanes in dreams, you often meet what is unbidden and spontaneous in you. This may be disturbing, because it may come in the form of a wolf or animal that you feel you cannot control. It is important to find some sort of working relationship with such an animal.

COUPLE

This symbol depends a great deal on the dream. It can suggest your parents, a marriage or a relationship. It is certainly about a relationship or partnership of some kind. Whether the indication is positive or negative depends on the couple in the dream.

COUSIN

The weaknesses or strengths you see in this cousin are being used to illustrate those things in yourself. (*see* Family)

COVER

Usually we cover something to hide or protect it. It can also link with feelings of inclusiveness or togetherness if you cover yourself and someone else. If you are covered in something, for example, dust, oil, etc then it suggests a condition you are in that will need defining by imagining yourself in the situation and taking note of what you feel.

COW

This represents femininity, motherhood or female sexual feelings. It can also suggest lack of intelligence.

CRAB

This symbol evokes fear or strong emotion causing tension within, especially abdominally. This may be due to fear or guilt of sensual pleasure. It may also represent outer hardness or cynicism covering inner softness, or outer hardness and greed in life. If the crab is threatening someone, it points to a desire to cause pain to others. Being nipped by a crab may indicate psychosomatic pain or illness.

CRATER

This refers to the responses left by something that hurt you in the past. It can be a memory of an old hurt, old emotion or pain, or a frightening situation. If volcanic activity is involved, then it is a deep hurt with unexpressed emotions.

CREAM

This shows good times or pleasure, unless you have an allergy to dairy products. It may then suggest irritants you are taking that appear to be pleasurable.

CREATURES

Sometimes we dream about creatures that are not like any animal we know, perhaps they are ancient, or mixtures of plants and animals. These can represent our fear of things, such as bacteria, or illness due to micro-organisms. Occasionally, they may even represent what such an illness is doing in the body. But frequently they point to the wonderful cellular activity and processes in your body, or the unconscious activities of the mind.

CREDIT CARD

This often links identity or social power and can represent the ability to move around and pay your way. It can link with feelings of ease and relaxation that can be destroyed if the credit card is lost or stolen, or if you are in debt. (*see* Money)

CRESCENT

A symbol of femininity, intuition, and receptiveness. A crescent moon suggests an ending or new beginning.

CRIED/CRY/CRYING

This is usually a direct expression of feelings experienced in the dream. But occasionally you can cry in the dream without knowing why, and then it usually links with emotions that you have not allowed yourself to express, and which have been pushed out of sight. If possible, it is best to let these surface.

CRIPPLE

This symbol is possibly a portrayal of the attitudes in yourself that stand in the way of you living a satisfying life and fulfilling your potential. It may also suggest past hurts that have crippled you and that you are trying to heal. (*see* Body, Leg, Right, Left)

CROCODILE *see* Alligator.

CROSS

Starting with its most popular uses, it can depict a trial we face in life, the cross we have to bear. It can also mean completion or finality, even death. In Christianity, the cross also has many meanings. It represents the religion as a whole; Christ's suffering; people's suffering in the name of their religious beliefs; the strength of one's beliefs; or it can be a sign of goodness

dream messenger

"Falling dreams" may be seen as fear of losing control, but they can also signify letting go of control. When you fall, you have to let go, and this can show that it is sometimes necessary to let old attitudes and perspectives fall away.

and power to ward off evil. The symbol of the cross also means the difficulties in surrendering individual will to the will of the community/communion.

CROSSING

If you are crossing a road or a river in your dream, it suggests that you are making a change of some sort. The change may be in connection with a relationship or a way of life, such as moving from being single to married, or moving into employment. If there is danger involved in any way, it shows the fears and difficulties you are meeting in making the change. When you see a friend cross a river and you cannot, this sometimes indicates their death.

CROSSROADS

The crossroads relates to making decisions and a convergence of different desires, or it can be the need to choose a direction, and therefore a turning point in life. Alternatively, it may represent indecision, a fear of not doing the right thing.

CROW

This symbol shows a fear of death, bad luck, or possibly failure. A crow is known as a messenger, so it is sometimes interpreted as a warning of death, marriage, or impending important and difficult events.

CROWD

A crowd in a dream usually means it is an important dream, for all the many parts of self are involved in its subject matter. Common idioms also illustrate other possible meanings: three's a crowd; playing to the crowd; the in crowd.

CROWN

This can mean success, experiencing new dimensions of your mind, enlightenment, or it can also refer to your father if the crown is on the head of a man.

CRUCIBLE

This is the center of our turmoil, tension, or the forming of awareness of the changeless. In it our nature is transformed.

CRUCIFIXION

This may represent some sort of masochism or self-torture, possibly through guilt. It can suggest the giving up of your own will for something beyond yourself, to do what others want. It can even suggest that you are a scapegoat, especially if others are crucifying you. An occasional meaning is that it shows that if you can accept the misery of human life, you can also transcend it. (*see* Cross)

CRUTCH

This can relate to compensating for feelings of weakness, a lack of confidence or vulnerability in your personality. It can be an attitude or courage that you automatically adopt to get you around in life while you are healing from a physical injury.

CRYSTAL

This depicts the human sense of the eternal or your wholeness. It can also be rigid views or emotions or crystallized opinions or habits. (*see* Jewels)

CUBE

This represents your physical existence. It is also linked to the number 4, and stands for stability, strength, and physical expression, so therefore it also relates to the body. The square or cube is an enclosure in three dimensions, like our body, so that in its center hides a fourth dimension—the mind or our personal awareness. The cube can also indicate orthodox patterns or the establishment. (*see* Numbers)

CUL-DE-SAC

This is generally taking a direction that leads to barriers, or indicates no way of further expression or it may suggest a pointless effort. It can have definite sexual implications, sometimes representing the inside of a woman's legs. In this case, it suggests a no-go sexual experience or desire. There is no way of getting out of it.

CUP

This shows receptivity, or openness. In some way you are offering yourself or being offered something. For example, a woman offering a cup could suggest sexual openness.

CURRENT

A current is the outer flow of circumstances or events as they influence you or pull you along. It is the inner pressure of desires, the direction of the inner life, or it can be the influence of inner tendencies.

CURSE/CURSED/CURSING

This usually refers to fears that an evil influence is attached to your life. Such fears become expressed in the image of a curse. It can also point to the influence of past action and that arising from your forebears.

CUTTING

Mostly this symbol deals with how we make a break in a relationship or an activity. The ties that bind us to others and to duty are invisible but powerful, and are made real in the dream by things that might bind or link us with others. One young woman dreamed of cutting off her breast, which suggested she was trying to cut out the living process that was letting her become a grown woman. So cutting can also relate to dissociating from growth and aging.

CYCLONE

This links to powerful emotions or influences against which you can struggle. Such influences may produce enormous change.

DAGGER

This is a fear of being hurt or a desire to inflict hurt. (*see* Knife)

DAM

This is a repression of emotions or a damming up of feelings. It can even be the controlled release of such emotional energy.

DANCE/DANCING

This symbol is a spontaneous expression of inner feelings. It can also encourage contact with the divine. If you are dancing with someone, it usually shows a loving relationship, or it can be the prelude to a new sexual relationship. If the dance seems awkward and unnatural, it shows there is a lack of harmony with your dancing partner.

DANGER/DANGEROUS

There are many things we may feel are dangerous, such as falling in love, changing employment, or moving. Your dream of danger may be showing you what you do not acknowledge as causing anxiety. If the danger involves someone you know, it is most likely revealing your anxieties about that person, or your fears of losing them, a fear of their death or a fear of them hurting you. You therefore need to define just what the dream is portraying as dangerous. These types of dreams seldom predict the future.

DARK

This denotes a lack of understanding, something that is difficult to grasp or which is obscure. Dark can also mean ancient, worn dark with age, and can relate to depressing feelings. A woman with dark hair sometimes represents intuition. Similarly, a dark-skinned person in a dream can be parts of yourself that are difficult to understand, and the obscure ways in which they influence you. Dark water suggests powerful emotions not yet defined or understood. Dark colors indicate feelings that are emanating from your unconscious, or it can be unhappy feelings. (*see* Aboriginal)

DAUGHTER

Dreaming about your daughter often relates to how you feel about her. Is she an adventurous, creative person? If so, then dreams will usually be depicting your own feelings of creativity and risk-taking. Is she an introverted person, or anxious? Are you worried about her? If so, then the dream is either about your own urges to withdraw, or your feelings of concern for her. She can also represent what is happening in your relationship with your partner.

In a mother's dream, your daughter can represent the companionship you feel with her. She can be the image representing the difficulties you feel with her. Do you feel your daughter is competing with you for male attention? Is she representing yourself at that age?

In a father's dream, your daughter usually represents your feelings, your more feminine or receptive side. So problems in the dream can suggest you have problems allowing your feelings to develop. A daughter can also depict whatever difficult feelings you have about mistakes you have made in the relationship, or self-recriminations you experience. When she starts dating, dreaming of her may also highlight your struggle of losing her to another man.

DAWN/DAWNING

This is the beginning of understanding, illumination, a new beginning.

DAY

This relates to being aware and active, or to a new beginning. The time of day can be important: the morning suggests the start of things, opportunities, or youth; midday indicates middle age, the central point of experience, or full awareness; the afternoon relates to the winding down of activities, the ending of things. Daylight in a dream usually depicts a particular mood. So a bright day suggests positive feelings and a dull day some despondency. A day is also a period of life that begins and ends. (*see* Night)

DEAD

Seeing something dead in your dream suggests you are realizing that some part of yourself, or your feelings, is no longer expressed fully. In fact, you may have killed that part of you by denying it, repressing or freezing it from normal life. The "death" may be related to a painful experience. But even so, it still means you have made a decision, perhaps unconsciously, to shut out that part of you. Death can also relate to a lost opportunity or potential. Dreaming of someone who is dead, a relative or a loved one, is quite common. After all, the person, such as a husband or wife, will have played a big part in your life. So their influence is still very much alive in you.

Dreaming of a dead husband or wife—Many dreams of dead people come from women who have lost their husbands. It is common to have disturbing dreams for some time afterward; or not be able to dream about the husband or wife at all; or only seeing the partner in the distance. In accepting the death, meeting any feelings of loss, grief, anger and continuing love, there are usually painful dreams. But these resolve if the feelings in them are expressed. (*see* Death)

DEAF

There may be a desire not to know what is happening to you, or something you are feeling. Or you may be frightened of hearing something that could hurt you, or to learn things about yourself that you do not wish to face.

DEATH

This is an everyday part of life. Dreams often use death to illustrate leaving something behind, such as childhood or a relationship. Also parts of your feelings sometimes die. Our love for someone may die, for example, and so our dream illustrates this with a death, perhaps of that person. Some teenager's dream of their parents dying as they start to become independent. This is a form of killing the dependence they have on their parents as a means of growth. This can happen in some relationships too, where deep down we know we want to break free from that person.

Death is also something we sometimes create into a frightening specter. It is something we all face. So some dreams in which we actually die are a means of experimenting with meeting death. If we do not do this, if we are frightened of death and have not worked out a relationship with it, then we will not live daringly. But in our dream life, death usually holds in it the promise of change or regeneration in some way. What is dead may also depict what is past. It therefore carries traditional experience and wisdom. For example, the farmer today unconsciously uses the collective experience of humanity in farming. What innovation he does today his children or others will learn and carry into the future after his death. (*see* Dead, Illness)

DECAY/DECAYED/DECAYING

This points to something in you which is not alive, or which has been deprived of expression. It could be something you do not allow to be acted on or acknowledged. It might even indicate a part of your body needing attention.

DECOY

This symbol is the means you employ to lead others to believe something you really do not feel or think. It can be a self-deception in regard to what you feel. For example, a man who has a job with a high wage may convince himself that he likes the work, but really hates it. This can also be a warning, either of a trap you have created to trick someone, or one you sense is there to catch you.

DEEP/DEEPER

Most of your body and mind processes take place unknowingly. Going deep underground or into water usually shows you becoming more aware of what is taking place in these usually unconscious parts of yourself. It can also mean you are becoming more aware of the past influences from family and culture, out of which your present personality was, or is woven.

DEER

This is the gentle harmless aspects of your involuntary or instinctive functions. It may also refer to your sensitivity that can be hurt or wounded by aggression and cynicism, or by other people's criticism. Sometimes it is used as an image of lovesickness. In a man's dream, the deer may represent a woman who he is pursuing.

DEFECATE *see* Feces.

DEFENSE/DEFEND/ DEFENDED/DEFENDING

This suggests you are being, or have been, defensive in life or relationships. There may be an underlying hurt creating this defensiveness.

DEFORMITY

This frequently illustrates the results of early childhood experiences that damaged your natural development. This can also relate to adult traumas that injured your personality in some way. It is helpful to visualize working with the dream character and give it loving acceptance. It then moves toward normal growth.

DELL

This is a quiet retreat contained within yourself. It is a way you have found of creating inner quiet. It can also be the female sexual organs.

DEMOLISH/DEMOLISHED/ DEMOLITION

This indicates the breakdown of ideas, philosophies, emotional attitudes, or established ways of life. It can also be a threat to hopes you have cherished. There can be a feeling that another person is undermining you by being critical, arrogant, antagonistic, or aggressive. It can show major changes in your inner or outer life have been, or are being, undertaken.

DEMON

This symbol denotes the things in life and yourself that threaten you. You may feel an urge is sinful, so you repress it. Your dream then presents it as a demon, not necessarily because it is devilish, but because that is how you see it. So a person who has feelings of guilt about sex may represent them as a demon threatening to possess them. A demon may also show guilt, hatred, feelings of uncleanness, aggressiveness, desire for love, and so on. (*see* Devil, Satan)

DENTIST

This may represent a fear of pain. Or it can be connected with the mouth—the things you say, your opinions, or anger. The dentist is sometimes associated with fear of sexual abuse. (*see* Teeth)

DEPART/DEPARTED/DEPARTING

This symbol suggests you are leaving an old way of life or a relationship. It may also depict a search for something new, or change. Such a departing may reflect becoming more independent of parents or a lover. If you find work or a relationship difficult, the departing may show you wanting to escape demands. It can sometimes be death, perhaps when you see a spouse walking away from you, or departing on a journey. This is not necessarily a prediction, but a confrontation with what can happen.

DESCEND/DESCENDING/DESCENT

This is a regression into more youthful ways of looking at things, or it can be immature behavior. This may mean you are meeting the effects of a childhood hurt or betrayal. It can also indicate a period of depression or feeling low. In some dreams where there is intense fear, it can show an aversion to falling or descending from favor, power, or authority. It suggests coming down to earth from a more idealistic, fanciful, or visionary viewpoint.

DESERT

This indicates a lack of feeling, intellectual aridity, skepticism, or doubts. There may be uncertainty about yourself, life, or the future. You may feel lonely or worry about being deserted or having no change in your life. It can also depict a woman's infertility. It shows the wilderness that our outer lives can present to us, creating a terrible thirst and hunger for certainty and real experience of our inner being. The desert can also represent all the so-called logical, intellectual, arid opinions, beliefs, speculations, and biases we hold that bring no real satisfaction.

DESK

It may represent work, creativity, or tasks you are working on. If you use it to write letters, it can also link with communication. (*see* Table)

DESTINATION

This is where you are aiming to go in life—consciously or otherwise.

DEVIL

This relates to all those desires, ideas, or habits in your life that you feel or believe are wrong. It can also be aspects of your own natural urges that you have repressed. It is all the things that you are not master of, and which can therefore influence you against your will. For example, you may not be master of anger, emotions, hungers, or ambitions, and these may lead you to do things that deep down you do not wish to do. While the results of these tendencies may seem devilish, at the same time they offer the opportunity of wrestling with them and developing strength and awareness. The anger or urges can seem as if they are strong enough to control you, so you represent them as an external force pushing you to some sort of evil. In each of us there is also the potential for creativity or destruction. This is especially noticeable in connection when our fears are connected with illness. Such a fear, if based on imagination rather than a real cause, can still cause illness. In this sense our own mind can turn against us. Your undirected fear may be pictured as the devil or an evil entity. (*see* Demon, Satan)

DEVOUR/DEVOURED/DEVOURING

If you are being eaten by a creature of some sort, this shows you being deeply influenced by urges that you feel will rob you of your will or direction in life. Being swallowed by something huge may be something quite different. We all have a sense of universal life around us. This is so huge that when we become aware of it we sometimes feel threatened, as if it will take away our personal identity. This happens every night in sleep, but we are used to that. It is only when we go into such a loss of self with some awareness that the fear may start to arise. If you are devouring something or someone, it suggests that you are being possessive, overbearing, or deeply insensitive to another person's needs. You may, of course, be absorbing something fully.

DIAMOND

This is something in your experience that is valuable and lasting. Sometimes the diamond depicts the materialistic aspect of human nature, for example, "diamonds are a girl's best friend." (*see* Jewels)

DICE

This is something you are gambling with, or depending on chance for a result, or the situations that life deals you.

DIE *see* Death.

DIG/DIGGING/DUG

Mostly this represents delving into your memories to uncover what is buried there. But it can also be self-improvement without looking back.

DIGEST

Dreams use the experience of physical digestion to represent the way we integrate ideas and experiences. This also applies to relationships in which we absorb a great deal of the other person's traits or ideas. (*see* Food)

DINNER

This indicates satisfaction and fulfilling your needs. If shared with others, it shows your connection or relationship with them. It can also relate to gaining nourishment. (*see* Food)

DINOSAUR

This shows your present personality and body has arisen from processes and experiences that are millions of years old. The dinosaur, or a prehistoric animal, often depicts this ancient past out of which your present self has grown. The dinosaur can also depict instinctive urges, or your feelings about being a devouring monster.

DIRT

This represents a sense of what is unclean, or of being unclean in mind or body. We have to realize, however, that dirt is only misplaced earth, which can form the material for growing vital things. (*see* Earth)

DISAPPEAR/DISAPPEARANCE/ DISAPPEARING

This indicates forgetting or losing sight of something, or maybe wanting to be rid of it. Occasionally, it can depict a transforming power and the magical world of the mind, where thoughts, feelings, and memories constantly appear and disappear. If so, it suggests something that is emerging from the unconscious.

DISC *see* Circle.

DISINFECTANT

This is used in dreams to represent healing, of removing fear, or feelings of guilt and being dirty. It is sometimes linked with pain or burning as a cleansing power. So the painful experiences of life are healing, as they force attention to the cause of pain. They make us adjust, or let go of emotions, desires, and attitudes that have caused trouble, but which we would never have let go of otherwise.

DITCH

This is an unknown situation that can cause you to fall or fail. It is a hazard of which you need to be aware. If it is a drainage ditch, it can be about the way you release your feelings. The word also associates with leaving a partner, so it can link with being ditched or ditching.

DIVE/DIVING

If you are not showing off or challenging yourself in your dream, then it is probably indicating that you are taking a chance, or entering something new and unknown in life, and perhaps facing some fears in doing so.

DIVINING ROD

This means an intuitive realization, or it can mean intuitive directions.

DIVORCE

This can suggest that you are angry with your partner, or that you fear for your marriage. It can also suggest a difficulty with your feelings and intellect. Occasionally, this indicates the future, because you sense a parting.

DIZZY

This depicts losing your sense of balance in relation to others or the world. It is a fear of falling/failing, a sense of strain, or being on the edge of falling in love, out of love, or into inner consciousness. Sometimes, this image describes being in situations that are going too fast or too intensely, and require too much input.

DOCTOR

This symbol represents your healing forces. It may also be intuition or self-knowledge about the state of your body or mind. It can be your feelings about, or need for, an authority figure. It can also be your fear of illness or death.

DOCUMENT

This usually indicates an important idea, or some information that you are about to discover about yourself.

DOG

In general, the dog in your dream represents strong feelings or urges that are only slightly friendly or proper. If you have loved dogs and been loved by them, then it can depict this love, or caring, given or received. Consider the context in your dream: a dog may represent faithfulness, doggedness, a dirty dog, or unclean feelings or urges, usually sexual. It is often used to represent a person who threatens you emotionally, such as a father or marriage partner, who shouts, barks, and rages, or shows their teeth. In this case, it refers more to feelings induced by the attack. Or it can depict, your own anger and aggression. The dog is generally thought of as male, while a cat is considered female. It therefore also represents male sexuality, adventure, or aggression. As a dog sees in the dark and has keen ears, it is sometimes a symbol of intuitive knowledge. It also represents instinctive life, so it shows a person who lives without much feeling or thought, like an animal. The dog may be a guide into the unconscious, or land of the Dead, not unlike Egyptian symbolism. (*see* Animal)

DOLL

This symbol frequently represents yourself when you were a baby, or it shows your feelings when young. Many dreams including a doll show it being savagely beaten or injured. In this case, it can show how hurt you felt in your own childhood, or perhaps it means you are angry and need a target that will not hit back. Occasionally, in a woman's dream it can mean you want to be cared for like a precious doll.

DOLPHIN

The dolphin depicts the sense of beauty you may feel about the deeply natural and mysterious life in and around you. It may, therefore, show you things about life that actually come from deep within your unconscious mind. So this symbol can represent your intuitive knowledge. (*see* Fish)

DONKEY

This represents your hard working and long suffering body, or your automatic or instinctive body responses or processes. The ass or donkey may also show your body as a beast of burden, or that you are living as if you are only a dumb working animal.

DOOR

This indicates opportunity or the openings that life offers. It also represents the possibility of entering new challenges contained within you, or the realization of new feelings, or new ideas. The door can also be a barrier that is placed between yourself and others, or yourself and life. The opening or closing of the door represents the movement of your feelings and attitudes. Death is sometimes spoken of as the other door, with birth being the first. The door also represents a threshold between one feeling or condition and another. Sometimes, it can link with your sexual feelings when you allow yourself to "open" up emotionally to a special partner or lover.

dream messenger

Garden dreams hold key messages about what is growing or ebbing in your life. They tell if you have worked at cultivating your abilities, watered your creativity, or improved the quality of the "land" you inherited.

DOUGH

This is money and the possibilities inside us. Dough can turn into bread or pastry, indicating the raw material from which you can create something else.

DOWN *see* Descent.

DRAGON

This symbol shows parts of your sexual drive or feelings that are untamed and fiery. The dragon can also represent the power and magic of your unconscious mind. But to get the "gold" or treasure, you have to meet and deal with those wild forces contained within yourself first.

DREAMING

To dream that you are dreaming, can mean a lack of attention to everyday affairs. It can symbolize a contact with the innermost contents of your being.

DRESS

This usually depicts your feminine qualities, and shows how these are being expressed at this time. (*see* Clothes)

DRINK

This connects with your feelings of thirsting or longing for something. It also denotes satisfying longings, emotionally, physically, or spiritually. It also shows you absorbing something, taking something into yourself. Most things have some effect on how you feel, so it points to a change in some way.

DRIVING

If you are driving, you are maybe deciding your own direction in life. Driving carelessly indicates a lack of responsibility socially or sexually and a need for more awareness. Driving without a license indicates a feeling of guilt about your way of life or social conduct. It can indicate not daring to test yourself against social standards, so you may be hiding a sense of inadequacy. When someone else is driving, you are probably being influenced by them.

DROWNING

This shows you feeling anxious about something. It usually links with strong and difficult emotions that are hard to move beyond.

DRUGGIST/DRUGSTORE

This symbol possibly links with concerns about your health, or some form of healing taking place. The pharmacist may depict your own insight and wisdom about your health. (*see* Roles)

DRUGS

This symbol depends on what drug appears in your dream. Take time to define what you associate with that drug. For example, you may link morphine with a way of hiding pain, ecstasy with letting go of control, and prescription drugs with various illnesses or conditions.

DRUM

This can indicate your heart, pulse, or a unifying or motivating influence. It sometimes links with masturbation or sexual intercourse. In some dreams, the drum is a means of timing, or of being in or out of time with events.

DRUNK

This can either mean you are feeling out of control, or that you are being unreasonable. It occasionally means you are filled with power from inspiration, or from a connection with a more expansive sense of yourself. If you dream of driving when drunk, this shows you out of control in your life and that perhaps alcohol is dominating you. (*see* Alcohol)

DUMB

If you cannot speak in a dream, this is an inability to express inner feelings.

DWARF

This represents unconscious forces, or the powers that work on your being to keep it functioning. A dwarf may also represent a part of you that has been held back in development because of fear, pain, or guilt. If you dream you are a dwarf, it may express the feeling or fear that you are small, insignificant, or undeveloped.

DYING *see* Death.

DYNAMITE

This can show explosive emotions or a threatening or explosive situation. (*see* Bomb)

EAGLE

The eagle can represent several things: it can point to the powerful, strong hunting instinct you have in business, or in being a providing parent. It can depict protective strength, a male figure, or relentless energy. Because the eagle has an extraordinary far-reaching and inclusive gaze, it can link with your mind's ability to expand, far beyond your immediate senses and concerns. The looking back can include years of experience, and an overview of what you have learned. It can therefore represent an inclusive vision. Occasionally, the eagle can be threatening in a dream because the wider awareness may make you feel as if you are "carried away." Being lifted into the unknown can bring unnecessary fear. (*see* Bird)

EAR

This symbol shows you being open to your feelings and intuition. It can also indicate the existence of rumors.

dream fact

Around 3 percent of adults may suffer from apnea. This treatable condition can interrupt sleep up to 500 times a night without the sufferer being aware of it. This leads to unexplained tiredness and inefficiency. Snoring can be of the effects of apnea.

EARTH

This suggests the things that are a constant background to your life, which sustain you and give form to your experiences. These include your body, the processes of life, your family or cultural background, and the basics of belief upon which you stand. But earth also depicts the past, the fallen leaves of your experience from which soil and new structures of self are built. Digging into the earth is digging into your history, and in its layers you find the story of the evolution of consciousness and your life. (*see* Earthquake)

EARTHQUAKE

This points to great anxiety. This dream often occurs when enormous personal changes are taking place, perhaps coming to the surface from the unconscious.

EAST

This is the indefinable but known source of your personal awareness. It is the mystery of birth and existence. It sometimes represents what you know unconsciously but have never made conscious.

EATING

This indicates satisfying your needs or trying to do so. Occasionally, it refers to what your body needs to eat or avoid eating. If you are the one being eaten, it may suggest you are consumed by some passion, such as sexual desire or burning ambition. (*see* Food)

ECHO

This represents your inner response from outer action. It may suggest the effect of what you do in life, like reaping what you sow. It can also show how the importance or impact of things that are glimpsed in everyday life can be missed or overlooked.

true dream story

For Victor, the need for spiritual experience became an overriding drive. He consequently spent long hours in prayer and meditation. Then in a dream in which he was searching for God, a beautiful hare told him to give up his search and live an ordinary life. The hare said that what he sought was already within, and would emerge through everyday experience. This symbol became a lifelong totem for Victor.

ECSTASY

This reflects a state of being in accord and harmony. There are no discords, conflicts, or divisions of self. This is different from elation, which may be experiencing one sphere of the emotions.

EEL

This represents the male sex organ or sperm. (*see* Fish)

EGG

These are possibilities, things that can develop and grow if nurtured. They are latent abilities and tendencies, good and bad. They can also represent hopes. Eggs have been used since ancient times to represent your complete nature. In this case, it is similar to the chrysalis. The egg can represent the female ovum, and life in the womb. (*see* Chrysalis)

EIGHT

This is usually associated with generation, degeneration, and regeneration. The number eight is seen as a climax where an aspect of personality that is outworn opens up to new development. It is a sort of death or degeneration that develops the seeds of the future. It is known as the sign of death and rebirth. When you look at the symbol of the figure eight you can see that the downward loop drops and then doubles back to rise positively again. (*see* Numbers)

ELASTIC

This is your power of flexibility and your ability to hold things together or to give support to other people.

ELBOW

This is a support: an idea or hope that gives some help or perhaps flexibility in expression. Idioms include: bend your elbow; elbow room; rub elbows with.

ELECTRICITY/ELECTROCUTED

In general, this symbol relates to your energy in

all its aspects—mental, emotional, and spiritual. This energy, like electricity, can be positive or harmful. For example, the emotional energy of fears and long-held grief can cause illness. In some dreams, the electricity is seen as frightening or threatening. This is because there are levels of your own potential and feeling you are not handling well. You may be feeling a lot of self-criticism for instance. The electricity can also be "shocking." This suggests that some event or feelings are painful. If an electric motor is burning out, be careful about dealing with your energy and emotions.

ELEPHANT

This is the great power of the unconscious processes of life, not just in your body, but also around you. Your relationship with the elephant shows how you are dealing with this enormous force. The elephant may also connect with sexual intercourse or sexual energy.

ELEVATOR *see* Lift.

ELEVEN

The term "eleventh hour" represents last-minute activity or last desperate efforts. It also represents strength to face and control instincts, which gives us liberty from them. It is two on another level. Eleven is the matrix, or mold, within us, which receives and restores form after the pattern we have created or experienced in the past. (*see* Numbers)

ELF

This is a force that is active in your unconscious. (*see* Dwarf)

E-MAIL

These are feelings to do with connection and communication. (*see* Letter)

EMBLEM

This probably relates to what you deeply, but perhaps unconsciously, identify with or you have links to. For example, you may identify with the culture of your parents if you are an immigrant, or you may connect with a certain type of person. So the emblem in your dream can show your strong psychic strengths. It can be a link with your inner confidence.

EMBRYO

This is something unknown developing in the unconscious, or growing inside. It is vulnerable because it has not yet sufficiently developed to be expressed outwardly. Or it can be a regression to early levels of consciousness or a desire to live in womb-consciousness.

EMERALD *see* Jewels.

EMIGRATION

This indicates changing habits or ideas. It is the search for self, or a change of direction in life.

EMPEROR

Sometimes this figure, like a king, represents feelings about your father or an authority figure. It can be your need for approval or parental blessing, or what feelings or needs rule you. A ruling figure like this also can represent the "whole"—the will of collective humanity. (*see* King)

ENCIRCLE/ENCLOSED/ENCLOSURE

This can indicate protection or defensiveness,

depending upon the dream. Either way, the enclosure and what it is made of was built by your own attitudes and your own fears. (*see* Circle)

ENCYCLOPEDIA
This relates to information, memory, and sometimes prestige or learning. (*see* Book)

END OF THE WORLD
Dreams featuring the end of the world can reflect anxiety about the future, such as many people experienced with the Cold War. Even though such a war never happened, the anxiety surrounding it dogged many people's lives for many years. End-of-the-world dreams can also show the person that enormous changes are occurring that will eventually produce major shifts in the way they live and feel about themselves.

ENEMA
This may be a memory of infant experiences that have left deep-rooted terrors. It can also be inner cleansing of outworn habits.

ENEMY
The enemy in a dream is usually a representation of our struggle with our own self-doubts, fears, and weaknesses. It particularly depicts something that is causing conflict. (*see* Shadow)

ENGINE
This represents your energy, or your heart and central drive, especially if it is a car engine. Also it can represent the life processes in the human body, all the things that run by themselves.

ENTER/ENTERING/ENTRANCE
This represents something new happening, perhaps an opportunity or a new experience. A secret or magical entrance illustrates an attitude or a psychological "stance" that reveals a new part of yourself, or an inaccessible side. (*see* Door)

ENVELOPE
This represents the body, surroundings, protection, or a means of hiding something.

ERUPTION
This is the emergence into your waking life of processes that usually only take place in your unconscious when asleep. These powerful activities may be disturbing, but are healing.

ESCAPE
If you escaped in your dream, then you know a way to emerge from your fears, attitudes, or beliefs that are holding you back. Negatively, however, sometimes we escape from something to run from difficulties or avoid growth. (*see* Prison)

EUNUCH
This indicates you are without sexual feelings, or they are blocked.

EVE *see* Adam and Eve.

EVIL
The word evil is "live" spelled backward, as devil is "lived" spelled backward. In dreams, the sense of evil often depicts things that you have so repressed that they are no longer alive and healthy. They therefore need to be brought to

the surface and expressed. In fact, they need transforming love. So frightening or shameful sexual urges, for example, may appear as demons in your dreams.

EXAMS/EXAMINED/EXAMINING

If your dream relates to exams or being examined, it usually points to some uncertainty in yourself, or some sort of search for deeper understanding, if it is positive. If there is anxiety in the dream, it may relate to feelings about yourself that you learned at school, due to exams and their results. If you are being examined, it can also show you looking at yourself to see who you are. If you are examined by a doctor, you may have health concerns or something that needs attention. Or, it can mean that you like being looked at and touched.

EXCREMENT *see* Feces.

EXECUTION *see* Death.

EXPLOSION

This may represent anger. (*see* Eruption, Dynamite)

EYEGLASSES *see* Glasses/Spectacles.

EYES

This symbol is your ability to see or realize things. Eyes also represent consciousness and knowledge, or curiosity. In such cases, this symbol often means to look at yourself. Many eyes indicate greater awareness, intuition, psychic abilities, and your innermost feelings.

dream messenger

Feelings in your dream are the basis of its meaning. The images are clothing to make the subtlety of your motivations and feelings more obvious. Try to recognize what part those feelings are playing in your waking life.

Looking into someone's eyes shows intimacy and understanding. Loss of sight in the right eye indicates not seeing what is going on. Loss of sight in the left eye connotes not seeing what you are feeling or having no "in-sight." Idioms include: all eyes; apple of his eye; right before my eyes; turn a blind eye; bright-eyed; eye candy; and catch your eye.

FAÇADE

This is the "front" that you show to the world that perhaps hides a very different inner self. (*see* House)

FACE

This is similar to façade, but in dreams it often symbolizes an outer expression of inner or unconscious feelings. But it usually represents the part of you seen by others, whether you are aware of it or not. A face, as in a photograph, can depict memories and the feelings associated with that person, or with the type of person shown. It can also mean you are faced with something, or are confronting something.

FACTORY

If you work or have worked in a factory, then this symbol links with your feelings and experiences of that time. It can also depict the way your life may be formed by the artificial and mass-produced things we have or buy. Instead of love and real family connections, we may exist in an artificial world that is surrounded by junk foods. The factory may also suggest industry and productivity, or the working of your body's processes.

FAILURE

Often a sense of failure arises in a dream because you have been comparing yourself in some way. Therefore, it is helpful to consider exactly what the comparisons mean or provide. You may also have experienced some competitiveness. Another thing to consider is whether the failure in the dream was "because" of something. In other words, did it happen because you took a wrong direction, or because you went along with a particular person? In this case, try to define what the "because" factor is in your everyday life.

FAINT

This suggests losing energy and enthusiasm, or feeling overwhelmed by a situation or relationship. (*see* Dizzy)

FAIRY

This represents natural forces or processes, such as electricity, gravity, cohesion, magnetism. The unconscious tends to express such forces pictorially as images.

FAIRGROUND/FAIR

What you are experiencing at the fairground shows your feelings about the enormous range of differences and activities you observe in human society. It therefore depicts the range of human circumstances: from rich to poor people, midgets to giants—it shows you the "swings and roundabouts" of life. A fairground can also suggest a colorful façade. (*see* Carnival, Market)

FALL

This usually refers to memories. old age; the autumn of one's life, or old age.

FALL/FALLEN/FALLING/FELL

Most often this symbol illustrates some threat that has arisen in your life from such things as uncertainty, loss of a relationship, money, work, or death of a close contact. What happens in the dream illustrates your drop in confidence, or your feelings of falling from power, grace, or love. Maybe you have lost confidence and so get the sinking feeling of the fall. It can even suggest falling in love, the fear of not being in control, or the wonder of "free fall." (*see* Stairs)

FAMILY

The meaning of this symbol depends enormously on what your relationship with each member of the family was or is. There can be everything from loving support to brutal arrogance. And then each person has different characteristics. So the dream content will help define this. But to generalize, the family represents the many things you learned or that are engraved on your nature from exposure to life in and with your family. Many of these things are still active in the way they influence your responses and decisions. So sometimes a family member represents one of these responses. For example, a woman who did not want a waste disposal unit in her sink later realized it was because she grew up on a farm, where no waste was ever thrown away as it was food for animals. (*see* Brother, Father, Mother, Sister)

FAMOUS PEOPLE

We can often project many of our own unlived or unacknowledged weaknesses and strengths onto famous people. So the person in your dream, may represent a particular quality or weakness; your own potential, or the desire to be noticed or given attention. If you think of the person in a particular role or scene this will probably be the major clue to what they represent. So, for example, it can be the lover who leaves you, the father who makes sacrifices, etc.

FARE *see* Ticket.

FARM

This usually has to do with your relationships, with your natural urges—the basic drives that motivate you, such as sex, survival, social hierarchy, parenthood, or the more down-to-earth side of yourself. It can also represent the area of your basic animal tendencies or emotions, where territorial fighting or perhaps fighting over a mate are expressed. Seeing yourself as present in a farmyard can also represents efforts to deal with all your sensual, aggressive, or animalistic urges.

FASTING

This symbol indicates withdrawal or turning away from your natural urges or it can also be not taking in what society is offering you.

FAT PERSON

This relates to overemphasis on material values. You can feel very weighted down by cares. Or it can suggest jollity or sensuality. It can also mean defenses used against anxiety or feelings of inadequacy. In some cultures it simply indicates being healthy. Becoming fat can suggest pregnancy or carrying more weight.

FATHER

This figure represents the feelings you have about your father, the characteristics in your nature that have arisen from this relationship, or an authority figure. He can also be a teacher or someone who greatly influences you. Alternatively, he can show your own positive, protective qualities: how you relate to the "doer" inside you, your physical strength and protective qualities, your will to be. The negative aspects of the father figure are introverted aggression, dominance by fear, uncaring sexual drive, or feelings of not being loved.

FAUCET

To turn on the tap refers to tears, or the emotions that produce tears, but a tap may also refer to how you control your emotions, or what you can get from within yourself.

FAUN *see* Fairy.

FAX/FAX MACHINE

In the same way as the telephone, this machine is connected with communication and perhaps intuition, where the sudden and perhaps unexpected emergence of information occurs. (*see* Telephone)

FEAR

To feel fear in a dream means that you have not yet developed abilities to cope with what-ever symbol is causing the fear. One of the wonderful things about dreams is that if you work with them, they gradually show you how to deal with the parts of your personalty that need to grow or heal. They show you how to meet the parts of yourself that need release, or to be understood or re-evaluated. If you persist in trying to meet all your fears, then your dreams will gradually take you on an inner journey to increase your emotional strength. You will be able to face your fears more readily, and in fact gain some power and instruction from them. You can do this by meeting each of the dream situations that involves anxiety using visualization techniques to work through what is being shown to you.

FEAST *see* Food.

FECES

Occasionally, this symbol indicates something you have produced and created, something visible that has come out of you. It also suggests the corruptible parts of human nature that become manure for new growth. Feces can even represent money, riches, or fertility. In another sense, to pass feces with feelings of relief means to get rid of worries, tension, or sexual repression. To be covered in feces may suggest a fear of being outwardly repulsive, or to harbor self-destructive thoughts and feelings. To play with feces suggests a return to infantile behavior, but it may develop in the dream into a question of what to do with them or how to use them. This is the beginning of using our basic earthly nature to creative ends, and to shaping and developing our inner self. (*see* Manure)

FEE

This indicates the price to be paid. For example, the price of maturity is greater responsibility. Or the price we have to pay for not living in harmony with our innate nature is sickness or unhappiness. There is a Spanish saying, "Take what you want in life, and pay for it." The fee can therefore symbolize what you will have to pay for your desires, aims, and activities. (*see* Fare, Ticket)

FEET

Your feet depict your contact with reality, your foundations, hence the saying "keeping one's feet on the ground." So observing what it happening with your feet in your dream will show if you are "grounded" or not. Walking with bare feet can suggest either that your path in life is more difficult at the moment, that you are more in contact with the situation you are in, or that you are suffering some impoverishment. At times, the foot can depict beliefs which underpin your actions, your basic feelings, and so on. It can also show your direction —the way you are going. Kissing the foot shows it as a symbol of lowliness, earthiness. Putting your feet up depicts the meaning of labor or work.

FEMALE

Seeing a female in dreams often represents the

soul solution

Norma dreamed she was looking at a goose carcass. Within it were two fluffy, beautiful goslings. The dream was a turning point, helping Norma to accept that her youth was ended and that a new life could emerge out of the loss of the old. Further dreams helped Norma find fullness in age that she had not found in youth.

more feeling, intuitive, irrational part of yourself. If it is someone you know, she probably symbolizes your opinions and feelings about her, or what emotions she has led you to feel. (*see* Girl, Woman)

FENCE

This indicates a barrier, or a difficulty felt in yourself. It is either something that bars your progress or expression, or it is used as a protection from things outside yourself, or from things getting at you. If you are sitting on the fence, it shows you attempting to avoid a decision or action. In many dreams a fence or wall also suggests social barriers, the attitudes and feelings people express to keep others at a distance, to keep a separation between those of different social, religious, or economic opinions. This sort of fence may also depict tension or conflict, as was expressed by the Berlin wall that was built between two opposing powers.

FERRY

This can indicate the change from one situation or environment to another, or connection in a relationship. It may suggest work if you often use a ferry in such a way. It is sometimes connected with death or a new life. It also represents the means of moving beyond emotions that barred progress or development, such as a child's feeling of being dependant on parents, or pain felt in a relationship. So the suggestion is that you are leaving something behind on the far shore.

FEVER

This can be a sign of bad health, or a symbol of great stress and intense emotion that is burning out its own causes and getting rid of the worries or insecurities that produced it.

FIDDLE *see* Musical Instrument.

FIELD

This shows your feelings of relaxation, or your natural feelings. Fields also suggest freedom from social pressure, and the feeling you have about yourself when away from other people, with your own natural inclinations. A field can refer to an area of activity, or a particular aspect of your life. If the field is in bright sunshine, or it is overgrown, then it may suggest a particular feeling state.

FIGHT/FIGHTING

This generally expresses angry feelings that you may have been holding back when awake. But it can also, like a war scene in a dream, point to an area of conflicting feelings or interests that you are harboring. Occasionally, a fight can also express feelings not so much of aggression, but of struggle for what is right for you—a fight or battle for your "space," a fight against urges in yourself, or influences coming from other people. This can also indicate a fight for independence. (*see* War)

FILM *see* Movie, Cinema.

FILM STAR *see* Famous People.

FILTH *see* Feces.

FIND/FINDING/FOUND

This is the realization of something, such as when you find the solution to a problem. It can also mean change, perhaps finding a new direction or relationship. Sometimes what you find is a clearer realization of your own identity or qualities, or facets of yourself that can be nurtured and developed.

FINGERS

This suggests how you manipulate things. They are therefore expressive of intricate skills. We also use fingers to indicate things, hence the idiom "put a finger on him." Fingers are also what we grasp objects with, so they indicate our hold on people and objects. In many dreams, fingers are also involved in sex play or even represent the penis. If it is the wedding ring finger, then it can depict your marriage or state of it. Idioms about fingers are: wrap around her finger; at your fingertips; point a finger at; work your fingers to the bone; butter fingers; sticky fingers; burnt fingers; can't put my finger on it; cross your fingers; lift a finger.

FIRE

This indicates burning love, fiery passion, emotional fever, pain, or purification. Fire is a tremendous energy that we learn to use even when quite young. So it can refer to how you use powerful emotional energies that can support or destroy. Therefore, fire can show an emergency or a sudden and difficult change. Like all energies, fire can warm, produce power, purify, and bring about chemical change, or it can consume, destroy, injure, or run amuck. It is therefore often used as a symbol for your relationship with your own powerful energies—sex, anger, ambition, and fear. Like our own life process, fire needs to consume and destroy to stay alive. Fire can also stand for suffering of a mental or even physical nature. Or it can depict the destruction of things, as happens when you are angry. Standing in, or being in flames, can therefore suggest either purification, the burning out of old attitudes or experiences, or deep personal suffering. In mythology, to use fire for selfish ends has often produced terrible guilt or reactions, probably because it shows a selfish expression of the life-giving energy. Sometimes, fire can give you advance warning of illness.

FIREMAN

This represents those of your qualities capable of dealing with your energies, burning desires, or emotional emergencies. (*see* Roles)

FISH

A fish represents the living processes of thought and feeling that go on under the surface of your mind. To fish is therefore to seek and bring to light your inner feelings or transforming realizations. Fishes depict the ideas, feelings, treasures, or sustenance of our inner, unconscious life. To be swallowed by a fish, similar to Jonah and other legendary heroes, represents a period of deep and sometimes difficult introversion. At such times we see under the waters of the unconscious and know what it is like to live in the irrational. But if the quest is based on a trust in your own wholeness, your integral part in the whole, then you survive this irrational state, as Jonah did.

You can also fish for compliments or information. Or something can be fishy, not quite right. Fish can also have a sexual significance and may represent fertility, prenatal experience, or life in the waters of the womb. A woman's dream of a fish or many small fishes in a bowl or small tank can represent pregnancy.

In the Christian mysteries, the fish signifies Christ or the collective consciousness of humanity. In the English language, some idioms illustrate the possible ways fish may be used in your dream. Someone can be called a "cold fish," indicating an unfeeling person. You can be a "small fish in a big pond" or vice versa. You can be a "fish out of water" or a "queer fish."

FISHING

This suggests someone who creates a receptive state of mind that allows usually unconscious insights or processes to become known. You can also "fish" for ideas, compliments, or information. A fishing rod can indicate male sexuality, personal power, or feelings of impotence. But if you love fishing, it can simply mean relaxation. In general, the rod indicates pulling something out of the unknown.

FIST

This usually shows anger or the personal strength of grasping or holding. It can also depict tension or restrained feelings.

FIVE

In the same way that the five-pointed star is similar to the human body, five has come to represent human consciousness in the body, and the hand. Sometimes, it is called the number of marriage because it unites all the previous numbers—1+4 and 2+3. It also connects with the five senses. The alchemists called it quintessence, because it arises from the other four elements—earth, air, fire, and water—and the four aspects express themselves in a fifth quality: life and consciousness. (*see* Numbers)

FLAG

This symbol depends on your feelings and connections with the particular flag. But in general, flags depict the characteristics of a nation, a group of people, or an organization like the Red Cross. Sometimes, a flag can be seen as a warning.

FLAMES

Similar to the process of life, flames consume in order to exist, so the flame can represent your own life energy. It can also represent a spark or flame passed on from one person to another, as a candle lit from another. This suggests an influence, something ignited in you from another person. You can also have an "old flame," meaning a past lover. Flames therefore depict the mystery of life, or self-awareness, passed from one person to another, in the same way as culture itself is passed on. (*see* Fire)

FLASHLIGHT *see* Searchlight.

FLESH

If human flesh is represented in your dream, it suggests the vital life processes that keep you alive. Flesh is deeply linked with sensation, pleasure, and pain in a personal way. It may in some dreams suggest a part of you that is linked with another person. So if that person leaves, that part of you is torn out. Flesh is the most sensitive part of you, so it relates to your feelings. It also represents your physical life and the urges of the body. Any marks on the flesh show what your life has created—your fate or karma—and suggest something that you carry with you as your fate or destiny. It can also be saying that one of your experiences has marked you. The story of Cain and Abel illustrates this. Seeing any flesh that is eaten away indicates that life is draining you or you are under great stress. (*see* Body, Meat)

FLOAT/FLOATING

This symbol often appears in dreams where the dreamer is getting close to someone of the opposite sex, if some aspect of sexual feeling is present. It can show how you can go beyond the usual boundaries of your beliefs and physical senses. Floating on water suggests that you are deeply relaxed, are being indecisive, or that you are allowing yourself to be carried along by events. (*see* Flying)

---

instant interpreter

Dreaming in color has special significance. It shows intensity or importance. It is like highlighting things to attract your attention. This is especially so when red appears in dreams—then the intensity is increased. When you see red in your dreams, it shows that there are very important feelings being dealt with.

FLOOD

This represents powerful and difficult emotions that are making you feel swamped and threatened by their intensity. The flood can, of course, be a release of positive feelings, such as love or affection. In any case, floods can enrich your growth if they are handled well. In many dreams about a flood the dreamer is anxious about showing and displaying positive energy. (*see* Deluge)

FLOOR

This shows your support system or your physical life; how you can be floored or overcome by events that happen to you. Lying down on the floor and finding it difficult to move represents being overpowered by intense life experiences or your present situation or your environment. For instance, seeing a first floor or second floor can suggest a different situation where the dream's events are actually taking place.

FLOWER/FLOWERS

This symbol shows growing or the growth that is going on, the opening out of your abilities or feelings, in the same way that a flower opens from a bud. Flowers can also indicate a type of spiritual energy, such as the Chakras of Indian philosophy. The context of the dream is also very important as flowers can also represent a sense of beauty or love. They are used to express warm feelings, such as giving red roses to a lover; they can also relate to sexual activity as the act of losing your virginity is called deflowering.

FLUID *see* Water.

FLUTE

This instrument suggests harmonious feelings. It relates to expressing yourself well, or the spontaneous expression of your unconscious mind. Some folklore and mystics say that God plays us like a flute. The flute's shape can also have a sexual significance. So it can relate to "the play" of passion.

FLYING

This can have many meanings, depending on the dream. It can indicate that you are flying or fleeing from something that is difficult to face. This is usually an aspect of your life that you avoid by using distractions, such as your social life or media entertainment. You can also become over-idealistic, religious, or live in a fantasy world. If you are flying you do not have your feet on the ground, so it can suggest either that you have found a positive expression of your energy, or that you have lost a practical grasp on what is happening.

Flying is positive when you are not fleeing from something. It indicates independence and the ability to deal with your emotions or fears. This type of flying suggests the desire to rise above things, to attain greater heights, to break free of limiting or cultural viewpoints. Freud explained all flying dreams as showing sexual desires, representing intercourse, or life in the womb, which in some cases is true. But flying also represents ambition, abstract thoughts, and the ability to rise above your fears. Flying in a plane or alone can be an attempt to gain insight into your future or your potential. From the air we can see forward and back. We can quickly review where we are heading, and work out the best possible direction in which to go.

FLYING SAUCER

Dreaming about an Unidentified Flying Object (UFO) is probably a meeting with the complete "you," or an awareness of parts of your mind that are usually unknown to you and therefore alien. This may include a brush with infinity or eternity. And as this awareness is an enormous and unusual experience it can be expressed as alien contact, a UFO, a round light, or something outside your usual life. This new experience, or new way of knowing yourself, is emerging. So the UFO experience often happens before life changes, so you first need to reflect or meditate on what type of changes are occurring inside you.

FOG

This relates to uncertainty, mental ignorance, or an inability to see ahead or understand. It also represents inner mental stagnation. It can show you weighed down by too many intellectual queries, doubts or objections. It may also show your desire to hide your real motives behind a fog of self-deceit.

FOLLOW/FOLLOWING/FOLLOWED

Whatever you are following in your dream indicates that you are being influenced by what you are pursuing or what you are looking for, depending on the dream's content. If you are being followed, this may show who or what you are influencing, or what is coming into your life. It can also be some aspect of your life that you are avoiding.

FOOD

This symbol can represent anything you depend on to sustain or strengthen you mentally or physically. To eat excessively may represent a hunger for affection, self-confidence, sex, or recognition. It may hide a fear or feeling of loneliness and emptiness. It can also connote the things you experience. In eating, you digest what you take in, so food can show what you are taking in emotionally, intellectually, or physically. Your reaction to what you eat shows what is happening to you as you absorb the food. Something might sicken you, for example, or make you strong. Food is the building material of the body, and can be the symbol for experience—the actual building material of your personality or mind.

Food or eating plays a large part in the ceremonies of many religions throughout the world. This is because it portrays your connection with the rest of life, your total involvement with creation. So eating food in this way acknowledges this communion with life and how you commune with other humans. (*see* Eating)

FOOT *see* Feet, Left, Right.

FORCE

This can be an expression of hate, aggressiveness, anger, or energy.

FOREIGN/FOREIGN COUNTRIES *see* Abroad.

113

FOREST *see* Jungle, Tree.

FORGE/FORGERY
This represents a lie or deceit. (For forging metal, *see* Blacksmith.)

FORTRESS *see* Castle.

FOUNTAIN
This is the flow of life that exists within you. It can also be an influence that springs from deep within that can satisfy your overall needs, or cleanse any negativity, and possibly heal you.

FOUR
The symbol of four is the square or cube, representing stability, earthiness, strength of a physical nature, permanency, or how you make things happen in your life. It is the symbol of the four points of the compass; the four elements—earth, air, fire, and water; the four functions—sensation, feeling, thinking, and intuition. Four, perhaps depicted as a square, often shows a sort of physical harmony in your body, or indicates a feeling or sensation of being complete. (*see* Numbers)

FREEWAY
This symbol shows the more direct approach to your goals. If the freeway appears to be blocked, then perhaps it indicates feelings of frustration or things at the present time that are blocking your energy.

FRIEND
Friends are deeply important to us, and a dream friend can represent the important factors that a friend represents: emotional and economic support and the sharing of love and interests. But friends also represent your human state. So they will represent whatever characteristics that friend displays, far example, generosity, caution, courage, anxiety, sexuality, shrewdness, and so on.

FROG
This symbol reveals the processes that led you to transform from a tadpole/sperm into an air-breathing frog/adult. The frog is therefore a guide into your unconscious world. It is here that many unknown processes are at work.

FRONT
This symbol relates to what you are aware of, and what other people see about you, or what you are doing. This has the same meaning, whether it is the front of a house, a car, or yourself. It is the "front" or façade you use when you meet other people or encounter situations. It is also the part of you that takes most of the impact from relationships and events.

FRONTIER
This symbol indicates you facing changes in

dream messenger

Speaking animals are very often messengers communicating great wisdom or solutions to a pressing problem. They embody your intuition and perception. This is especially so if the animal has white or brightly colored fur.

your life or self. It suggests decisions you are making, and can show you undertaking new life experiences or gaining new insights into yourself. (*see* Border)

FROZEN/FREEZE

This represents repressing your emotions, and possibly becoming cold emotionally and sexually, to be unfeeling, sometimes in a painful way. It can also mean you need affection or warmth.

FRUIT

This shows what has come out of everything you have done—basically the fruits of experience and work. It may at times link with diet or health. Sometimes, it also shows fruitful activities, so it can depict children or fertility.

FUEL

This indicates drive or motivation, or whatever has "fuelled your drive." Basically, it refers to energy and resources. But the energy may be dangerously explosive, and this may be symbolized by gas/petrol.

FUNERAL

This can reflect any concerns about death, perhaps because someone close to you has died. Death is an important aspect of your life, and dreams use a funeral to explore the subject and find greater completeness and healing. Sometimes, we dream of seeing someone we know buried when we want them out of our life. So this can be a reminder that we want to make a break. Very occasionally we can dream about the funeral of a close relative or friend because we have a premonition of their death. It is a common dream to watch your own funeral. It not only allows you to define what you want to do before you die, but it also shows you what you feel about death. Often this is a great healing. Of course, such a dream may also be a cry for attention or sympathy. If you see yourself being buried, you may be leaving behind an old way of life or part of your personality, or feeling "burned" by events. (*see* Death)

FUNGUS

This can indicate a feeling that something is not healthy, perhaps a relationship, for example. It can be a sense of something decaying or being unhealthy.

FUR

This usually suggests that you are experiencing stronger feelings than usual. (*see* Animal)

FURNITURE

This is your inner contents: your beliefs, opinions, and attitudes. If the furniture is from an old home, it relates to things you felt, or a relationship you were in at that time. It relates to domesticity—the disciplines and restraints you use in a relationship or in your home life. (*see* Bed, Carpet, Chair)

FUSE

This refers to part of your nature that will break down if you become too stressed. When things fuse together in your dream, it shows a combination of their characteristics, for example, male and female if you see a man and woman blend together.

GALE *see* Air, Tornado.

GAMES

These often indicate your skill in dealing with life and relationships. But similar to life, some games are dangerous and some hold good rewards. Such games as tennis are especially associated with relationships, and they can indicate superior/inferior feelings too. So the game being played may well be a way of exploring what is a useful stance to take in your life situation, or in a sexual relationship.

GANG

This shows a meeting with your fears. It may represent aggressive tendencies, or parts of yourself, and may also suggest your particular need to conform to a group or follow a leader.

GARAGE

The meaning depends on how you see the garage or if you actually have one. What do you use it for and what do you feel about it? It may depict stored memories, your special skills, or your tools. If you see it as full of garbage, it can suggest things you need to release. Or is it a place of creativity? If it is an auto-repair garage, it indicates a need for personal care or "repairs" to your ambition, drive, or perhaps the ability to motivate yourself. (*see* Car)

GARBAGE

This is the unwanted aspects of your own memories or self, the things you want to get rid of, the things you don't like or of which you are ashamed. It is your discarded ideas or opinions.

GARDEN

This symbol reveals what you are doing with your latent possibilities. It is pointing out whether you have cultivated your abilities or buried them. A garden is sometimes a place of love in a dream. In which case, it can connote what is growing or dying in your relationship. Another garden theme is connected with activities we do in the garden, such as playing with pets or gardening chores. The pets show what is growing in the area of your natural urges, and the gardening represents what you are doing there that is visible socially. (*see* Digging, Pool)

> **dream fact**
>
> While working with victims of recurrent nightmares at Montreal University, Tony Zadra, Ph.D., found that "rehearsing the nightmare" while awake, and changing it, brought a healing resolution. Zadra says, "It's the change that counts—it dismantles the dream and pries loose its hold on the dreamer."

GARDENER/GARDENING

These are activities or attitudes that lead to personal development and the flowering of your potential or abilities.

GASOLINE

This shows your emotional or sexual energy. (*see* Fuel)

GASPING *see* Asthma.

GATE

This can be a barrier or boundary, possibly the feelings that keep us out of someone else's garden or house. The opening and closing of such a gate points to the feelings of permission or refusal we give ourselves. It may also refer to the boundary or gate between the conscious and unconscious mind. If it is open it allows selected memories to penetrate, while a closed gate prevents a massive flooding of impressions. The gate can also symbolize the passage from one part of life, or level of maturity, to another. Therefore, to stand before adolescence, parenthood, or death may be shown as facing a gate in a dream. (*see* Door)

GEESE/GOOSE

This shows freedom, your soul, wanderlust, foolishness, or group conformity. Sometimes, the goose is a symbol for a lifelong relationship.

GEM *see* Jewels.

GENITALS

These denote your sexual feelings, fears, desires, plans, or hopes of a sexual nature. Sometimes, they refer to your gender as a whole. Some dreams show you with genitals of the opposite sex; this indicates that mentally, or in your psyche, you can be anything. You are, in your wholeness, both male and female. (*see* Penis, Vagina)

GENIUS

This may represent feelings of inferiority or superiority, or even be similar to the Guru, depending on the dream. In the positive sense, it depicts your potential. (*see* Guru)

GERMS/MICROBES/VIRUS

These indicate an anxiety or unconscious worry, or something invisible that is damaging your health. Depending on the dream, the germs or virus may suggest that you are absorbing a bad influence from another person. You may also be fearful about your health, or know intuitively that you are getting a viral or bacterial infection. Sometimes it suggests "dirty" feelings that are disturbing you about something that you have done or in which you are involved.

GERMINATION

A part of yourself that has been quickened to life and growth by some influence, such as love, interest, change of heart, understanding, or personal growth.

GESTURE

Most gestures we make in dreams depict an inner state of being. To understand them, it is best to imitate the gesture to see what it expresses. For example, there are the typical gestures of fear, anger, and tenderness. A gesture may also be a way of communicating something that has not been put into words or is not clear. Occasionally, a gesture or posture is a way of changing your inner state. For example, taking a positive posture or making a confident gesture may shift you from feelings of uncertainty. (*see* Posture)

GEYSER

This indicates that your emotions are under extreme pressure or that your feelings are about to explode.

GHOST

A ghost represents an old memory, an old fear, or something from the past that haunts you or comes back to you. It may suggest a guilt, a fear of death, intuitive knowledge, dread of the unknown, or things that you have done or tried to bury and forget. In Eastern terminology, it may be your karma, the accumulated results of actions and thoughts. Occasionally, the ghost is a contact with the dead.

GHOUL

This is usually a repressed part of your life that haunts and terrifies you. When explored, it usually turns out to be images describing a frightening event that happened in childhood or in the past, or buried fears.

GIANT

If you are the giant, then it may mean that you have feelings of power over others, or if you are a big person; it may also suggest that you feel inferior and that you are making compensations. If someone else is the giant, then it may symbolize your relationship with them, and may indicate feelings of inferiority, lack of power, or fear. Take the trouble to understand what the other person signifies. Apart from their size, they may represent one of your emotions, fears, or ambitions that have become too big for you to handle and have increased to giant proportions. A giant in a dream can also depict feelings you had about parents who in your childhood were giants, physically and emotionally.

GIFT

If the gift is from someone you know, it shows what you are receiving from that person in the way of support, love, or understanding. The gift itself will define what this is and if you want it. If you are giving a gift, then in some way you are giving yourself. In some dreams when a woman receives a gift, it can point to pregnancy.

true dream story

Phyllis Atwater, an Idaho housewife, experienced a dream while apparently clinically dead. She relived her whole life, and says, "For me it felt like a total reliving of every thought I had ever thought, every word I had ever spoken, and every deed I had ever done; plus the effect of each thought, word, and deed on everyone and anyone who had ever come within my environment." This totally transformed her approach to life.

GIRDLE/CORSET

This indicates sexual restraint, or holding back outer pride or vanity that does not bring inner changes. It may also suggest being in control, or unconsciously holding yourself back and creating a social corset, for example.

GIRL

A girl usually represents your feelings, young sexuality, or vulnerability. But it depends what age you are and what gender. If you know the girl, it most likely points to her most pronounced characteristics active in yourself. If you are a male, it can refer to feelings about a sister or to your emotions. If you are a female, it can be depicting your sister if you have one, or yourself at that age. Dreaming about a young woman with your man suggests that you are worried about how lovable you are, or you have suspicions about his fidelity.

GIRLFRIEND

This symbol can reflect concerns, feelings, or issues promoted by your relationship. An ex-girlfriend in your dream suggests the feelings, difficulties, or hopes you are left with from the relationship. Alternatively, it can be the positive things gained.

GIVING

The art of giving and receiving is fundamental in any relationship. You can give time, support, money, sex, and information. So giving in a dream usually indicates some sort of relation-ship. But you need to define who or what is in the relationship and what is being exchanged. This will clarify what you are giving, receiving, or rejecting. (*see* Receive)

GLACIER

This may be pointing to some emotions that are frozen in a past attitude. This can relate to an old hurt that has never healed.

GLASS

This is the unseen but evident barrier that we often encounter in daily life. For instance, the social taboo against walking in the street undressed.

GLASSES/SPECTACLES

This is your ability to "see" or understand something clearly. The glasses may suggest a way of dealing with your difficulties in how you appear to others. (*see* Eyeglasses)

GLOVE

This symbol indicates being insulated against the world. It may be an invitation, like a dropped glove or handkerchief. It can also indicate a hand that does not have any life in it. Sometimes it means protection, or avoiding contact, or something that does or does not fit in some way. (*see* Clothes)

GLUE

This represents feelings, a sense of duty, or love or fears that keep you "glued" to a partner or job, for example.

GNAW

If you see a rat or mouse gnawing away at something, it indicates that you are dealing with or processing a worry of some sort, something that keeps attracting your attention. If there is gnawing at a bone or food, it suggests attacking a problem or situation, or it can also link with a hunger for something. (*see* Eating)

GOAL

This represents your aims and ambitions. The goal may also refer to the purpose of your unconscious drives. There can also be a link with winning (success) or losing (failure), such as in a sport.

GOAT

This symbol often depicts foolishness or the urge to break out. It can also refer to argument or "head butting," and can refer to being consumed by sexual urges.

GOD

There are many possibilities here. It may refer to a set of emotions that you use to deal with anxiety. For example, you may have a belief that a higher power is in charge and that you are okay in the world and can escape responsibility. It may be a parent image from early infancy, or it can refer to a set of moral or philosophical beliefs you hold, such as self-judgment or something/someone you worship. It can also be a sense of the collective awareness that lies at the deepest level of human consciousness.

GODDESS

If you are a woman dreaming about this symbol, it is most likely about your potential as a female or the connection you feel unconsciously with women as a whole. It also depicts the power of love and life that can have a transforming influence in your own and other people's life. If you are a man dreaming of a goddess, you may be connecting with your feelings as a child about your mother, or confronting the power of a woman's passions and creativity. It often deals with your ability, or lack of it, to love and meet the full flood of a woman's sexuality and longings.

GOLD

This indicates attitudes or parts of your character that are of great value. It also suggests something that does not tarnish or change with time, or something that relates to the changeless part of you.

GOLF *see* Games.

GORILLA *see* Ape.

GOWN *see* Clothes.

GRADUATION

This suggests the tests you meet and the skills you develop in life and relationships. It also represents achievement, an entrance into a new life, the gaining of adulthood, or the skill leading to adult independence.

GRAPE

The juice of the grape is its life that it gives you freely. It is the blood of its being that it allows to flow and gives to you. It does this to perpetuate its seed. But this act of survival is done in a way of self-giving, which is why the grape and its juice have become symbols of the eternal life, and the love that flows out to us from life. The grape, therefore, also symbolizes our relationship with life. It is an image of the pleasures of the world: drinking, sex, and wealth. Conversely, in Christianity, it links with the blood of Christ, which means the essence of human experience, the collective human wisdom. (*see* Alcohol, Coffee)

GRAVE/GRAVEYARD

This indicates your thoughts and feelings regarding death. It may relate to your family's attitudes or traditions. Sometimes, but not often, such a dream is about contact with the dead. But more frequently it relates to things in your life that you have "buried." It can also refer to melancholy feelings about life or feeling "different" from other people. It can even be a relationship that we think is "dead and buried." (*see* Burial)

GRAY

This suggests a serious attitude or lack of vibrancy. It is sometimes associated with business: worldly activities lacking human warmth. The idioms "gray world" or "gray area" depict the way dreams use the color. (*see* Colors)

GREEN

This may indicate a process of positive change or some kind of personal growth. Strangely enough, this color is often found in dreams about peace and heaven. This suggests it is linked with feelings of relaxation and well-being. When dark green appears, this may refer to negative intentions or depressive attitudes—even sickness, envy, or jealousy. (*see* Color)

GREENHOUSE/GLASSHOUSE

This can depict the tender, growing parts of yourself or others, or perhaps overprotected things.

GRENADE

This relates to anger, violence, or explosive emotions. (*see* Bomb)

GROUP

This shows how you feel about being one of a crowd, and the strategies you use for dealing with a group. For example, you may be a follower, a leader, an introvert, or an extrovert.

GUARD

We guard our language, our thoughts, and our actions. The guard can symbolize the morals, social pressures, or fears that are used in this way. It may also represent a fear of losing some-

soul solution

Steven and Miriam dreamed about a blue-eyed baby, but this seemed unlikely as blue eyes were not in their family, and she had not wanted children. As Miriam said, in the dreams "He seemed to be continually reminding us of his presence." So they decided to become parents and Miriam gave birth to a blue-eyed boy.

thing, such as respect, love, social standing, or virginity. It can also suggest protection, perhaps a guardian. (*see* Police)

GUIDE
This relates to the principles that guide you in life. They may be a worthy or unworthy guide, depending on the principles or desires by which you are directed. The guide may also be an animal, in which case see it under its specific heading, or it may be an intuitive guidance.

GUILLOTINE
This is a very graphic image of losing your head, or being cut off from feelings or the body's needs. (*see* Body, Head)

GUITAR *see* Musical Instrument.

GULF
Is there something separating you from a person or a situation? The gulf may even be a feeling of some kind that has caused the rift. (If the gulf is huge, *see* Abyss.)

GUN
This can be a sign of an urge to hurt someone. It may also signify fear of being attacked and hurt by others, or a sense of inadequacy when facing aggression. For some people, the gun relates to feelings of power and strength to meet the world. It is a confidence based on an exterior object. The gun can also represent aggressive or frightening sexuality.

GUNPOWDER *see* Dynamite.

instant interpreter

Anything that transports you, such as a truck or train, shows your ability to get somewhere in life, to motivate yourself and others. Who you travel with reveals what attitude you have to those who share your endeavors. And "breakdowns" are just that—the fears and feelings that interrupt your journey.

GURU
This represents your connection with the wisdom of the collective unconscious in the way that it relates to your life. The guru is not so concerned with physical welfare, but with the realization of your potential and your life as it connects with the whole and the changeless. So in dreams the guru will usually guide you toward greater self-understanding, deeper relationships with him or herself, and instruct you in any necessary disciplines of mind and body. There will be an unfolding of the inner meanings of ancient scriptures. The guru really represents your own awareness within the wider awareness beyond the physical senses. So as a dream series develops, if you reach the stage of illumination, you will wake up as the guru, or merge into her or him, or be absorbed in his or her consciousness. The guru is you.

GYPSY
This indicates intuition, psychic faculties, or irrational aspects of your feelings that are perhaps pressuring you toward things you don't want, or it can be about the unacceptable aspects of yourself or others.

HAG

This sometimes represents grasping, evil, or emotional tendencies. Alternatively, it can hide the old wise woman of instinctive or natural wisdom.

HAIR

This symbol occurs a great deal in dreams, as head, face, or body hair. Head hair usually represents your character and gender. The style, length, even the hair color suggests the different mental attitudes, characteristics, strengths or weaknesses being portrayed. Hair can also represent your thoughts and intellectual life, or the transformation of sexual feelings into sympathy, fraternal love, protectiveness, or union with the life process. If the hair is growing on unusual parts of the body, it often shows an emerging of your natural and instinctive feelings. Idioms include: hair of the dog; hair standing on end; fair-haired boy; get in your hair; get out of my hair.

dream facts

During your teens your dreams center around:
1. Becoming independent of parents;
2. Developing the skills in relating to the opposite sex and wider society; **3.** Meeting the strong tide of sexual drive. Therefore your dreams can help refine and develop these areas of important personal growth.

HAIRDRESSER *see* Barber.

HALL

This indicates a point of unity, a coming together of things, or a connection with new people and ideas. It can also represent an important change, such as occurs when getting married, or achieving social acclaim.

HALLWAY

The hall or passage in a house may depict how you relate to other people, or how much you let them into your life. It may also suggest the connections between the different parts of you, such as different interests or talents. Occasionally, the hallway in a woman's dream indicates her vagina.

HAMMER

This suggests power of a material or physical nature. It is the threat of aggression. It may also refer to the male sex organ, or sexuality in its physically, forceful, unsympathetic aspect. Or a hammer can express your desire to make something secure.

HAND

This relates to your deeds, outer creativeness and power in the material world. It represents what you do outwardly. So you can have a helping hand, or it may be a grasping, wringing, or heavy hand. It also depicts self-expression—

how you relate to life, your ideas, opportunities, people, your children, or situations. The hand is your extension of power, it is your ability to give, take, wound, heal, support, or to do something. Losing a hand can suggest not being able to do or create something, or to express yourself positively. If you are right-handed and it is your right hand, then it is the loss of ability to do things externally. If it is the left hand, then it represents a loss of confidence, or the ability to support your enthusiasm to act. (Reverse the context if left-handed.) (*see* Fingers)

HANDBAG *see* Bag.

HANGING

This relates to anything that hangs and its meaning depends upon the thing it is hanging by or from. So hanging in a dream shows a condition of depending for support on whatever is shown in the dream. It can also indicate connection or having a hold on something. If it is a person who is hanged, it suggests the awful repression of self-expression to the point of feeling dead or depressed.

HARBOR

This relates to feelings about being protected from the storms of life, but it also about partings or meetings. If you are departing from a harbor, then it suggests you are meeting new experiences and the ups and downs of such challenges.

HARE

This symbol indicates your intuitive abilities, your hardiness in life, or the irrational side of your character. (*see* Rabbit)

HAT

This is your mental attitude or opinions; your thoughts, philosophy, reasoning, or logic. It can be your different ways of thinking or even the different roles you take in life. The hat can also associate with roles, as with the hats worn by a police officer or baker. (*see* Clothes)

HAUNT/HAUNTED

Usually these are memories or wounds from the past that continue to cry for your attention, or influence you in detrimental or disturbing ways. If you are doing the haunting, it suggests you are unconsciously projecting feelings or wishes toward others, or have powerful connections with people or places that need to be dealt with.

HAWK *see* Eagle.

HEAD

You can lose your head, have a head for figures, or use your head. Usually in a dream, it relates to your mental astuteness, your intellect, or thoughts. But it is also often your attitudes and decision making. It also represents consciousness, awareness, or your controlling factor. In some dreams, it may help to think of the idioms about the head in your particular language. For example, in English we say "get ahead," meaning to improve your position in life, or "head-over-heels," which means to be madly in love. There are too many idioms to quote them all. (*see* Face)

HEAL/HEALER/HEALING

This shows parts of yourself that can allow your potential to emerge and bring about change, bringing the rest of your being into harmony.

HEAR/HEARING *see* Ear.

HEARSE *see* Funeral.

HEART
Mostly, dreaming of the heart represents your emotions and longings. But it can simply depict your sense of self. It also represents inner feelings, secret thoughts, or your conscience. You can take heart, and so carry on through difficulties, or lose heart and give up. In some dreams, the heart stands for worries you may have about your health. It may not be that you have heart problems, but simply that because of feeling down, your "heart" is not in what you are doing, so you have no zest for life. Idioms include: broken heart; eat your heart out; faint of heart; have a heart; put your heart into it; sick at heart; steal your heart; or heart on your sleeve.

HEAT
This symbol is about strength of feelings, passion, pressure, or a link with your state of health. Idioms include: if you can't stand the heat get out of the kitchen; dead heat; turn up the heat; getting too hot for you; hot piece of goods; or the heat is on.

HEAVEN
This may suggest you find life difficult, if so this is a compensatory dream. It may also be intuitive feelings about life after death, a retreat from life, or a meeting with your religious concepts, or even being in love or feeling deeply happy.

HEIGHT/HIGH
Sometimes, if you are at a height in a dream, this shows you having a wider grasp of your life situation. It may also suggest feeling isolated and distant. If something is higher than you, it suggests feelings of awe, or a sense of it being over your head or more powerful.

HEIRLOOM
This is good or bad tendencies that have been passed on from family, or been acquired from society. It shows powerful links with the past, possibly to do with talents or tendencies.

HELL
This represents difficult feelings about life and the world that you create out of your own fears and anxieties, or from anger and malice,

true dream story

Treasure Island author Robert Louis Stevenson said that his dreams aided his success as a writer. While experiencing financial difficulties, Stevenson spent two days "racking his brains for a plot of any sort." On the second night, however, he related how he dreamed a scene from which he developed the narrative for his story *The Strange Case of Dr. Jekyll and Mr. Hyde*.

jealousy, etc. Sometimes, it represents the fires of pain arising from past trauma and the connected feelings. People who have suffered birth trauma often see this in a dream as hell.

HELM (of a ship)

This shows will power, or the efforts made to direct your life. Whoever is at the helm symbolizes the directing influence of your life.

HEN

This suggests motherly feelings, or it can be something to do with being female or caring for the young. (*see* Chicken)

HERB

This indicates health, healing, or an influence on the way you feel or function.

HERMIT

This symbol represents the desire to retreat from worldly activity It can be an inverted energy and awareness, or possibly a difficulty with social relationships.

HERO/HEROINE

This suggests the courage to face or wrestle with problems or trials, as represented by the twelve labors of Hercules. You are the hero or heroine of your own life. It is you who face all the difficulties and heartbreaks, you who must develop all the powers and skills of survival.

HIDE/HIDDEN/HIDING

This symbol usually means the avoidance of something, such as feelings, or an awareness of something. But it also connects with not wanting to be seen or be involved. You can also be protective, or you can be hiding how you really feel about someone, or about your sexual feelings concerning a person. If you are hiding a body or object, it can be that you are not facing up to difficult feelings about them. Hiding from something dangerous or concealing a dangerous thing shows you are feeling threatened either by unconscious content or by an exterior situation.

HIGH /HEIGHT/HIGH

Sometimes, if you are located high up in a dream, this shows you having a wider grasp of your life situation. Alternatively, it may also suggest feeling isolated and distant. If something is higher than you, it can indicate feelings of awe, or a sense of being in over your head, or it can mean something more powerful. (*see* Height)

HIGHWAY

This is the direction you are pursuing. Each direction cannot help but lead you to a particular point in your life. Much of your destiny is created by your own decisions and predispositions. A road can symbolize any direction you have taken, or are thinking of taking. It may concern where a love affair, a marriage, or a business will lead you. In the dream you are looking at the possibilities of these roads and where they go. The condition and size of the dream road illustrates your views on the routes you have taken. (*see* Alley, Crossroad, Cul-de-sac, Freeway/Motorway)

HILL

This symbol depends on whether you are going up or down the hill. If you are going up, then it represents a challenge or a difficulty to be surmounted or avoided. The summit of the hill depicts your ability to gain a more inclusive view of where you stand in life and what possible directions you can take. Going down the hill can suggest things are easy, or conversely that events are taking a turn for the worse.

HIVE *see* Bees.

HOLD/HOLDING/HELD

This is a complex symbol. It may be that you are trying to control something, for example, when you hold your breath. You may be trying to control how you feel about someone or something. Holding something lets you manipulate or create something. So you need to define if what you are holding, or the way you are holding it in the dream, has this quality. Are you trying to protect something or someone by the process of holding? Or are you holding in a possessive way? This may mean an attempt at ownership and not sharing. Or is the holding a sign of responsibility, such as when you hold a baby? Or are you holding someone and expressing tenderness?

HOLE

This represents an error you may fall into, a difficulty you are facing, or a danger that confronts you. A big hole may suggest a descent into the unconscious or memories. A hole, especially with grass, foliage, or bushes around it, can represent the vagina. A hole can also be an escape route, so you need to define whether this is true in your dream. Holes in clothes or objects suggest faults, weaknesses, or even an illness. The saying "full of holes" suggests something that is not sound. If the holes are in your body, ask yourself what personal weakness is being looked at.

HOLIDAY *see* Vacation.

HOLINESS

This often suggests that you are meeting something in yourself that incorporates a great deal of your life experience.

HOLY PERSON *see* Guru.

HOME *see* House.

HONEY

This often represents the fruit of your labors, your hard work, the summary of your experience and/or work. Its mystical symbolism, arising from its use as a promise in the Bible, the land of milk and honey, suggests the reward for attempts you have made to transform yourself. Or it can be about facing your inner self and dealing with any upsets.

HOOK

This is something with a catch in it. You can be hooked on drugs, drink, or love for someone, or you can hook on to a good idea or useful opportunity. It can also suggest a question that is being posed.

HORIZON

This symbol represents the limit of your present perceptions.

HORNS

This suggests protective strategies, or the desire to hurt. It can also be the animal in the human, for example, the god Pan, and sexuality or the penis.

HORSE

The horse is a beautiful symbol that is found throughout human history, in all arts, and unconscious experiences. Basically, the horse represents instincts, energy, sexual desires, but also drives that have to some extent become "tamed" or directed. If the horse is wild and without a rider, it shows that these energies are strong enough to express themselves, despite the anxiety of your thoughts or moral conscience. If the horse is ridden, then it means such energies are being directed. But sometimes dreams suggest that although a horse is being ridden, it needs free rein, indicating excessive conscious control of your feelings, and the need to slacken your hold on yourself.

In folklore and religion the winged horse is mentioned. This symbolizes the sexual or instinctive drives that have not been repressed, but allowed, in conjunction with consciousness and reason, to develop all the higher possibilities that are latent within them. Physical passion and love can transmute into non-grasping or fraternal love and passion. This lifts consciousness, the rider, into higher realms of experience.

Finally, the mare represents a woman, the earth, femininity, receptiveness, fertility, and peace. The stallion, on the other hand, represents a male, firieness, masculinity, power, and virility.

HOTEL

This suggests new areas of yourself. It can be attitudes or a situation that may not be permanent. It can show luxury and ease, or a state of mind or being in which you are lodging, vacationing, or passing through on your way to somewhere else.

HOUND

This is something that persists, or hunts out your attention or fear.

HOUSE

This usually represents yourself, and the different activities or facets of your personality. Mostly the house depicts your body, but particularly the areas you can associate with your body. For example, the upper floor of your physical house/body is your head or mental attitude. So the upstairs may be associated with your attitudes, the downstairs with sex or reproduction. Because of this a cellar represents your unconscious mind, while the kitchen is about making life palatable or family interaction. The sitting room promotes relaxation and leisure activities; the library stimulates the intellect or wisdom; the bedroom is concerned with your intimacy, privacy, sexual life, and rest, or with the state of being awake or asleep to something; the attic deals with your idealism and high-mindedness, or perhaps your desire to get away from people; the toilet your relief from tension or parts of yourself that are unnecessary to you; the bathroom, your attempts to come clean with yourself, or it can be the removal of grime and dirt acquired from your mental or emotional contacts with life and people.

The roof depicts protection, security, shelter, or the family atmosphere of love and security under which you find shelter and comfort. To take someone under your roof is to share with them the family atmosphere and goods—yourself in fact. The foundations symbolize the basic attitudes and processes upon which your life is built. (*see* Basement, Stairs, Window, Glass, Door, Furniture)

HOUSEWORK

This indicates making changes to the way you live and feel. Depending on what you are doing, you may be clearing out old attitudes or things you have held on to, or adding new features to your life and personality.

HURT

This symbol indicates being wounded by what other people have said or done. Is there some event from the past that still hurts you in some way?

HUSBAND

This most likely depicts how you feel about the relationship with your husband at the time of the dream. Such dreams are usually deeply perceptive about the state of your relationship and what makes it work or fail. If you dream of a dead husband you are probably facing either the difficult feelings arising from the loss, or discovering the things left in you from your relationship.

dream messenger

Restraints and prisons in dreams show us how we have forged our own chains and restrictions through thoughts and fears. But such dreams help us remodel our imprisoning emotions and beliefs, creating greater freedom.

HYPNOSIS/HYPNOTIST

This shows you being influenced by the suggestions of who or what is hypnotizing you in your dream. It suggests becoming receptive and surrendering to the hypnotic symbol. Whether this is good or bad depends upon whom or what in the dream you are surrendering yourself to.

ICEBERG

This is usually the same as cold, or ice, namely that you may be holding back, or freezing, your feelings about something. Alternatively, you may have shut down your sensitivity, perhaps to deal with loss, pain or disappointment. Such a huge block of ice may mean that an enormous amount of your energy and creativity is frozen along with your feelings. The iceberg is often used in literature, and sometimes in dreams, as a symbol of consciousness. You are aware of only a small portion of yourself, just as the ice we see above the surface of the ocean is only a fraction of the enormous bulk of the iceberg beneath; much of who you are lies beneath your consciousness. (*see* Glacier)

ICICLE

This indicates repressed sexuality.

IDIOT

This suggests a lack of reason, or that some-

> ### dream fact
>
> Research has shown that pregnant women frequently dream of having a deformed baby, or forgetting to care for their child. Such anxiety dreams are normal, and can help to release stress. It was found that the more of these anxiety dreams a woman had, the easier the birth would be.

thing you are meeting is not logical. It may mean you are doing something stupid. Sometimes, it represents intuitive knowledge or insight. If this is so you will probably feel the wisdom of the person in the dream. (*see* Madness)

IGLOO

Sometimes suggests a cold and unloving home environment, or because of its shape, it may refer to a woman's uterus, perhaps suggesting frozen sexual function or feelings. (*see* Cold)

ILL/ILLNESS

Dreaming of illness is often a way of showing you that you have painful feelings that need to be addressed. Often these feelings were experienced, but not fully felt, earlier in your life and now need to be healed or released. At the very least they need understanding. But ask yourself if this is the way you get love, by being ill? Sometimes dreams about illness show the early signs of breakdown in your body. If you are having worrying dreams, have a check-up with your doctor. Tests have shown that men with serious illness have often dreamed about death, and women with such illnesses have dreamed about breakup and separation.

IMPOTENCE

This is often an expression of anxiety, or excessive use of the sexual function, so it will help to define clearly what triggers the anxious feelings. It can be fear of sexual dysfunction. Impotence can also depict a loss of manhood or womanhood, masculinity or femininity. It may also suggest feeling weak, or being unable to express yourself, or to impress others with feelings or ideas.

INARTICULATE

This indicates feeling of lacking power or authority when confronted by others, an inability to express yourself, or define ideas. It can be a fear of saying something stupid, of being thought a fool for your opinions, or it can relate to indecision or conflicting ideas, perhaps arising from criticism or punishment during your early years. Working through these problems with visualization techniques when awake can help. Or take the role of the inarticulate person in the dream and feel your way through the difficulty.

INCENSE

This is a prayer or an aspiration because of positive feelings. It is the cleansing or purifying of your inner self, or it can relate to the atmosphere.

INDIGESTION

This is an accepted idea or attitude that does not agree with you, or it is the inability to stomach something. It may be something that you have taken in, or perhaps something said to you that you did not see at the time was a poisonous

remark. Alternatively, the dream may indicate actual indigestion.

INFANCY

This indicates parts of yourself reflecting childhood experiences, behavioral patterns you have not grown out of, or it can also be control by your mother. Otherwise, it is the feeling of being a baby again, or the desire to be a baby and escape any adult responsibilities. (*see* Baby)

INFECT/INFECTED/INFECTION

This shows the influence of other people's fears, worries, or cynicism upon you, or your own negativity. It may also be a fear of being pregnant.

INFLATE

This suggests to "fill up" or be carried away by a sense of your own cleverness. It may also be superior abilities, knowledge, and power, or trying to achieve a lighter mood.

INJECT/INJECTION

This is something that is getting into your body or feelings that influence you. This may be

soul solution

A month after her father died, Janet dreamed she saw her father, talking and laughing as he sat with her sister on a bench. In the dream, Janet said to her sister, "Dad's so funny. Does he know he's dead?" "Yes, I think he does," she replied. For Janet the dream was healing, making her feel that her Dad was okay.

wanted or forced on you, or enter you without your awareness. There is often sexual meaning involved, so it can be sex, forced sex, or influences taken in during sexual relationships.

INQUEST/INVESTIGATION

This is an attempt to understand aspects of your life. It is also often an examination of all your past experiences.

INSECT

This may imply that something is subconsciously irritating you. Sometimes, it is to do with feeling insignificant. Occasionally, an insect also represents a certain aspect of sex. (see Bee, Spider)

INK

This can be something that has, or can leave, a mark on you, such as a blot on your character. It sometimes represents some unconscious content with which you are dealing.

INSIDE

This is something you are carrying about with you, or it can be feelings or memories that you carry with you. Basically, it is your own internal processes and feelings.

INTERNET

This is your connection with other people and the world, possibly at an unconscious level until you give it attention. It concerns your amazing possibilities and opportunities.

INVISIBLE

If you are becoming invisible, or appear out of nowhere, it suggests something relating to or emerging from your unconscious, or being forgotten. It can also mean that hidden influences are at work around you.

INVOICE see Bill.

IRON

This indicates strength, material power or force. It shows strength of will, perhaps unbending emotions and occasionally brutality. It can indicate that you are not allowing any emotional partnership, or it can point to hardness or lack of feeling. Rusty iron suggests you are dealing with something old or ancient.

IRONING

This suggests smoothing out a situation regarding your feelings or attitudes, or trying to get the difficulties or problems out of your feelings or social life.

IRRIGATE

This connotes allowing emotions or feelings to come into your life. This is a healing process that will promote positive growth and a new sense of yourself.

ISLAND

This can represent something that has come from the depths of your unconscious, but is now established in everyday life—a part of you cut off from others. It can suggest feelings of isolation or loneliness, or your attempt to be isolated from others because of your feelings about them. The island can also suggest the way you feel safe, independent, or trapped.

IVORY

This shows something precious or beautiful, such as an insight or personal quality, which has grown out of the push and shove of life experience. Black ivory is the unconscious aspects of the soul or personality.

JACKET

The style of jacket suggests what attitudes you are using to meet other people and deal with your everyday or social life. (*see* Clothes)

JAIL

This outlines feelings of being restrained by either your environment, morals, or philosophy. (*see* Cell)

JAR *see* Cup.

JELLYFISH

This is something that is floating just below the surface of your mind and feelings, yet you feel vaguely uncomfortable or anxious about getting hurt.

JESUS

One of the images portraying socially accepted behavior, which we are pressurized to conform to, is Jesus. Many of us meet pressures that are not visible but are deeply felt, social and economic pressure, for example, but such invisible but powerful forces are put into imagery by the unconscious dream maker. But Jesus can also represent your feelings and relationship with the Christian religion and its doctrines/dogmas. He may also depict your contact with your own potential that stems from your inner core. (*see* Christ)

JEWELRY

This usually represents love given or received, or the desire to be loved or noticed. It deals with relationships with others, or memories, or feelings connected with the giver, or the circumstances of getting the jewelry. Sometimes, it can be qualities you can develop or have achieved. If the jewelry has a particular history, such as a family heirloom, then it represents what you feel about or what you have gained from your family tradition. Because jewels connect with what you value, they can depict your sexuality. So losing jewels may mean a loss of virginity, or a loss of good feelings about who you are or what you are doing.

JEWELS

In general, a jewel is the emblem of eternity, representing your innermost self. However, each jewel has a slightly different significance.

Diamond: This is the hardest known material. It lasts forever, so the advertisements tell us. It represents the eternal core of your nature, beneath your shifting and transient personality. It is the gem or jewel at your center, representing your consciousness in the midst of change. A diamond can also represent human greed, hardness, being as cold as ice, or doing anything to achieve power. But is not often used as such in dreams.

Ruby: This represents the feelings, sympathies, and love arising from within rather than material values. It is the ability to reach out and to contact others.

Emerald: This shows the growth principle—the growth of consciousness, or an awareness transcending your own life and death, or harmony with life.

Pearl: This indicates value and beauty, from the depths of your being. The fact that a pearl comes about from irritation in a shell means it depicts the good in you that has come from difficulties.

Sapphire: This relates to feelings of peace, a reduction in material consciousness, and gives protection from evil sources.

Turquoise: This shows your ability to experience intuitive perceptions.

Opal: This suggests the dreams, longings, and the psychic world of the imagination and desires.

Amethyst: This stone is the bringer of dreams and visions. It heals and gives protection against being over-elated or being affected by inner influences.

Lapis Lazuli: This crystal promotes vitality and indicates a sensitivity to inner impressions.

JOURNEY

In general the dream journey is a comment on what is happening in your life, and how you feel about it. It may also relate to undertakings you embark on, and new experiences or ways of life you are entering. Your life and its events are the journey, and you can travel into spiritual adventures by taking the journey into marriage or parenthood, etc. The dream journey will show you what hesitations, fears, or strengths are helping or hindering your travels into the wonderful opportunities of your life.

JUDGE

This denotes your sense of whether you have acted in harmony with yourself, or with the people around you. The judge may be an inner self-criticism that you carry with you and need to reevaluate.

JUMP

This can indicate you are taking a chance or making a change from one situation to another. Jumping is sometimes linked with the start of flying and can suggest a powerful urge to go beyond your usual limitations.

JUNGLE

This represents the ancient, instinctive urges and processes that are alive in you, but often hidden. They include the most important directives in life— survival and reproduction. But the jungle of the unconscious also holds the hidden wisdom gathered from millions of years of experience.

dream messenger

Our ancient ancestors and modern hunter-gatherers dreamed of supernatural beings who guided them in community matters, healing, and prediction. We can receive the same from our dreams if we look to them for help.

K L

KEEL

This indicates basic strengths, or the basis upon which your life is built, but it also represents what holds you steady against any other opposing conditions.

KENNEL

This is the doghouse, so it may show you being shut out of your home and relationship. It is here that easily expressed feelings live. (*see* Dog)

KEY

This is the idea or state of mind that allows further realizations or experiences. It is also a symbol of the male sex organ.

KIDNAP

This relates to feelings connected with losing your freedom, or being forced in a direction by others or irrational parts of your own being.

KILL

This indicates you are suppressing or killing feelings, or denying conscious expression of parts of your personality. This may apply to the way you may "deaden" your feelings for someone in a relationship. (*see* Death)

KING

Dreams often use the image of a king to show a particular relationship with your father—the authority figure or ruling influence. The king can also depict the feelings you have about being ruled or directed by someone, or about your connection with the general influence of your nation.

KISS

This is an expression of love, passion, sympathy, or union. It suggests you are being more sympathetic or understanding.

KITCHEN

This is a place of transformation, where you can change parts of your nature. It also links with how well you provide for yourself or neglect your body's needs. It may portray you caring for others, or being in the mother role.

KITTEN

This suggests feelings of vulnerability or babyhood, of caring for someone or something vulnerable. It can indicate parental urges, perhaps protectiveness, and can also depict a baby, possibly in the womb.

KNAPSACK

This often represents karma, the load of positive and negative attitudes, resentments and habits that you carry from your past, or which you have inherited. It is also the wisdom, insight, and talents you carry, perhaps unconsciously, or alternatively it can be anything that seems to be a burden.

KNEEL

This represents being humble, a receptive condition of mind, or a state of awe. It can also be an acknowledgment of dependence, or even defeat.

KNIFE

This shows aggression, a desire to hurt or wound someone or to use cutting remarks. It can be the male penis. It is also your ability to cut through any existing restrictions or problems. (*see* Arms)

KNOCK

This symbol shows something is trying to get your attention, or you are trying to rouse someone. It may also mean that there is a change or something new coming into your life.

KNOT

This represents a problem, or a relationship tangle—a tangle of feelings. In Buddhism, there are three inner knots that have to be untied before Nirvana or Liberation can be reached. They are the knots of passion, emotion, and intellect that bind us to limited and illusory awareness. In daily life, we may be tied to our work, spouse, or to our mother's apron strings.

LABEL

This is a description or "label" you may be applying to yourself. So the contents of the label, or the words it contains, may be about a particular image you have of yourself, or feelings about the quality of something with which you are dealing.

LABORATORY

This may suggest the testing of something, or seeking insight and understanding. It also shows a logical approach that appraises what you are dealing with. Sometimes laboratory dreams indicate mistreatment of your own animal drives and needs.

LABYRINTH *see* Maze.

LADDER

This shows you attempting to get somewhere that is out of reach or difficult to attain. Perhaps it involves risks and anxiety. Depending on your feelings in connection with the ladder, it may show feelings of achievement through effort and daring. The ladder is sometimes a symbol of social success or failure, so if there are such feelings involved, you may be feeling strongly about your social or work standing.

LAGOON

This often depicts the unplumbed, and perhaps strange, depths, of your inner feelings and thoughts.

LAMB

This may refer to the childlike, dependent, vulnerable part of you. There are other possible meanings though, such as a new life. This can link with your own child or childhood, and with innocence. In Christianity, the lamb is linked to Christ. The innocence, purity, and weakness of the lamb have enormous power and can defeat evil. In ancient societies where sheep were bred, the spring lambs were a welcome sign after the often harsh and hungry winter—at last there was food. So the sacrifice of the lamb was linked with the feeling of being given life and redemption. (*see* Animal)

LAME

This is the difficulty, or lack of confidence or strength, you may face in making your way through life. It can represent any impediment in you that makes your approach to life difficult. Lameness can also represent uncertainty about how, or where, you "stand" in life. If you are right-handed, a lame left leg depicts weakness in your feelings and ideas from which you gain support. Lameness in the right leg suggests weakness in dealing with external activities. In the Bible, Jesus healing the lame man (Matthew 11:5) shows that the contact with your own wholeness enables you to face life with the energy and capacity that each event demands.

LAMP

This indicates becoming focused or achieving understanding. (*see* Light)

LAND

If it is undeveloped, it is the opportunities you make to create something from within yourself. This links with your own potential and gives you the opportunity to materialize what is inside you. If the land is developed or farmed, it shows the work you have done on yourself. It shows what you have made of your potential and heritage.

LANDSCAPE

A landscape can depict your feelings, moods, and attitudes. In dreams you create your own surroundings and environment out of your unconscious attitudes, fears, or wisdom. These surroundings, like your dream houses, show what attitudes or atmospheres you live in most of your life. So if you dream of a dismal scene, it suggests feelings of pessimism or depression; conversely a sunny bright scene displays optimism. (*see* Countryside)

LANGUAGE

This signifies communication and therefore can relate to understanding or misunderstanding. The process of dreaming is partly about verbalizing deeply felt emotions and bringing clarity. So a dream image is halfway toward this. Strange language in dreams is also a move toward clear awareness of what is starting to happen.

true dream story

Jose Silva, the creator of the Silva Mind Control Method, began his career because he dreamed several times of the numbers 343. Wondering what their significance was, he bought a lottery ticket beginning with those three numbers. Amazingly, he won $10,000. Jose says that for him the win was not the important thing—rather that it showed him the wonderful possibilities of the mind.

LANTERN

Unlike the lamp, the lantern usually signifies what shines out from you, perhaps as feelings, understanding, or wisdom. Also, it is the insights or understanding you use to guide you on your life's journey. (*see* Light)

LATE

This suggests that you are feeling that you have left something too late or you have missed out on something. Or perhaps you realize that you have not acted quickly enough to avert a situation or take advantage of it. It can also mean an avoidance of responsibility.

LAUGH

This symbol may be a sense of the ridiculousness of a situation you are experiencing. Laughing in a dream is also a way of dispelling tension, dealing with uncomfortable feelings, or it can even be a prelude to tears.

LAUNDROMAT

This is often to do with the way you feel transformed or cleansed, perhaps because you have met a good friend who changes your feelings. For some people it can be meditation or going to church. (*see* Washing)

LAUNDRY

If it is unwashed, it shows the attitudes or feelings that need cleaning up. If it is washed, it displays the changes you have made to your thinking and feeling. (*see* Washing)

LAVA

Powerful and burning emotions, probably arising from real emotional pressure or stress.

instant interpreter

Musical instruments or music in your dream are a way to become aware of subtle or creative impulses that are emerging. Just as a plant takes shape and color from a tiny seed, so you grow from the formless possibilities within you. Music is the expression of that flow toward life.

LAVATORY *see* Feces, Toilet.

LAWN

This symbol depends on what relationship you have with a lawn. It can link with something that needs frequent attention. It can be a visible sign of how you neglect or care for yourself, or be relaxed feelings. In some dreams it links with feelings of exposure or vulnerability.

LAWYER

This sign may connect with an argument you are having within yourself or with another. It may also be your rational approach to something.

LAXATIVE

This is something you are doing, or can do, to loosen up tension and release any emotional blockages, undesired feelings, or memories that currently exist.

LEAD

The metal—lead—suggests heavy feelings or a difficult situation that you are encountering. It may have a link with the alchemist's suggestion of turning lead into gold. In which case it means you have a situation that you have the ability to transform.

LEADER

If you are the leader, it suggests you feel confident about a certain direction you are currently taking. If you are following a leader, it shows an influence from something, such as an inner feeling that is giving you some direction at present in your life. The leader may therefore represent the confidence you gain from someone, from a special belief, or from whatever is signified by the leader figure.

LEAF

If the leaves are on the ground, they refer to things that were growing in your life and have now fallen away. This can also link with fall, and the end of a period of experience or growth. If the leaves are on a tree it suggests the part of you that is still growing or absorbing experience. If the leaves suggest spring, there is a link with a new period of growth or change coming. (*see* Tree)

LEAK

This suggests energy being lost, or expressing emotion without any control or direction. The energy leak may arise from any number of past traumas, and be using energy to keep them unconscious.

LEATHER

Sometimes this links with feeling tough, a "hide like a rhinoceros." It can also express instinctive feelings, or feelings about fashion or animals being used for food, clothing, or raw materials.

LEFT

If you are right-handed, the left hand nearly always depicts your less dominant or unconscious, or perhaps your supportive nature. It can also be things outside your awareness. This may be reversed if you are left-handed. There can even be a link with one side of your body, representing the feelings and attitudes you absorbed from your mother, while the other side can represent the feelings absorbed from your father. The play between left and right is sometimes used in dreams to illustrate the dynamic action between opposites in our own nature. (*see* Right, Arm, Leg)

LEFT BEHIND

If you are the one who is left behind, it suggests either that you feel rejected, or have a sense of not being the same as other people, or perhaps that you want to go your own way. If you leave someone or something behind, it may mean that you are ready for change of some kind. That is, ready to let go of something or someone that may have been important at some time. In some cases, this suggests changes in a relationship if the person left behind is your partner. (If what you left behind was your handbag or purse, *see* Bag.)

LEGS

This symbol indicates the attitudes or qualities that help you maintain confidence and the ability to be independent. Sometimes an event occur, or you receive news that knocks away your support or self-confidence, and dreams represent this by a problem or injury to your legs. Legs can also depict the ability to get on in life. Ambition, for example, may give us the drive and confidence to stand up and do something in life. If your business fails though, your ambition may crumble, which can be represented by your legs being kicked away from you. (*see* Left, Limping, Right)

LENGTH/LONG

A long kiss may be seen as a delight, but when length is represented it can also mean boredom. A long working day can indicate tiredness. So look to the content of your dream to see if the length suggests pleasure, importance, or something that is lacking impact in your life.

LENS

This connotes concentration, or focusing your attention or understanding. It may also represent something becoming bigger or more important, or gaining insight.

LEOPARD

Sometimes this represents libido or sexual drives that can appear as threatening. This type of animal also depicts anger or passion. It can also relate to a caring, protecting, or a quick, spiteful response.

LETTER

This shows a realization about something. It is usually about someone else, or news about yourself. It can be a hoped for, or feared, contact with, or expression of, feelings from someone. It can be a symbol used to express intuitive contact with another person. The letter may also depict the arrival of a new event.

LEVEL/LEVELS

Dreaming of different levels may be associated with feelings of class, superiority, worth, or power. Or they may suggest different levels of response, such as a mental response, a gut-level response, a sexual response, etc. In a building, they may refer to different functions, for example, the lower levels can refer to sexuality or the more physical side of your nature, and the higher levels can depict your emotions and your overall mental outlook. Levels can also indicate the fear and difficulty involved in making changes in your life or your current ways. Through analyzing what has appeared we sometimes realize that life has many other ways of "being."

LIBRARIAN

This suggests memory or contact with universal energy. It can be the creative or linking process of your mind.

LIBRARY

This denotes acquired wisdom or life experience. Sometimes, the books are very old, suggesting wisdom pre-dating this present life and experience. This is the meaning of Jung's theory of the racial unconscious, and equally that of reincarnation.

LICE

This indicates thoughts or sexual habits that are purely selfish or carry a health risk. It can also be a feeling that other people are like parasites. (*see* Insects)

LIFT/ELEVATOR

This shows the ups and downs of life, such as a rise or drop in status or your work situation, or your emotional highs and lows. So it can suggest shifts from emotional to physical sensations, for example. Lift dreams sometimes include strong feelings of rising sexual pleasure. So the lift can also depict the rise or fall of such feelings.

LIGHT

This depicts your ability to see, understand, or know where you are going and what surrounds and confronts you. This is powerfully illustrated by what happens in the dark, either in dreams or in reality. A noise in the dark can be terrifying because we cannot see its source, but light helps dispel fears and ignorance. This is why when we enter into darkness in a dream it symbolizes exploring the unknown or things we do not yet understand. Similarly, seeing light is the growing of realization, experience, and understanding. Light as a symbol, therefore, represents your consciousness, your awareness of individuality and personal realization. Light also holds in it the many invisible possibilities—the colors. This relates to your own unconscious talents and qualities. The idioms connected with light can explain some dreams. They are: bright lights; cold light of day; come to light; hide one's light; in its true light; lighter side; in a good light; see the light; light at the end of the tunnel; seen the light; turn a light on. (*see* Dark, Glow)

LIGHTHOUSE

There may be a warning in this dream of the dangers of unconscious elements that may wreck your life unless avoided. It can also suggest isolation.

LIGHTNING

This indicates a sudden discharge of tension in a possibly destructive manner. It can be a sudden enlightenment or realization, or a fear of fate or punishment from your conscience. It can also link to revenge or a sudden and disturbing change or release of emotions or sexuality.

LIMP/LIMPING

Limp in the sense of not being firm, suggests feelings of mild depression, loss of enthusiasm, or even sexual anxiety—the inability to respond to sexual stimuli. This afflicts both men and women and may be due to high expectations of sexual drive. (In connection with Limping, *see* Lame.)

LINK *see* Chain.

LION

This symbol appears in many dreams and usually signifies anger, anxiety, a desire to hurt, aggression, or a fear of these feelings in others or ourselves. We may be afraid of our own anger as it may hurt others in a way that will reflect upon our feelings and desires. The lion can often express repressed feelings of love that can become aggressive if they are not released. The lion and lioness can also represent images of strong parenthood. Seeing Daniel in the lion's den is a beautiful symbol as it represents how these feelings may be calmed and changed positively.

LIQUID

This represents the heart, or courage, that can turn to water, meaning that resolves have become soft. Or the heart can melt, suggesting a change of heart, or being open to sympathy. So liquid usually relates to change, to becoming soft, to realize your innate formlessness and flowing nature. Liquid also depicts the movement of feelings in your body. (*see* Water)

LIST

The list may be a personal reminder of things that need doing, so it may refer to changes you need to make in your life, or things to attend to at work or in a relationship, depending on the setting of the dream. The list may refer to personal qualities, a sort of summary of your abilities or potential. It may remind you of important thoughts, facts, or situations of which you need to be aware. A list in dreams may also present you with choices to make and refer to all the decisions that you are facing.

LITTLE

This relates to something your unconscious does not see as important. It can be feelings relating to childhood or the ability to avoid being noticed. It can suggest feeling small or insignificant.

LIZARD

The lizard usually depicts your most primal and built in responses, such as the

dream messenger

Many dreams are about keeping body and mind balanced. Like a news feature, we see only surface images unless we dig deeper. The message in the drama can be extracted by asking what the characters and scenes portray.

fight-or-flight response, the drive to procreate, territorial feelings, or ritual behavior. These are all part of your primitive brain functions and are very necessary. Because of this, the lizard, and more so the snake, can represent the very process of life in you. This life energy affects your functions and experiences. So emotions, for example, are a particular expression of this life energy. But emotions can be crippling when they are about fear, guilt, and self-incrimination. Therefore, the lizard or snake can also be shown as deadly or poisonous, and needing to be led in another direction. So the meaning is that your emotions and anxieties need some rechanneling.

LOCK/LOCKED/LOCKING

This shows a problem, often of a logical nature, that can be unlocked, if you have the key. It also represents the female sex organs. The lock or locking can depict emotions or tensions we use as a defense, or to stop you feeling something. It depicts an attempt to keep something safe or untouched by others, such as your beliefs or feelings. Locks or a process of locking can also occasionally suggest sexual tension. (*see* Key)

LOCOMOTIVE *see* Railway.

LOOK/LOOKED/LOOKING
This is being or becoming aware, or indicates your search for something.

LORRY/TRUCK
In the same way as a car, this symbol is your means of getting about in life, i.e a vehicle of expression such as music, drives, longings, or ambitions, but the lorry connects more with commercial associations or projects. So it may link with feelings of major change, commercial ventures, or moving.

LOSING/LOST
If you dream of being lost, it links with feelings of confusion, lack of direction, or conflict, of not understanding what is involved in your present situation. The dream environment you are lost in will define your confusion or conflict. Sometimes, this lost feeling arises because there are issues or changes in your life you have not or do not want to acknowledge. Losing something or someone probably relates to feelings about a lost opportunity, something that you have forgotten but need to remember, or the loss of an important personal quality such as confidence or virginity. People in middle age often dream of losing a husband or wife. It shows them fearing or exploring the possible death of their partner. It is not a prediction, only an awareness of a likely situation.

LOW
This is something that has escaped notice. Alternatively, it is something beneath you, or is morally unsound, cheap, vulgar, or depressing.

LUGGAGE
This suggest things, such as habits, attitudes, likes, and dislikes or longings, that you carry about with you, perhaps without realizing. It can also relate to past memories that you are still carrying around, or things that you value. It may also, of course, relate to feelings about getting away, going somewhere, or leaving.

LUMBER *see* Wood.

M

MACHINE

This represents things that are automatic, such as habits. It also indicates some form of reason or activity, such as when we say someone is like a machine. A machine may also represent your body's automatic processes, especially something like the heart that keeps pumping. In some dreams people use a huge machine to depict the relentless world activities that can, with apparent carelessness, roll over people claiming their life through illness or other calamity.

MADNESS

This sometimes arises from a fear of what lies beneath the surface of your mind and feelings. It can also represent the torment of a difficult birth, or the search for identity among shattered perceptions of the world and people. Dreaming of madness is sometimes an attempt to deal with, or express, pains and inhibitions that have upset you, and which need healthy expression. (*see* Idiot)

MAGIC

This is your conscious attempt to direct or control your unconscious mind—the eternal force of your being.

MAGGOT

This represents life or effects in your life that have sprung from parts of yourself that are no longer growing or properly proving life. The effects, however, are usually efforts on the part of nature to cleanse, heal, or deal with the situation. As an example, if there is a great deal of tension in your neck because of pent-up emotions, a dream may portray this part of your body as full of maggots. Maggots may also appear in a dream where there are fears about death or disease. This is because maggots often represent the negative view of death as the final decay.

MAGNET

This suggests attraction and repulsion. It can be the things you like or dislike.

MAGNIFY *see* Lens.

MAGPIE

This represents the desires caused by material possessiveness.

MAIL *see* Letter.

MAKEUP *see* Cosmetics.

MALFORMATION

This suggests that whatever is symbolized is not expressing its true characteristics.

MAN/MALE

The man in your dreams in nearly always an aspect of your own feelings, hopes, and fears.

Even if it is someone you know well, the dream image is never that person. It is certainly an image you have built from your memories, your views of that person, and also your likes, dislikes, and insights. The man is in general the polarization of thought, of activity in the world, of invention and doing. Even if you are a woman, you will dream of those qualities as a man.

If you are a woman dreaming of a man, the man may represent your relationship with a particular man, or men in general. It is therefore about your ability to relate to men. In this sense, the man portrays the power of your own womanhood, indicating whether you can meet male energy with your full female energy. The man can also represent your ability to question social conventions and to attack issues thoughtfully.

In a man's dream the male is an aspect of your own character traits. An old man may depict some aspect of the relationship with your father, or it may be a form of wisdom you have discovered, or feelings about aging. A half-human man shows the fundamental traits that have not been allowed to develop. Childhood training seldom allows these traits to grow gradually into the mature adult, as we are affected by upbringing. So the half-human sometimes comes through in an attempt to grow.

MANDALA

The mandala is a stylized shape, normally a regularly shaped square, circle, or even a star. In highly developed mandalas such as those used in Tibetan Buddhism, the center of such shapes contains a great deal of detail. Because it is an

dream messenger

Dreams help us define what burdens we carry from our inherited or developed tendencies. They show what problems we face, and the potential we have to deal with them. Often, they provide a map for our journey through life.

outline that can contain different details, it is used to represent the inner contents of the psyche, almost like a map of your being. Although we experience the mysterious life process daily, it is difficult for us to answer the question, "Who am I?" or "What am I?" with any lasting conviction. The mysterious essence of ourselves is met in dreams as a circular or square object or design: as the sun, a flower, a square garden with a round pond in the middle, or a circle with a square within it, a circle with a cross within, or a revolving or flying cross-shaped object. Classical symbols from all nations use this theme, and we can find it in the Round Table of King Arthur, in the center of which the Holy Grail appeared; the healing sand paintings of the Navaho Indian; the zodiac; the Buddhist wheel of birth and death; and so on.

MANSION

A mansion, like a house, shows all the different departments of your life. The bathroom relates to transforming the way you feel, and the library suggests mental growth, etc. The mansion is sometimes used to show just how big you are, how much you hold in yourself, and perhaps the amount of work you have put into becoming who you are. (*see* House)

MANURE

These are the things that you no longer need, but which can now be used to grow something new. The manure may be new ideas or a new encounter that stimulates growth. It may show too, how your personality is an almost organic thing that integrates bits of experience and ideas into its growth. (*see* Feces)

MAP

This is possible feelings of confusion and of indecision about your direction. On the other hand, if the dream is positive, then it can be an indication of what direction you feel is most productive for you.

MARATHON

This indicates participation in life, in the human "race." What happens may sum up your feelings about how you feel about life. It may also have connections with winning or losing. (*see* Race)

MARE

This is a female or fertility, the deeply physical and biological urges and processes that enable your body to exist. (*see* Horse)

MARK/MARKED

A mark suggests the influence that created the mark. We may be marked by certain experiences of life, or leave a mark through our actions. It may also have arisen by intention or by accident. The mark may represent a sense of ownership or a connection, as with a trademark. The mark may indicate quality or lack of it, for example, the mark of Cain or a goldsmith's mark.

MARKET

This often shows the everyday situations you face. It may also refer to your contact with the world in general, the hustle and bustle, the commerce of life, the commercial instincts, and the unsympathetic mob. So it includes the possibility of trade, buying and selling, perhaps of your skills or labor. In some dreams, the marketplace is where you meet a person who represents the highest in yourself. This may be in Christ or a being that you know is radiant with love.

MARRIAGE

This can be a desire for, or indicate problems in, marriage. What happens at the wedding shows your feelings about or difficulties in facing marriage. It can therefore clarify your difficulties and unconscious attitudes. But please do remember that dreams often depict your fears; they are seldom predictions. So learn from the dream to sort out your troubles. Don't use them to trouble yourself. Marriage appears in dreams often to represent the uniting of various parts of your being. For example, men often neglect their feeling values and live in their intellect, while for women the opposite can be the case. So, if a woman dreams of marrying a man it may represent the uniting of these two parts. It epitomizes a growth of sympathy and a relationship between parts of you that were previously not well related.

MARSH/SWAMP/BOG

This suggests any feelings that bog you down, hold you back, retard you, or undermine your confidence and well-being. Or you may be stuck in values or attitudes that are not helping your progress. Sometimes, the swamp represents the relationship existing between mother and child, or sometimes, though not so often, between father and child. The marsh here represents the difficulty felt in breaking away from parental control, the ties of emotional security. It can suggest, therefore, feeling stuck in a situation or relationship. The swamp can show despair or great uncertainty in a relationship.

MASK

This indicates hiding yourself. Or it may reveal a secondary personality, or characteristics that are not predominant in daily life.

MASS (in church)

This shows your approach to the sense of "wholeness," the communal whole or collective mind, or to Christ. (*see* Christ)

MASSEUR

This is a healing influence, the loosening up of rigid attitudes, tensions, preconceptions, or any repressions.

MAZE

This often portrays the things and feelings that confuse you. Sometimes you need to admit you are lost and need help. The maze can also depict the difficulties and confusions you face in becoming more mature.

MEAL/MEALTIME

This indicates taking in and absorbing life and aspects of the world, and being enriched by them. If you are with others, then it may reflect something about the way you relate socially to people. It could also be a sharing of life and experience with others. (*see* Food)

MEASURE/MEASUREMENT/ MEASURING

This may depict how long in time—days and weeks—something will be. It may be saying how "big" something is in your life, or even how you measure up to your own or other people's expectations.

MEAT

To eat meat in your dream is to partake of physical experiences or material values. Meat also represents sexual or sensual experience, physical strength, or prowess. We often say one man's meat is another man's poison. Here it represents your likes and dislikes, the characteristics and experiences of life.

MECHANIC

This is your means of dealing with habitual reactions to life. Your skill at dealing with problems, such as when you can't get going in the mornings, or on a project.

MEDICINE

This is healing energies that can be released into your conscious life, or positive changes that can be made to happen. Sometimes it means you are being made to, or need to, take something against your will.

MEDICINE MAN *see* Guru.

MEDITATION

If you dream of meditating, the dream often

defines a form of meditation that suits you. As a symbol, it portrays your approach to yourself, a way of dealing with stress, or an attempt to turn away from the external world.

MEDIUM

A medium may represent your intuition, premonitions; or it can relate to the dead.

MEET/MET/MEETING

This suggests the way you handle meeting other people or a relationship. The actions in the dream will define this. This is also about the way you meet and deal with the many different aspects of your own personality.

MENSTRUATION

This association depends very much on your age and gender. But if you are female, it can suggest emerging sexuality and childbearing, and any joys or worries you have about this. Young women often experiment in their dreams with menstruation and pregnancy long before they want to experience sex fully. It may refer to your acceptance or conflict with this powerful process of life working in you. In a sense it takes over your body as distinct from your personal desires. This calls for some adjustment, so the dreams may illustrate this. The dream may reflect concerns about pregnancy, or occasionally may reveal that you are expecting a baby. Lastly, the dream may show actual physical conditions needing attention. If you are worried about any such dream, check with your doctor.

MERMAID/MERMAN

This suggests love arising from the unconscious, or the unconscious drive toward reproduction, or seduction toward reproduction. In some cases, it can show your love of someone's image, rather than their actual being. A mermaid in particular depicts the inner image of womanhood, still held in, or emerging from, the waters of the unconscious.

MESSAGE/MESSAGES/MESSENGER

This is a way your unconscious makes you think about important things, or gives you information. It can also suggest intuitive insight into whatever the message is about.

METAL *see* Iron.

METRO *see* Subway.

MICROSCOPE

This is being aware of the underlying and unknown parts of your personality. It can possibly be an insight into how your body cells work, the intricate machinations of your mind, or it can be about your hidden feelings or responses—depending upon what it is that you are looking at through the microscope.

MILK

This generally refers to any feelings or needs that are connected with your mother or with mothering. If you are giving it, it means you are giving of yourself emotionally, nourishing someone or an aspect of yourself. Speech idioms give other meanings: don't cry over spilt milk; milksop; milk of human kindness; milking the system/business/person. (*see* Food, Drink)

MINE/MINING

The seven dwarfs of Snow White worked in a mine. They represent the unconscious physical and mental processes that support your conscious activities. The mine may be showing what resources you have within, as well as the state of these resources. If your dream shows an explosive land mine, it depicts your reactions that have been set in place in the past and can be triggered by present events.

MIRROR

This symbol has a great many levels of meaning. Basically, it is a looking at yourself, for better or worse. The face in the mirror may not match your own. In self-examination you may come across, or see, the worst or best parts of your personality. These are the things you do not usually see about yourself. The mirror appears in many religious books and in much folklore. Water was probably the first mirror and represents self-awareness.

MISTRESS

In the Jungian sense, this symbol shows an anima projection. It suggests being dominated or influenced by the projection of all our fantastic longings, imaginings, hopes, and desires for ideal love onto a physical and ordinary woman who is not such a wonderful creature. But as we long for her to be such, we project these qualities onto her. It may in fact be that the woman wishes to be regarded in this light, as a goddess, and so encourages these feelings.

In the legend of creation, before Eve, a being called Lilith was created by Adam's longings, but she was really only a phantom. Nevertheless, when Eve arrived, Adam's attention was still focused on Lilith. The same problem still haunts men and women.

MOAT

This suggests a defense used against others. Perhaps the "I feel ill" defense that may be used in a relationship.

MODEM

This in some way indicates how you communicate with others. It can illustrate problems you have with this. (*see* Telephone)

MONEY

In many dreams, money depicts your power to change things or do things, or it can be having power, even over someone else. It also links with personal potency and sexuality and self-giving, and what you pay for your desires or actions. It may depict what you value most in life, but occasionally connects with struggle or misery—to exist or to pay one's way.

instant interpreter

One very common dream is about neglecting a pet—for example, forgetting to feed a goldfish, or realizing there's only a few inches of water left in the tank. This reveals that we are neglecting a part of our own nature. We use pets to express this because they symbolize our natural urges in unnatural conditions.

MONGOOSE

This indicates attacks we make on our sexual feelings or on our strivings toward inner growth, or it can be the defense against anxiety.

MONK

This suggests changeless wisdom, or desires to leave the world. It can mean the influence of religious teachings on the unconscious. Some people may have been taught to dread hell, perpetual burning, and similar terrors. So the monk or priest may therefore represent the influences of the church's teachings. The monk may show the struggles you have with your sexual drive, feelings of guilt, and your personal wants.

MONKEY

Sometimes a monkey has the face of a man, or talks. In these dreams, tremendous power seems to accompany the monkey. This probably indicates the union of our instincts and intellect, which releases tremendous energies as conflict is removed. The monkey can also represent the flitting of interest from one thing to another, having no real intelligence, or being made to look like a fool. (*see* Ape)

MONSTER

Most monsters illustrate the effects of past traumas. Some such traumas may have arisen from events, such as having your tonsils out when young, being separated from your mother at an early age, or being involved in a war. In general, the monster depicts your personal fear, terror of death, failure, or impotence in the face of outer circumstances or inner urges. It can show attitudes, hates, and fears that have become monstrous and turned against you.

MOON

The most obvious association with the moon is love, romance, the sentimental, balmy experiences of life. It can also suggest youthful love and affection, the welling up of sentiments, and longing for the beloved. This is also linked with the irrational, the deep inner movements and urges within us, the tides of feeling, desire, or madness. It can suggest the pull and attraction of mysterious, dark, impelling desires, of women's strange, sensual, magical, and overpowering attraction, or vice versa. It can be all the unseen influences represented by the moon's effect on the tides. The new or old moon also symbolizes the woman's sexual organs, because of its shape. So therefore it represents femininity, irrational feelings, intuition, and lunacy. Because the moon is the companion of the earth and reflects the light of the sun at night, it is also used as the major symbol of intuition.

MORGUE/MORTUARY

This may depict parts of you that have died through being denied or not used. It may also reflect your feelings about death, or people you have known who have died. Or it can reflect parts of your experience you need to release and bury, or perform an autopsy on to understand them properly.

MOSAIC

This represents the countless fragments of experience and thoughts that may at first seem a meaningless jumble but, when seen from a wider awareness or perspective, become a pattern or design of beauty that represents life as a whole.

MOSQUE

This is surrender to the divine, or feelings about Islam. (*see* Church)

MOTH

Sometimes this represents those subtle fears that touch us in the dark. Or the blind urge to go toward something without any reasonable cause. (*see* Insects)

MOTHER

To dream of your mother usually signifies the feelings or pains you still feel in connection with her. A mother can represent all we want in a caring and loving relationship, or perhaps all we didn't get. Each of us has a fundamental, perhaps instinctive, drive to bond with a woman at birth. This has generated from millions of years of survival strategy. If that bonding does not take place, natural growth cannot, or does not, take place. So mother may represent this whole difficult issue of survival, and what happened in those early years of trying to become independent of such extraordinary needs.

MOTORBIKE

This is daring, youthful energy and unorthodox behavior. Sometimes, it also associates with sexual daring.

MOTORWAY *see* Freeway.

MOUSE

This suggests the activities within you that are not significant, but are irritating or subtly damaging. It indicates being small or insignificant, or it can be something that gnaws away at you. It can represent the sexual organs, a timid atti-tude, or fear, depending on your reactions when you see a mouse.

MOUTH

Dreaming of the mouth may suggest something to do with pleasure or gratification. It is also your hunger and sexual pleasure. The mouth represents the quality of the things you say, literally what comes out of your mouth in words. Not being able to open your mouth can suggest that you regret having said certain things and need to hold your tongue, or cannot express something. Idioms include: bite off more than you can chew; be mouthy; have a big mouth; or have a mouth like a sewer. When you are pulling things out of your mouth, it shows you trying to clear yourself of any emotions or attitudes that are not properly expressed. (*see* Chew)

MOVIE

This is sometimes a way of looking at a part of your behavior, or experimenting with feelings, as something outside of you, rather than confronting them as part of yourself. The theme of the film is usually important, because it will illustrate something relevant to your own life. In some cases it is an urge to escape from what is pressing in your life. (*see* Cinema)

MUD

In some dreams, as in a muddy road or swamp, the mud is simply the retarding aspect of your hesitations and fears. In other dreams, people search through or dig in the mud, which represents the cleansing of emotions caused by outer circumstances, the looking through the experience or muck of your life for its treasure, for often a flower or jewel may be found in the mud. Mud is like clay, a substance that can be molded, so it may indicate the "shaping" of your basic memories and emotions. Mud may also symbolize healing, as it contains all the elements of the past, which we need for completeness. Speech idioms include: Mud slinging; drag somebody through the mud; one's name is mud; stick in the mud.

MUMMY (Egyptian)

This is the attempt to preserve yourself as you are, instead of allowing the constant change, death and rebirth that life always brings. This only results in mummification or desiccation. The mummy may also appear in your dreams when a partner or someone very close to you has died, and there are still difficult feelings about them you need to resolve.

MURDER/MURDERER

This suggests a repression of your feelings or areas of your life. A man may kill his love for a woman because she does not come from a wealthy family. Or we may kill our feelings because we are ashamed or feel guilty about them. We may kill a creative streak in ourselves because of feelings of incapability. The murderer is a representation of a fear that is threatening to, or is, killing our feelings and energy. A trauma can often lead to murderous rage, which is held deep in the unconscious and is only represented in some dreams. (*see* Death)

MUSCLE

This represents physical strength, a sense of being outwardly forceful and impressive, masculinity in its physical aspect. Some muscle dreams actually refer to what is happening in your muscles.

MUSIC

This indicates harmony in yourself, or feelings that are harmonious and emotions that heal and soothe, or stimulate and rouse you.

MUSICAL INSTRUMENT

This symbol shows how well you are able to express your flowing feelings and spontaneous creativity. In some dreams it links with what you feel about sex or your genitals, and how well you can express your pleasure and those feelings. If it appears as a large and complex instrument, it may be depicting your mind.

MUSTANG

This suggests youthful sexuality, aggression, or nonconformity. (*see* Horse)

soul solution

Alissa dreamed of a child reaching feebly for help from beneath heavy robes. She realized that the child represented her own needs for recognition and cries for help when young. Alissa saw how she had numbed herself to meet everyday needs. It led her to care for the part of herself she had denied, to reach out more fully for her needs as a woman.

N O

NAIL

This is binding power or the strength to hold together in the same way as a common belief binds people together of opposite temperaments. A nail may also represent, as in Christ being nailed to the cross, the painful links that bind us to our body, our earthly experience, our pains and trials.

NAKED

This suggest revealing your feelings, thoughts, and reactions that you usually conceal. You may disguise dislike with a smile. If you are not pleased to meet someone, you may hide your feelings with courteous behavior, shaking hands, but a child will usually refuse to talk to, shake hands, or associate with someone they dislike. Their real feelings are therefore naked to view. To be naked in a dream may show either a fear of, or a dcsirc for, people knowing your real feelings. It can also be a fear of being disclosed, or a discovery of your real self. Some dreams in which you are naked show extreme self-consciousness about other people seeing you. In other cases, the dreamer enjoys being on view, likes people, or the doctor, looking at them. Sexual feelings are often a part of these dreams. (*see* Clothes)

NAME

Your name summarizes you. So changing your name can suggest a change in the way that you see or express yourself. Someone else's name can depict your feelings and intuitions about them.

NATION

This indicates characteristics that are symbolized by people as a whole. (*see* Abroad)

NAVEL

This is a symbol of your outer connection with your innermost feelings and being. It also represents a sign of dependency, perhaps on your mother, or on the life process on earth.

NEAR/NEARER/NEAREST/NEARNESS

When something is near you in your dream, it shows the strength of your feelings about it, or how aware of it you are. The nearer it is, the more strongly you feel about it.

NECK

You can stick your neck out, which means to take a risk, or have a lot of nerve or audacity. These meanings have arisen possibly from the head being severed in execution, or hanging, or strangulation. The neck is a weak point, and to offer it suggests confidence or fearlessness. So the neck may depict a certain attitude, such as confidence or caution. It is also the point up to which we can be easily immersed in water; beyond that point there is danger. So it can depict what we can take in life, and what is more than enough, which is suggested by the saying, "up to one's neck in it." Problems with the neck often refer to the way it can act as a bottleneck, or of a traffic jam for deeply felt emotions. In such a case you need to examine what feelings are persisting, what emotions or words you haven't allowed yourself to say. As your neck connects your head (your mental capacity) with your body (your feelings and sexuality), dreaming of it may refer to a split or non-connection between these two main areas of your being that needs to be investigated.

To be strangled in a dream may be caused by breathing difficulties, or feelings of being unable to express yourself easily or to say what you really feel. Some relationship situations leave people feeling that life is being choked out of them. To have your head cut off is to have your thinking abilities divorced or removed from your feelings.

NECKLACE

This is a symbol of power, authority, an augmentation of personality, social attractiveness, or it can denote a charm or an amulet. It may also represent the things you hang round your neck, such as a millstone, obligations, difficulties, or setbacks. It may link to the person who gave it to you and your relationship with them. (*see* Jewelry)

NEEDLE

This indicates sharp pain, self-searching, or the male sex organ. It is the ability to mend things,

dream messenger

Some dreams let your mind leap beyond its usual boundaries. Research at Maimonides Medical Center, Brooklyn, showed that people often telepathically connect while dreaming. They may foresee the future and solve life problems.

such as a relationship or situation.

NEIGHBOR

This probably depicts the qualities you feel they have; neighbors may be helpful or grumpy. Or it may be used as a male or female symbol. (*see* Male/Man, Female)

NEST

This is the female sex organs or the womb or womb consciousness. It indicates protection, relaxation, warmth, home, or homemaking, parenthood, or a nest egg.

NET

This is the subtle aspects of emotions, words, or a relationship in which you may get trapped. It can be attitudes in yourself or others that may trap or imprison you. It can also be the ideas and beliefs you hold that entangle you in conflicts, and which can restrict your response to life.

NEWS/NEWSPAPER

This symbol is something that is commonly known. It can be thoughts or memories that you are becoming aware of, or already know about. It can also be consciousness as distinct from unconsciousness.

NICKNAME

This probably associates with feelings you have, or memories that are connected to the person or people who gave you the nickname. It can also be whatever you feel about the name. (*see* Name)

NIGHT

There can be many different associations with night in your dream. So try to define what you are feeling. Some possibilities are: not understanding clearly what is going on around you, anxiety about being in the dark, feelings of freedom because you are no longer on view in the light, relaxation and mellow feelings, intimacy and freedom to express yourself. (*see* Light, Black)

NINE

This relates to the fact that all numbers rise in series of nines and then begin again, and that human babies are born in the ninth month. So seeing the number nine symbolizes the completion of a process, or stage of growth. There are also, in some mythologies and religions, nine orders of angels or forces. (*see* Numbers)

NIPPLE

This represents infantile feelings of longing or hunger, mixed with sexual feelings of pleasure. (*see* Breasts)

NOON

This indicates your active waking life, the height of your waking consciousness, your ego

and rationalism. It can also suggest being halfway through life—middle age.

NOOSE

This connotes feelings about being caught or trapped, or a desire to catch or trap. It can be a fear of, or desire for, death.

NORTH

This can sometimes depict the "north" and "south" of your body—your head and genitals. If you live in the northern hemisphere, it may suggest darkness, unconsciousness, cold, or a situation that leads you to seek the light and warmth. Sometimes, it indicates death or frozen emotions. If you live in the Southern hemisphere, it suggests light, warmth, life, and positive growth.

NORTH STAR

This is your guiding star or guardian angel. The star that guides you through your life's journey. It can also be intuition.

NOTICE

This literally means to notice or to be conscious of something.

NUMBERS

These are difficult to define and are very often only connected with personal associations. They may refer to a particular year of your life, a number of a house you lived in, a date that something happened, how many children you have and their order of birth. They may also draw your attention to these events and emotions surrounding them. Sometimes they may refer simply to multiplicity or size—a crowd of events, a big experience, or a many- faceted realization. However, since humans first counted numbers have had a fascinating, mysterious and even magical significance. In this way, early humans discovered inner qualities in numbers, or possibly unconscious wisdom. Dreams often use numbers in the same way. (*see* also the separate numbers: One, Two, Three, etc.)

NUT

This shows a fool. It is also the symbol of the inner self, or the kernel of truth.

OAK

This is usually strength, endurance, or shelter. (*see* Acorn, Cross, Tree)

OAR

This is a means of steering your life through the influences or currents that try to take you off course. It may also have a phallic significance due to its in and out motion. It can be used as word play for whore.

OASIS

The oasis brings the possibility of being alive and fertile in the middle of aridity and where there is no growth. It may suggest finding or losing a sense of well-being. (*see* Desert)

OBSESSION

We can be possessed or obsessed by all manner of things. We might not be able to give up smoking, for instance, or someone else's needs may overpower our own. Even the act of love can be seen at times as a form of obsession, during which we are carried away by a torrent of feelings. Dreams tend to depict such feelings as an obsessing influence.

OBSTACLE

This suggests you are facing some difficulty that you feel is blocking what you want to do, or is opposing or restricting your freedom of action. The barrier can be external or internal, so you need to consider or meditate on what it is in your life that is leading to this obstructive feeling.

OCEAN *see* Sea, Water.

OCTOPUS

If you are the octopus, it may symbolize the desire to seize another in your emotions and possess them. Or it may represent fear of being possessed by such emotions, either in you or in another. One psychiatrist, Hadfield, has pointed out that a baby at its mother's breast often seizes upon her in this way while suckling. So sometimes the octopus represents feelings you have about your mother. The octopus can also represent terrors that drag you down.

OCULIST

This is the aspect of yourself that attempts to improve our view of things, or gives us a false view. (*see* Eye Glasses, Spectacles)

OFFER/OFFERED/OFFERING

To offer something in a dream, or be offered something, usually depicts some sort of change, perhaps one in which a decision has to be made about whether you are going to accept or not. It may also suggest extending yourself, or being reached out to in some way. This may involve some level of risk or exposure to rejection or being used.

OFFICER/OFFICIAL

This mostly symbolizes the part of you that is in control of a particular part of your emotions. A love for a husband and children may act as a controlling factor on desires to have a good time with others, or over innate laziness. A fear of being a nobody may direct ambitions and plans. Sometimes, it represents a feeling of confidence or wholeness that brings authority to guide and direct. It also associates with any dealing you have with authority, and what this brings out in you. So it may refer to your father in some way. It can therefore show how you "authorize" or judge your actions.

OGRE

This symbol generally indicates temper, anger, or a lack of sympathy or understanding that devours or crushes others. Or it can be a symbol of the same thing in others, and how we relate to it. This may be a childhood impression of a parent.

OIL

This indicates how we can pour oil on troubled waters, be an oily or slippery sort of person, or be well oiled. The word is sometimes used to mean flattery, unctuousness, cunning, or working well. It can mean the removal of friction, argument, and disagreement. In parables, it is referred to as resourcefulness, forethought,

and as a symbol for the soul.

OINTMENT

This is a healing or soothing influence or feeling. It can indicate feelings to do with care and contact, or in some cases it may associate with injury or illness.

ONE

This is the first number and cannot be divided. It symbolizes you as an individual, a beginning, or something separate. It is the first manifestation, something that is so basic and fundamental that it cannot be divided. It represents the first cause. You can divide into any number leaving that number unchanged. It therefore represents the power of the unchanging, for example, a hundred divided by one is still a hundred. (*see* Numbers)

ONION

This may represent crying or tears, or something we find difficult to face. It sometimes

true dream story

Lucy dreamed that she was standing at the foot of an ex-boyfriend's bed, watching him sleeping as she had in waking life. In the dream, Lucy felt love for her ex-boyfriend and wanted to reach out to him to touch his soul. Many women have a passionate need for "soul" love. The frustration of not receiving this causes such dreams, and sometimes creates a love for someone who doesn't warrant it.

represents the layers of your personality. Its symbolism possibly arises from its layers going into a center. Onions have also been used as a symbol to ward off the devil, as with garlic.

OPAL *see* Jewels.

OPERA

This sometimes depicts either the dramatization of your inner feelings, the drama of your life, or the stage of life, or the stage of development reached. (*see* Stage)

OPERATION

This can indicate an inner attitude that may be sick, but which is being sorted out. It may also show a fear of illness, or memories connected with an actual past operation.

ORANGE

This color suggests warmth or wholeness. It shows the influence of the mysterious process of life and life energy. The fruit depicts satisfaction or fruitfulness. Because of its color, orange is often used as a vibrant sun symbol. (*see* Color)

ORCHARD

This depicts a sense of possible growth and fruition in your life. It may be that things have already reached fruition, or that your efforts are leading to growth, depending on the season shown in the dream. (*see* Garden)

ORE

This indicates latent possibilities you are developing through personal effort. It can also link with deep levels of your memory or

unconscious psyche that are being brought to your awareness at this time.

ORGAN

This shows your different feelings and responses that can be stimulated by situations. It can be the wonderful possibilities of mind or spirit.

ORIENT *see* East.

ORPHAN

This is the fear of, or feelings about, being unloved. It can be a feeling of being misunderstood, insecure, or homeless, either in mind or body. It particularly links with feelings or fears of abandonment by the person you love.

OSTRICH

This symbol normally relates to sticking your head in the sand because you do not want to see what is happening.

OVARIES/OVUM

This denotes childbirth and any feelings or fears you have about it. The ovaries also depict fruitfulness or sterility.

OVEN

In common speech the oven is used as a symbol of the womb, for example the phrase "one in the oven" refers to pregnancy. It is also a symbol of the crucible or melting pot, where life changes are made. The oven is a magical instrument because we put in one substance that may be inedible and out comes something quite different. It therefore represents transformation.

OVERCOAT

This indicates protective attitudes or feelings. It is the feelings you show in public. It can also mean not displaying any intimacy. (*see* Clothes)

OWL

This is about intuition and intuitive wisdom because of the owl's ability to see in the dark and turn its gaze in any direction. It sometimes represents a fear of the dark or your inner self, or of death or the unconscious—the latter being synonymous. Because of its ease with the dark unconscious, the owl in your dreams can sometimes act as a guide or adviser.

OX

This represents the earthy, practical, service-giving, and sexual parts of human nature. (*see* Animal, Bull)

OXYGEN

This is energy or life-giving forces.

OYSTER

This symbol represents silence, tight-lipped or secretive behavior, or it can mean hiding a secret beauty. It may also represent the body, or material existence, in which your psyche develops in the same way as a pearl, through irritation, and is trapped by its restrictions. In some dreams, it depicts the protective shell closed around your inner feelings or sexuality. Eating oysters is thought by some to stimulate sexuality, so it could be a symbol of this. And there is the saying "the world is my oyster," suggesting that we can find riches and beauty in life once we open the shell. (*see* Clam)

P

PACK/PACKED/PACKING

Packing can connect with leaving home, becoming independent, or being rejected. So analyze your feelings about the last time you packed your bags or house goods as your dream probably looks back at those feelings. It can associate with holiday feelings, and so gives a sense of ease. It can also link with making changes or wanting to change. Packing somebody else's bags may therefore mean you want them to go, or you want them to go away with you.

PADDLE *see* Oar.

PADLOCK *see* Lock.

PAINT

There are many sayings that illustrate how paint can be used in dreams. We can paint the town red, paint too rosy a picture, whitewash everything, paint too clear a picture. These sayings suggest releasing pent-up high spirits, being too optimistic, trying to cover up mistakes, or being too honest. Painting can also mean self-expression, showing your inner self, hiding the condition of things with a veneer of paint, or putting a new appearance on things.

PAJAMAS/PYJAMAS

These represent your intimate feelings. It is the part of you only shared with people to whom you are close. It often indicates a feeling of closeness to someone emotionally or sexually. (*see* Clothes)

PALACE

Your dream palace may be indicating that you are exploring, or beginning to become aware of, the qualities and potential you have inherited from your cultural upbringing and forebears. It may also suggest class roles and privilege.

PAN

If this is a cooking pan, it may link with the care you give to yourself or your family, with everyday life and its needs, or it may represent some sort of receptive situation. A cooking pot is similar to an oven. It can also mean a receptive part of you that receives new things and is open to change. (*see* Cook, Oven, Food)

A chamber pot refers to what you need to discharge, either emotionally or physically. It may also refer to the female genitals.

The god Pan suggests some loss of yourself, or abandonment to natural urges, such as sex.

PANTIES

This represents your hidden feelings—your sexual feelings and desires. (*see* Clothes)

PANTS

Very frequently these depict your sexual feelings, your desires, or what you may be hiding of yourself. (*see* Clothes)

PAPER

This is possibilities, communication, ideas, or self-expression. If the paper has writing on it, it depicts connections with the past, or with other people's ideas and wants if it is their writing. Otherwise, it shows memories or an awareness of thoughts and sentiments you may have forgotten. Paper can also suggest something valueless. Sometimes the word "paper" refers to a project or essay, so it may link with college or work. Paper may be used as a container, so it can suggest contents, or something you have wrapped up inside you. (*see* Newspaper)

PARACHUTE

This is a skill you use to overcome the fear of falling or failing. It therefore suggests a feeling or a technique to deal with anxieties. (*see* Fall)

PARADISE

This may suggest that you are feeling in harmony with yourself. It can also indicate that you have been practicing some form of meditation, and you have felt the timeless state within yourself. The experience of being in the womb is often felt to be paradise.

PARALYZED/PARALYSIS

This is an expression of how fear paralyzes you. Sometimes we become paralyzed because our unconscious fears come to the surface, or urges that we fear arise. We can also be paralyzed by a sense of guilt, a sense of inadequacy, or ignorance. When Jesus healed the paralyzed man he said, "Thy sins are forgiven thee." This suggests the paralysis arose from a sense of guilt. Sometimes, while dreaming, a person experiences a profound physical paralysis. This occurs because while you dream your brain switches off the voluntary muscles. If you then become semi-awake and attempt to move, it can feel as if you are paralyzed. The resulting fear causes deeper paralysis. If this happens to you, remember that the cause is a temporary loss of control of the voluntary muscles. When you realize this, you can wake slowly without anxiety.

PARASITE

This symbol represents fears, thoughts, and feelings that diminish well-being. For example, while relaxing, a man saw a dark and frightening shape leave the region of his heart. The man had suffered an illness and now feared a weakness concerning his heart. The dark shape was an embodiment of this fear, sapping his energies in the same way as a parasite. It can appear in dreams as a demon or incubus, and represent our own terrors, fears, thoughts, and desires that are out of harmony with our innate energy. We unconsciously give a shape to such subjective feelings as anxiety to make them more understandable. Often, we do not believe the enormous effect anxiety has on us, especially when we repress it with drugs, such as alcohol or nicotine.

PARCEL/PACKAGE

This is usually a memory, idea, or experience you have not explored or opened to your consciousness. It can be unused talents, ideas not applied, or loving words you have not said. It is also the silent gifts of love and support received from others that you may not have appreciated.

PARK

This represents relaxed feelings, depending

upon whether the park is light or in darkness, etc. It is also the way you relate to other people or society. A national park depicts your sense of who you are without social restraints or training—your natural self.

PARKING LOT/PARKED/CARPARK

A car often represents a resource you use to get somewhere in the outer world, and the parking lot suggests leaving behind or accessing this skill or attitude. These are the skills or attitudes necessary to achieve goals in life. So it may indicate a switching of attitudes or roles.

PARROT

This suggests copying what others do or say. (*see* Bird)

PASSAGE

This is a way of making a change, or the restrictions you accept to arrive somewhere. It can be the difficulties you face in growing or changing. The passage, like a tunnel, can sometimes depict what you met in being born. It can also link to the rectum (the back passage) and the vagina (the front passage). (*see* Corridor)

PASSENGER

If you are in a car, it suggests you are following someone else's lead. It can be a dependence on other people's decisions, energy, or drive. Or it can be a mutual direction being taken, for example, in a business venture. (*see* Car)

PASSPORT

This is a symbol of travel, of change, of your integrity or identity. It also relates to feelings of confidence about being accepted, facing authority, or going beyond your usual limitations or boundaries.

PATH

This is your life's direction, the ideas that govern where you are going. If you enjoy caring for others, you may go along the path of healing or medical practice. The path, therefore, shows the direction of your predominant feelings. To lose the way, or go off the path, is to lose contact with or become confused over your best interests, or to miss seeing the direction cues around you. So a well-worn path shows your habitual direction.

PAY/PAYING/PAID

In nearly all the dreams studied that refer to pay, the action is to pay for something such as a fare or goods. Few of them include being paid. This suggests that pay and paying depict concerns about wanting to, or having to, give something of value, either to get something, or to deal with a situation. The payment can therefore refer to what you have to bring to a situation to make it work or to get positive results. If you are being paid, it shows the results of previous effort, or the reward for who you have been, what you have done, or are doing. (*see* Money)

PEACOCK

This connotes pride, what you show outwardly, an attempt to impress. It is also renewal and vanity.

PEARL

This represents a beautiful personal quality that has developed through trials. Pearls can also represent loss or pain. (*see* Jewels)

PEDESTAL

This is to place apart, to separate, to place above other things, to idolize, value, or worship.

PEGASUS *see* Horse.

PELVIS

In general the pelvis relates to your sexuality and feelings, or difficulties in that area. In a woman, it more specifically connotes the ability to conceive and bear a child. (*see* Body)

PENDANT *see* Necklace.

PENIS

In a man's dream, this represents the sexual urge or the male sense of identity. It is all of the male polarity, including the glandular and emotional disposition. What is happening to the penis in the dream relates to the male identity. It is therefore often depicting a man's own power of self-expression, his potency in expressing himself, and capability in the world.

The genitals predispose his body toward male sexual characteristics. They bring a certain creative explosiveness to his personality, they create urges toward fatherhood and loving his partner, and desires to help his family if he is emotionally healthy. The positive side of these drives is for him to expect his partner to meet his power with her own dynamism.

Femaleness or maleness must not be confused with personality. The conscious personality is a very flexible and shape-shifting thing. It can be male or female in quality, no matter what the body gender. But in dreams, the female is the receptive, creative aspect of this shape-shifting personality. The penis in a woman's dream, represents a desire for a mate, her relationship with her own male characteristics, such as ambition, work capability, and the ease or difficulty in sexual relationships.

PENTACLE

This often represents the human body, or the subtle eternal life of the person. (*see* Five)

PEPPER

This represents a stimulant, being hot tempered, heated feelings, or desires to heat up an affair.

PEOPLE

If there are several people in a dream, it usually depicts the way you relate to other people or the different aspects of yourself. It can also be about your social skills or difficulties.

PET

This can have several associations, but is generally about caring. The caring can be a need to care for or love someone or something. The pet is also often a source of unconditional love in our childhood, and so can represent that. Pets are also dependent creatures and the dream can indicate feelings of dependence, especially by children who know what it is like to feel dependent, and have that need neglected. (*see* Animals)

PERFUME/SCENT/SMELL/ODOR

This depends entirely on the odor, and what emotions surround it. For example, you can say "I smell a rat," or "something smells fishy," or "the whole situation stinks to high heaven." A perfume can remind you of a particular person and trigger your feelings about them, or it can evoke particular memories or special feelings or moods. Odors often represent feelings of attraction or repulsion. They can link to fresh or stale food, or be associated with the act of living or dying. They can also represent feelings radiating from you, or from what you sense intuitively about others.

PERSPIRE/PERSPIRATION/SWEAT

This indicates the presence of strong emotion: being deeply moved, excitement, fear, or very intense feelings. If you are worried about your body odor in the dream it suggests that you are ill at ease about how other people feel about you.

PETROL see Fuel, Gasoline.

PETTICOAT

This represents your inner feelings that few people see. Sometimes, the symbol depicts sexual feelings, or even the "aura" of a person. (*see* Clothes)

PHANTOM *see* Ghost, Demon.

PHARMACY/PHARMACIST
see Chemist.

PHOENIX

This shows that we all may have to release a new self after the death of the old. (*see* Death)

PHOTOGRAPH

This is usually about memories and all the feelings connected with the person or situation it depicts.

PHYSICIAN *see* Doctor.

PIANO

This is an expression of yourself in some way. (*see* Musical Instrument)

PICTURE/PAINTING

This is your works, the things you have done, the picture you have painted of your possibilities and inner world. It is an expression of any subtle realizations or intuitions you have. (*see* Photograph)

PIG

This shows someone being low, greedy, or having no refinement. But because of the sow's ability to suckle enormous numbers of piglets, it may also symbolize sustenance of a material sort, or motherhood. Being pigheaded relates to stubbornness. Generally, it represents sensuality that is lost in material vices. It can sometimes mean the power of material experience.

PILL

This is something you can take in or reject that can influence you in some way. The pill can refer to the contraceptive pill and birth control. The idiom "a bitter pill" illustrates another meaning, that of facing a difficult experience.

PILLOW

This suggests restful, relaxing thoughts and feelings. It indicates the softer parts of you, or it can be someone you want to hug or hit.

PIMPLE

This relates to irritating inner feelings that have come to the surface. It can be worries about how you appear to others, or it is a personality trait that is not healthy.

PIN

This is how you connect to things, for example, as in the phrase "you can't pin that on me." It can mean good luck or minor hurt, possibly from someone else. It also links to painful sex.

PIPE/TUBE

Pipes sometimes represent connections, the passage of feelings or influence between people. A large pipe or tube may depict a difficult way out of a situation, or big social connections. Crawling through a pipe suggests

soul solution

Clive had suffered from a lack of praise from his father. His subsequent avoidance of authority figures had led him to miss out on many opportunities. When Clive dreamed he was in his father's shop, helping a man who had been shot in the left arm, he was able to meet the pain from his past and move toward greater accomplishment.

feelings or fears of being hemmed in, being trapped in the narrow straits or difficult circumstances. It may also represent birth, either symbolically or as intense emotional memories. A sewage pipe indicates the group unconscious—the negative feelings of society.

PIPE SMOKING

This suggests masculinity, adulthood, assurance, calm, patient and peaceful feelings, or possibly fears about cancer.

PISS

This is letting go of tension or deep emotions. It can be feelings of relief or life flowing through you. Dreams where you try to go to the toilet but find it mysteriously locked may be due to the need to pass urine during the night. (*see* Toilet)

PISTON

This represents force, energy, or the penis.

PIT

This is a possible difficulty you may fall into if you are not aware. It can show you being trapped in the pit by events or circumstances that have come about because of attitudes and desires. It can also be problems or feelings of being imprisoned and buried by your life.

PLAIT

This is the inner strength that comes from uniting parts of yourself into one aim or direction. Plaited hair may suggest youth or girlhood. (*see* Hair)

PLANE *see* Aeroplane/Airplane.

PLANET

You may use a planet in a dream to suggest a subtle influence touching your life. A planet may also suggest a different lifestyle or experience, perhaps through a relationship or change.
Sun This is your center, the source of vital energy and life. It can be consciousness and awareness, or warmth and uplifting moods. (*see* Sun)
Moon This represents subtle, half-seen influences in your life and love. It can also be strange moods. (*see* Moon)
Mercury This indicates intuition. It represents the universal mind or knowledge of all things. It can also relate to changes, or be a reflection of change, as with mercury in a thermometer. Therefore, the god Mercury, can be a guide.
Venus This is love, motherhood, receptivity, feminine loveliness, and gentleness to which a man can turn and find strength and inspiration. It is the wife and mother of God (Mary), a man's wife, or possibly Eve from the Garden of Eden. It can also be emotions, feelings, sympathy, beauty, harmony, and love.
Mars This is an expression of energy through activities. It can be destructive, or add vigor to

creativeness. It is masculine and aggressive. It is an energy that is ruled by passions.
Jupiter This planet relates to growth and preservation. It shows a huge benevolent nature. It is the soul becoming free materially. It also links to wealth, prosperity and good fortune.
Saturn This connotes slowness, a retarding influence, or emotional coldness. It is the ruler of fate and time, so it is your kismet or karma.
Uranus This is change, fluctuation, or the sudden reversals in life.
Neptune This links to psychic ability, emotions, your inner self, death or rebirth, and the unconscious mind.

PLANTS

Depending on the plant, this shows something growing in you, or it is your experience. It can sometimes represent your children and their progress. If the plant is shriveled, it shows a lack of life energy in some area of your life.

PLATE

This refers to having "a lot on one's plate." It means having a lot to cope with or get through. A plate with food can depict what is in front of you in life, what you have received or earned. It may also suggest your needs or appetites. At one time a plate was a symbol of status, when only the rich had china or silver.

PLATEAU

This often appears in the dreams of people who have reached mid-life. It suggests reaching a place where they can rest, as there is less need to keep climbing in search of security or a better job. It can also mean there is no change, or things are more even and certain.

PLAY—in a theater

This is often a way of bringing a theme to your attention. The theme often refers to something important. The play may also be a way of exploring things, such as a relationship or a dangerous situation. This allows you to practice dealing with it. It can also be the "play" of thoughts or emotions. The play is usually happening in the public eye, so it may include the theme of being seen, being liked, or judged.

PLAYING

This shows a way of experimenting and practicing skills without too much risk. So we can play at flirting, for example, and find out what works in finding a partner. Dream play often has this element of trying out things without commitment, or being creative. The tremendous number of idioms containing the word "play" show the many possibilities of the action in dreams— there are too many to list.

PLUMBING

This is the flow or control of your emotions. A burst water pipe may therefore represent being very emotional. Or it can depict an actual physical ailment, possibly in the intestines or the "water works"—the urinary tract. (*see* Tap)

POCKET

This indicates your memory, your inner reserves of vitality or money, your capabilities or tools. It is also what you possess or carry through life. It sometimes depicts the vagina.

POCKETBOOK *see* Wallet.

POEM/POET/POETRY

This is your imagination that may, through inspiration or intuition, express your deepest feelings, which may be hidden to the more conservative, conscious side of you. (*see* Proverb)

POISON

This is a warning that you may be taking in something that can harm you mentally, emotionally, or physically. This may be in the form of words, thoughts, or substances.

POLICE/POLICEMAN/ POLICEWOMAN

This is the discipline put on our actions, and therefore our social code, our sense of right and wrong, or how we wish to appear in the eyes of others. The policeman does not necessarily represent your most important directions, but only social or moral codes. These, like the country's laws, can change arbitrarily and be replaced by others. The policeman is, therefore, most often a symbol of how we feel about outer and social relationships. He often links with ideas or feelings about punishment, and behavior influenced by needing to conform to orthodoxy or uniformity. The policewoman is similar to the policeman, but gives more of a feeling of personal connections, sympathies and feeling values than from conscious or unconscious feelings of wrongdoing or guilt.

POLLEN

This may suggest hidden seeds of ideas or even sperm. But it can indicate invisible irritants, such as allergies, or even criticism that attacks you.

POOL

This is the inner world of your mind and imagination. It particularly links with looking into yourself and becoming aware of what you are feeling or daydreaming. Sometimes, if you are in the pool or remember being in the pool, it may be referring to a time, perhaps in the womb, when you felt connected with all living things through a shared awareness.

POP STAR *see* Famous People.

POSTER *see* Newspaper.

POSTMAN

This is a part of yourself, or a realization that brings something to your notice. It represents hopes and how you communicate.

POSTURE

This is a major way a dream communicates

meaning. It expresses things you may never have put into words. Therefore, postures and movement in dreams express how you think beneath the layer of your everyday life. Because there are so many postures you may make in your dream, it is impossible to list them all. You can arrive at their meaning by taking on the quality of the posture, or exploring the movement, to see what it feels like. Then take time to put it into words so that you make the subtle feeling more conscious and known. (*see* Movement)

POTATO

This depends more than usual on the dreamer's own associations. Do you regard the potato as fattening, starchy, forbidden, enjoyable, messy, or what? (*see* Food)

POTTER

We can potter around, which suggests doing nothing in particular. Objectively, it may depict an attempt to shape the raw material that is your life. Subjectively, it suggests outside influences.

PRECIPICE

This is a fear of falling or fear of failure. It can be a difficulty in attaining your goal, if you are at the bottom. It may be confrontation with great change, or a leap into the unknown, or something that makes you anxious. It is also the sense of the enormous expanse of the mind and spirit. (*see* Cliff, Fall)

PREGNANCY

If you are physically pregnant, it relates to this state, and the fears, hopes, attitudes, desires, and your physical condition regarding it. It can also depict the development of a new approach to life, a new outlet of expression. If you are pregnant, don't be too worried by anxiety dreams about the baby as virtually all women have them. Only worry if they persist. A doctor can check to see if you are just being anxious or intuitive. Research has shown that frequent anxiety dreams actually reduce tension during delivery.

PREHISTORIC/PRIMEVAL

This represents deep levels of the unconsciousness. It is levels of your being that developed in past ages, but which are being given to you as a physical and mental heritage. We feel these as instincts, or as profoundly strong reactions to situations. It is the part of us that makes the hair stand up at times when we sense something we do not understand.

PRESENT

This depends very much on who or what gives you the present. It may be about love or recognition. (*see* Parcel, Package)

PRIEST

This depends on your attitude toward priests and your experiences of them. It may represent religious aspirations or possibly a sense of sin.

PRINCE

This is conscious (or in a woman possibly unconscious) intellectual or masculine qualities. Sometimes, it depicts the attitudes and qualities in us that search for truth, which try to find their way through personal difficulties, or which attempt to direct or use our physical and mental heritage. A prince often represents the best in a man, and an ideal male in a woman's dream.

PRINCESS

This is your conscious (or in a man unconscious) emotional, intuitive, or feminine qualities. Sometimes it is the inner self, your receptive nature. It can indicate beauty and love. The princess in a woman's dream can depict her inner strength to deal with difficulties and problems.

PRISON/PRISONER/IMPRISONED

This is often feeling imprisoned by your inability to cope with circumstances, moods, or relatives. You can feel trapped by inadequacies, fears, or ambitions. It can be any limiting inner or outer influence. You can be imprisoned by an idea or a fear, blaming others for your situation, or it can be a moral code. Try and discover what you are doing to hold yourself back.

PRIZE

This suggests a gain in self-understanding or insight through your endeavors. It can be achieving something valuable, or a desire to win, or be superior. It can be a fear of losing or feeling rewarded. It is occasionally intuition about forthcoming acclaim. It can also be that you are seeking praise and recognition.

PROVERB

Many people dream of a popular proverb, or a sentence from a poem, hymn or song. This is because it summarizes their feelings, desires, or inner feelings as depicted in the dream.

PSYCHOANALYSIS/ANALYST

This frequently shows your own intuitions or insights into dealing with your personal difficulties or dilemmas. (*see* Analyst, Guru)

PULL/PULLED/PULLING

If you are pulling something, it shows you being active about a problem you are confronting—you are pitting your will against something. If you are being pulled, it suggests an influence that is affecting you in some way. Perhaps you are being pulled by your emotions, or you are attracted to someone.

PUNISHMENT/TORTURE

This may be showing the way you punish yourself or feel pain because of the beliefs you hold or the standards by which you live. Sometimes, it illustrates the struggle between your natural impulses and your social training or conditioning. Torture, in the same way as crucifixion, can indicate that you are arriving at a new freedom or inspiring future. (*see* Hell)

PUPPET

This suggests being controlled by another's whims, or being controlling in the same way. It can also indicate you are being made a puppet of your own desires, by a love of whisky, religious ideas, or betting, for example.

PUPPY

This symbol often depicts all the things we love or hate about babies and children, such as their spontaneous and thoughtless behavior and exuberance. It can also represent a baby, or desire for a baby, or feelings about your childhood. Like a baby, the puppy is deeply dependent and can be neglected. So the starving puppy in your dream shows the neglect of your own lively enthusiasm, or how it was neglected in childhood.

PURCHASE/PURCHASING

This usually links with decision making. It may also be dramatizing the way your actions are directed by internal and external influences, such as other people's suggestions or pressure. It may indicate the way you relate to money, and whether you use buying things as a way of dealing with stress.

PURSE

This often links in some way with your own sense of identity. It can also depict your feeling of confidence or being capable, so losing a purse in your dream can bring difficult feelings. In some dreams, the purse is a magic container and can represent the mysterious creativity of the womb (*see* Bag or Purse). The idiom "hold the purse strings" indicates being in control of your finances.

PUSH/PUSHED/PUSHING

If you are pushing, it shows your positive action. It may involve opposition in some form, depending on the dream content. But pushing can also mean being in control, or even venting anger. Occasionally, it is about making stand or holding your ground.

PYRAMID

In popular association, this represents the dead, or the mysteries of life. Its shape, however, can speak to the unconscious mind in a different way. Having a square base, it represents physical stability, while its triangular sides symbolize the material connections with creative processes or the hidden side of life.

dream messenger

Studying the dreams of traumatized soldiers, Dr. W. H. Rivers found that men remained sick if they repressed their memories. As he helped them to let traumatic memories surface and be felt, the nightmares faded and their mental health improved.

QUARTZ *see* Crystal, Rock.

QUEEN
These are your feelings connected with your mother. It can be your ruling passions, or a desire to rule over others emotionally, or to be respected. It is also your need for recognition and acclaim.

QUICKSAND
This relates to feelings of hopelessness that swallow up all plans, hopes or efforts. It can be a fear of losing ground in competition with others or be about emotions that engulf you.

RABBI
This is a symbol of your attitude to your religious tendencies, or to Jewish religious ideas.

RABBIT
This suggests vulnerability, sexuality, and sometimes an object of sacrifice or killing. This is because it represents your own vulnerable feelings and hopes that you may have "killed" in some way. The rabbit hole depicts the journey into yourself and what you may discover within. (*see* Animal, Hare)

RACE
This depicts feelings of competitiveness, questions of capability, worthiness, success and failure, or a fear of losing or being inferior. It can also show your passage through life, your participation in the human race, and how you feel you have performed. What you do in the race, how you feel, may show what you put into your life and creativity. If you are in a marathon, it depicts all human expression. The marathon expresses human participation, from comic actions to fantastic struggle. It therefore represents the drama of human life, with all its possibilities. What you do in the marathon shows how you choose to "run" your life.

RADAR
This represents your basic intuition.

RADIO
This connotes entertainment, news, or communication with others. It can be intuitive knowledge about what is happening around you.

RADIOACTIVE
This relates to powerful energies arising from within that seem to threaten your conscious self. It can be contamination, or harm through unconscious influences, such as unnoticed emotions picked up or radiated from others, which have influenced you negatively.

RAFT
This is a flimsy philosophy, or half-formed ideas to cope with life. It can be a purposeless relationship. Or it can be a lifesaving change in yourself.

RAILS/RAILWAY/TRAIN/STATION

The rails themselves represent orthodoxy, the accepted or habitual way of going about things, or moral values. Hence the saying: "someone has gone off the rails." The train often depicts the train of events that carry us or other people along, or a direction we choose to take along with others. The engine depicts the energy you put into your activities or direction. The carriages are the events or influences, or things that happen: the train of experiences or events that follow in the wake of your actions. They can also be the compartments of your life.

A train or railway station depicts your efforts or desires to get somewhere, to go on a journey, to find fresh territory, new friendships, opportunities, or understanding. It can suggest travel for new experiences or self-development. Self-analysis is often symbolized as a journey. Leaving someone behind or being left behind suggests feelings about losing someone or being left. The train journey shows your journey in life, since it connects with the direction other people are taking. So it can at times also relate to aging and the stages of life that we all experience.

RAIN

Generally, rain symbolizes emotions or a release of feelings. If the rain is gentle, it is usually a relaxing experience and suggests a release from ideas and intellect. If it is a downpour and storm, it is feelings that may make you withdraw, for example, when you are sad and grieving over a friend's death. If the land is flooded, then our common sense is lost to sight in the emotions that are released, and danger may threaten. But rain may also show a return of normal feelings after a long spell of dry intellectualism or a drought of feelings.

RAINBOW

This is a promise of good things to come, an agreement, a harmony between yourself and your whole being.

RAINCOAT

This relates to attitudes that protect you from difficult emotions, worry, or outbursts, especially other people's. (*see* Clothes)

RAM

This suggests tenacity, masculine strength, toughness, leadership, and power. It can be a man's strength. The sacrifice of the ram is a surrender of this strength to the guidance of your inner self.

RAT

This can refer to underhanded activities carried out without admitting the real motives, such as sex without love or for material gain.

dream messenger

Shadowy and unrecognized figures often appear in dreams. Sometimes they denote parts of your nature that you avoid or repress—or, at the least, fail to express. In other dreams they help to define attitudes that can transform you.

Idioms include: to be a rat, smell a rat, or rat on someone. A rat is also said to represent time gnawing away at your life, leaving emptiness. It can depict what we most hate or what we feel is repulsive.

RAVEN

This represents death, fear, or the unknown. It is the dark intelligence, the forces in life that seem to have intelligent direction, yet which are not visible. It can be the negative aspect of your father.

RAZOR

This is sharp intelligence. It is the ability to cut through useless or misleading information to get to the real issue. It can depict the thin dividing line between extremes, wisdom and folly, life and death, genius and irrationality, the inner self and the universe.

READING

This is realization, thinking, looking at yourself, reviewing ideas, considering something, memorizing data, or memory. It sometimes shows a way of escaping into fantasy.

RECEIVE/RECEIVED/RECEIVING

This is usually about receiving something, such as feelings from a relationship, or ideas that prove to be helpful.

RECORD/RECORDS

Paper or filmed records usually indicate memory or stored information. If they are lost or hidden, then you may have forgotten or not accessed them before. (*see* CD for musical records)

RECTUM *see* Feces.

RED

In many dreams, this links with experiencing strong feelings, even to the degree of horror. So there are probably some issues that are worth exploring when red suddenly appears in your dream. Red also represents your primal emotions, the earthy side of your nature, and your sexuality. It depicts your strength, your vitality, and also your power to heal. Because of its known association with traffic lights and brake lights on cars, it may sometimes be used as a warning, or a way of saying "stop" or "no."

In Africa, red ocher is still called the "blood of the earth" and used in different rituals connected with death and renewal. Because red links to blood and health, being alive, and the process of childbirth in women, ocher and the color red often indicate strong and powerful forces that are working within you. On the other hand they can indicate emotional pain. (*see* Colors)

REFLECT/REFLECTING/REFLECTION

Reflections from a mirror or water, especially if they show your face or body, usually represent the image you have of yourself or how you feel about yourself. Sometimes what you see is an unconscious image from the past that needs some reevaluating. Ask yourself where those feelings or that image arose from and then you can re-appraise it.

REFRIGERATE/REFRIGERATOR

This suggests cooling off in some respect. It can relate to feeling cold emotionally or sexually. Or it can be a relationship on hold.

RELATIVES

In dreams, relatives usually depict family values, a way of life, or particular feelings or responses. A great deal of your personality came about from the close or difficult relationships you experienced when you were a child. You developed extremely powerful feelings to deal with what you needed and what happened to you. For example, a man who was placed in an orphanage when young learned to get love from whatever females he could make contact with to stop himself from becoming deeply depressed. As an adult, he may still experience a drive to have several women to whom he can turn when in need. In some ways relatives in a dream can show aspects of what you are doing now in your relationships and activities. So look for such issues as security, attraction or repulsion to males or females, introversion or extroversion as a way of life, dependence or independence and their many levels of growth or action, sickness or anger as a means of getting love, and so on. (*see* Brother, Sister, Father, Mother)

RENT

This relates to the amount of confidence you have in your ability to meet the demands of life. What are the events of your life asking of you, and how are you dealing with the basic living process? If you are receiving rent, then it is dealing with what you expect or receive from others.

REPTILE

Any reptile in your dreams may depict your basic reactions to that creature, such as like or dislike, attraction or repulsion. But in many cases reptiles, such as snakes or lizards, are used to portray your very basic instinctive responses to life, such as the fear reaction, flight or fight response, the sexual drive toward reproduction, territorial display, and ritualistic social behavior, such as shaking hands, bowing, etc.

The reptile also frequently shows how you are dealing with such enormous flows of emotional or nervous energy. For example, fear is a great protector, but in human life, because we can keep stimulating our response with our imagination or words, it can become overactive, making us ill. A lion may chase a gazelle, but if it escapes it doesn't spend days shaking or drinking alcohol to cover its fear. In a few minutes it is quietly grazing again. A human in such an encounter can replay a scene over and over again. So you cannot become fully mature until you learn to meet these ancient drives and integrate them into your everyday life. So it is important to develop a working relationship with the snakes, lizards, and frogs in your dreams. (*see* Snake, Alligator, Frog)

RESCUE/RESCUED/RESCUING

This relates to an intervention or action that has brought about a radical change in you, possibly from real psychological or even physical difficulty. It is worth defining what brought about the change, so you can use it in the future. Rescuing someone else or an animal suggests efforts you are making, or have made, to preserve something important to you.

RESTAURANT

This indicates sociable and relaxed feelings, or being with, or away from, family and friends, depending upon the dream's content. It can also relate to a search for a partner or emotional needs. But as this is a public place, there may be elements dealing with your social interactions. (*see* Food)

RESTROOM *see* Toilet.

REVOLUTION

This suggests major changes in yourself, in your viewpoint, understanding, activities, or in your overall desires. It can also show some conflict between major parts of your personality. For example, some people often act rationally, suppressing their true feelings. This is akin to the Russian and French aristocracy dominating the working class—the result can be revolution.

RHINOCEROS

This relates to being dominant or using your influence. This also applies when you want to use someone sexually.

RIDE/RIDING

If you are riding a horse or an animal, it shows your relationship with your own spontaneous drives such as fears, feelings, or sexuality. Also, it can connote how you relate to your body and its needs and processes, indicating whether you are in harmony with it or driving it too hard. (If you are riding in a car or train, *see* Car, Railway.)

RIFLE *see* Gun.

true dream story

John dreamed that he was looking for a private bathroom. He found himself seated at last on what he thinks is his own private lavatory in rather a swanky sort of place. A waiter appears and sets up a banqueting table over him, sets the table, and then places six people around him. Such dreams usually suggest that there is not enough time alone, perhaps due to too many family or work responsibilities.

RIGHT

If you are right-handed, the right foot, arm, leg, eye, ear, all symbolize conscious attributes as opposed to the unconscious. This symbol may also suggest right as opposed to wrong. For those who are right-handed, the right hand is the active, creative, dynamic hand. The left is the passive, supporting, or female helping hand. When we knock a nail in, the right hand does the work, while the left holds the nail, and so on. So it suggests that the right side of our body represents our active, conscious, extroverted, and male aspect. (*see* Left)

RING

This depicts your relationship with the person who gave it to you, perhaps the reason it was given, or the feelings that drove you to buy yourself a ring. It can also represent the state of your marriage, engagement, or, if you bought the ring yourself, how complete you are as a person. (*see* Circle)

RIVER

The river depicts the richness or poverty of your life energy, the flow of feelings and creativity. Air and water continually flow through you, and if that flow dries up you die. Your life processes, expressed as feelings, can carry you along, sustain you, or sweep you away. If you are drowning, you may even feel overwhelmed by the torrent of what you feel. The river can be associated with a snake because of the way that it curves. Sometimes, it represents the passage of time. Going against the river's current is to go against your inner flow, or it may be an effort to find the source or to get back to the womb.

Dreams often use crossing a river to mean great changes. If you are trying to cross the water, it means encountering emotions as you change. Seeing someone going across or falling into a river often refers to your feelings about death. A stagnant river shows some restrained feelings or restricted sexuality, or that you are holding your feelings back.

RIVET

This suggests binding connections or your relationships in life. It can also be depict a sexual organ.

ROAD *see* Highway.

ROBOT/ROBOTIC

This can suggest that what you are doing is automatic or that you are not thinking about it. It can also depict actions or a relationship that is undertaken without emotion, or alternatively something in which you are not getting involved.

ROCK

This suggests solidity, strength, basic foundations, or steadfastness in the face of storms, problems, or emotions. The rock has often symbolized security, refuge, and protection on a physical or social level. It can represent rigidity or being unmoved in the face of opposition. Inwardly, it signifies faith to help you through turmoil. Mentally, it represents the ability to understand and not be moved. If the rock you see is sculpted in any way, it shows what you have done with your life that will last through time.

Rocks or stones are the nearest material things we have to eternity: They evolve by pushing up from the depths of the earth. In the shape of upright columns, they are often used as phallic symbols. Rocks are placed upon graves to symbolize the spirit outlasting the decaying flesh. As symbols of eternity, they are used to mark places where holy experiences have happened, or where a person contacted the divine.

In temples, a rock was always the original altar, the contact with eternal life, the place upon which you sacrificed or surrendered your body.

dream fact

The word "dream" is derived from the middle English word *dreme* which means "joy" and "music." The film director Luis Bunuel found such richness in dreams that, should he have twenty years left to live, he would want "two hours a day of activity, and the other twenty-two in dreams."

ROCKET

This is the energy and drive you direct into enthusiastic activity. It can also suggest male sexuality. In either case, it suggests taking care about where the rocket is directed. (*see* Spaceship)

ROLE/ROLES

This indicates the various people who appear in your dreams, and the roles they play are usually representative of the many and varied aspects of your own personality, along with the talents and stances you take. It is, therefore, helpful to stand in the role of the characters and describe who you are, and your capabilities as this defines your own possibilities.

ROOF

This symbol represents the attitudes or strategies you use to keep yourself feeling secure. It shows the family atmosphere under which you live. So a hole in the roof will suggest something that has attacked your sense of security. (*see* House)

ROOM

This is an atmosphere or particular situation. Depending on the dream room, it can be a condition or possibility. A big room suggests your opportunity to do things, while finding a new room in your house is the discovery of new talents or possibilities in yourself. (*see* House)

ROOT

This relates to your origins, your basic consciousness, or things that you are tied to by necessity, love, or connections. It can also be your connection with family or heritage from your forebears.

ROPE

This relates to connections you make with others that are binding, or an attempt to bind something or someone. It may also suggest restrictions and limitations.

RUBY *see* Jewels, Blood.

RUDDER

This shows the principles that guide your actions, the decisions that you make, or the emotions that control your decisions.

RUG *see* Carpet.

RUINS

This can point to any aspect of your past. So it can refer to an old relationship now in ruins, or attitudes or a way of life that existed for you in the past. (*see* Castle)

RUNNING

This is trying to escape from an emotion or fear, or it can be rushing toward something. It connects with fitness, if you jog to exercise. In a few dreams it expresses a sort of surrender to the joy of living and existing.

S

SADDLE

This is to impose your will on something or someone, or to be imposed on, or saddled with, something. If you are thrown from the saddle, it can be feeling out of control or sudden change.

SAILING

Whatever happens to you in the boat suggests how well or how badly you are meeting the changes, the tides and storms, or calm waters of your life. If there is someone else with you in the boat, it shows how you are dealing with a relationship, or group project.

SAILOR

This is your means of coping with emotions. It is your desire to change, to move, to see more of life. It is also your ability to cope with life.

SAINT *see* Guru.

SALAD

This is taking in feelings and influences that are alive to create personal growth. (*see* Food)

SALOON *see* Barroom.

SALT

This represents value, goodness, luck, taste, or the spice of life. It is something that transforms your experience, but it also preserves. When Lot's wife looked back in the Bible and was turned into a pillar of salt, it represented her desire to stop change or growth. Salt here depicts stagnation and preservation of the past.

SAND

This is time, the incessant wearing away of things, the multitudinous aspects of life governed by time. It can be small irritations or abrasiveness, or a difficulty in progressing or making headway. (*see* Desert)

SATAN

This represents the power of material values in life. It is the things in life you cannot control, such as anger, sex desires, ambitions, fear, worries, etc. It is the things that lead us against our innate link with the rest of living things. (*see* Devil, Evil, Demon)

SATELLITE

This is communication with others and with your whole being. It is the link between your changing and unchanging nature. Sometimes, it is a feeling of being isolated or disconnected, such as when you are in a relationship and all your activities have to center around something or someone.

SAUSAGE

This denotes the male sex organ or it can be your sexual feelings. It can also relate to all your material values.

SAW

This represents energy to reshape old attitudes, or it can be masturbation. It can also be criticism, a questioning state of mind, or cutting remarks.

SAXOPHONE

This is self-expression, or spontaneity.

SCALES

These indicate balance, justice, fair play, or careful judgments or decisions. Scales on fish may represent your shining thoughts and feelings.

SCARECROW

This suggests having no life, no spirit, feelings, or worth. It can also be an illusion.

SCHOOL

This indicates your feelings about learning. It is the attitudes and strategies you learned at school, such as interrelationships, class structure, competitiveness, authority, group preferences, habits of behavior, or reactions developed during those years. A classroom suggests a connection with study and a relationship with authority. Sometimes, there is a lot of stress connected with self-evaluation and taking exams.

SCIENTIST

This is your analytical mind, or an attempt to measure life, to discover its usefulness, and how to apply it. It may symbolize an intellectual attitude. It can also be your creative curiosity.

SCISSORS

This is your ability to shape things or cut through barriers or connections with others. It sometimes also suggests aggression, a sharp tongue and the ability to hurt or damage others. (*see* Castration)

SCORPION

This connotes bitterness, or the sting of bitter remarks. It can be your negative emotional energy turned inward to hurt you, or outward to "sting" others.

SCREW/SCREWED/SCREWING

This is sexual intercourse, or the male genitals. It is the effort to make things secure, or an attempt at security.

SEA

This means to be at sea or lost. Whereas a river has a male significance, the sea is the mother into which the male enters. It is *mer* or the mother of consciousness. Life began in the sea, in the depths. Like the sea, our blood contains salt and is our inner sea. The sea represents universal life, the collective unconscious, where all experience is stored, or the infinite cosmic mind. The surface is conscious life, on which the ship, or you, floats, supported and surrounded by uncharted depths. To dive into the sea is to dive into yourself, to look beneath your consciousness. The seashore is the point

instant interpreter

Life is an expression of energy. In dreams anything that moves or flows, such as flames or water, shows how you are expressing your energy. Your dreams show if you are blocking yourself, going with the flow, directing your energy, or fearing it. You may even be creating something that is beyond yourself.

where all our elements meet. The sea holds in its depths, or floating somewhere, vast treasures of all the things that humans have ever done. So it can wash them ashore and bring them to our notice.

Because the sea is mother and the united consciousness, or the unconscious, it relates to birth and death. To come up out of the sea is to be born, to become conscious. To cast yourself upon, or under, the waters is to let go of the world and your individuality, and to connect to your origins and death. (*see* Fish, Mother, Water)

SEAL

In the same way as the sea, this represents the inner energies rising within. It depicts the emergence into your conscious life of your deepest life energies, which in Eastern terminology is the kundalini. Sometimes, it depicts birth, emerging from the waters of the womb.

A seal on a document depicts a trust, a security, a sign of integrity, which we can abuse or use as power.

SEAM

This is connecting with others. It is the strength of beliefs or convictions, the weak point of attitudes or philosophy.

SEARCH/SEARCHED/SEARCHING

This often relates to lacking or missing something in your life. Sometimes you have to search for its cause. Ask yourself what it is that you have lost or what you are looking for.

SEARCHLIGHT

This is your ability to see things that are normally hidden or in your unconscious. It is focused attention, or concentration on a particular issue. It can also be meditation or the search for something. It can be trying to understand and make your feelings conscious.

SEASONS *see* Spring, Summer, Fall, Winter.

SEAT *see* Chair.

SEAWEED

This refers to growth, or ideas that emerge from your unconscious. It may also suggest feelings and influences that you get mixed up in and threatened by, such as when you go swimming and your leg gets caught in the weeds.

SECRET

This is something you know inwardly, but have not yet recognized outwardly. You may know in your heart that someone does not care for you, but because you so badly want them to, you may refuse to recognize this.

SECRETARY

This is the background of activity upon which creative work can take place. It is the orthodox side of you that lends a hand in the development of your creative or changing personality. In a woman's dream, it may depict your feelings about the other woman.

SEDATIVE

Sleeping pills may represent attempts to cover up worries, fears, anxieties, painful emotions and thoughts. It can be an attempt to push these problems into your unconscious. Alternatively, it can be something that is putting you to sleep.

SEED

This is stored influence and experience from the past. It is your potential for a new beginning, or new growth. Seeds can also represent the sperm or ovum. (*see* Acorn, Germs, Eight)

SELL/SELLING/SOLD

This possibly relates to the economic value you place on things, or your struggle to survive. It may reflect and comment on business activities or life-changing decisions.

SEMEN

This depicts manhood or potential, life's essence or personality. It is stored power. It can also link with pregnancy or parenthood. (*see* Seed)

SETTING

The setting of a dream is important in that it shows what attitudes or fundamental life situations you are dealing with. If you think of how the opening scenes of a film tell you so much about the tone of what is to follow, you will grasp this aspect of dreams.

SEVEN

This can refer to yourself at that age, or to the cycles of life—7, 14, 21—years, and so on. It can sometimes indicate your subtle nature. So it can be the influence of your invisible inner rhythms on your physical body, the cosmic keyboard of harmonic vibrations or energies that bring about your existence. (*see* Numbers)

SEX

This relates to sexual dreams that usually express hidden desires, or the appearance of sex can relate to problems in this area. Sex is symbolized in many dreams, but where it appears directly it shows that the dreamer is more easily able to accept his or her sexual urges and pain. It is therefore important to understand the setting or drama surrounding the sexual element. This will give information about what is happening with your sexual feelings and activities. Our psychological and sexual nature, like our physical side, never stands still in development unless a pain or problem freezes it at a particular level of maturity. Therefore, our sexual dreams, even if our sex life is satisfactory, show us what growth or new challenge is being met.

SHADE/SHADOW

This suggests feelings of being in the shade, or being obscured by somebody else. It may be wife, husband, or parents who link with our feelings of being in their shadow. Usually something is standing in our way, in the sense of not enabling us to see the light or gain understanding. A shadow is also a symbol for our unconscious activities that can control our actions. So a shadow can depict inner feelings that are seldom expressed. A shadow can also be a sign of coming events, the shadows cast from the future. This is because we often see someone's shadow before we actually see him or her.

SHAMAN *see* Guru.

SHAMPOO

This depicts the effort to forget or get over something or someone. It can express the effort to deal with longings, ideas, or emotions, or to cleanse sexual feelings. (*see* Hair)

SHARK

This is a trickster or swindler, or it can be a desire to swindle. It is a threat from within, such as a desire to hit or hurt someone that may destroy you or your self-respect. It can be a fear of death, fear of the collective unconscious, or loss of your inner self. It is therefore the power of the unconscious, so it is also its protectiveness.

SHARP

Something that may hurt you. (*see* Razor)

SHEEP

This is being easily led. It can be a sign of being abused, or of accepting advice and help, conformity, or vulnerability. In Christian culture, sheep are often linked with the man and woman in the street and the care of them. (*see* Lamb)

SHELL/SHELLFISH/ SHELLS

This sometimes represents you or your inner self. Or it can be the shell you crawl into for protection against the world. (*see* Oyster, Clam)

SHIELD

This is your desire for protection, or to protect.

SHINING OBJECT OR PERSON

Anything that gives out light in your dreams has a special significance. The enormous potential we each have can be thought of as a trapped source of light. This light sometimes

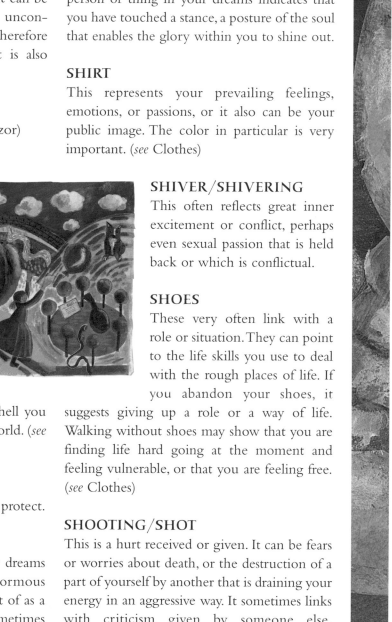

expresses itself as our feelings and attitudes constantly shift and change. This is because certain attitudes, states of mind, or particular ideas form a transport for this light. So the shining person or thing in your dreams indicates that you have touched a stance, a posture of the soul that enables the glory within you to shine out.

SHIRT

This represents your prevailing feelings, emotions, or passions, or it also can be your public image. The color in particular is very important. (*see* Clothes)

SHIVER/SHIVERING

This often reflects great inner excitement or conflict, perhaps even sexual passion that is held back or which is conflictual.

SHOES

These very often link with a role or situation. They can point to the life skills you use to deal with the rough places of life. If you abandon your shoes, it suggests giving up a role or a way of life. Walking without shoes may show that you are finding life hard going at the moment and feeling vulnerable, or that you are feeling free. (*see* Clothes)

SHOOTING/SHOT

This is a hurt received or given. It can be fears or worries about death, or the destruction of a part of yourself by another that is draining your energy in an aggressive way. It sometimes links with criticism given by someone else.

SHOP/SHOPPING

This suggests exploring the possibilities in life, the decisions that you can make, the variety of attitudes or activities you can choose from, or it can be something that you are searching for or that you really want.

SHOVEL/SPADE

This is exploring your unconscious, or the techniques you are using to uncover your past or what is unconscious and therefore buried.

SHRINK

This connects with losing power and presence, or changing relationship to things. It can show a return to childhood feelings or perspective. The shrinking of other things suggests they are becoming less important or less powerful to you.

SICK

If you are vomiting, it indicates the feeling of having thought, felt, or expressed things that do not agree with your emotions. You may be trying to discharge disturbing but usually unconscious feelings or personality traits that you adopted, but which feel foreign to you. If you are sick, *see* Illness.

SIDE

Something on the side connotes something that is not a real pleasure, or real work, not your greatest goal. It is not confronting you, but it may be a support in some way. It is in fact a "side issue."

SIDEWALK

If it is on a specific street, you know it links with your feelings and experiences of that place. In general, it depicts the ease or anxiety you feel about being among other people, or being open to the opportunities and dangers of life. But the sidewalk is also a place of reasonable safety from the dangers of the road, so it is about your skill in traversing the risks of daily life.

SIGN/SIGNED/SIGNATURE

This is your agreement. It is the mark you leave in the world, or what you want to happen. It is your subliminal influence.

SILVER

When it is silver hair, it suggests age and mellowness, perhaps influences from the past. It often has to do with feelings emerging from deep within, perhaps because of the way it reflects and mirrors things. (*see* Moon)

SING

This suggests a sense of harmony with others or yourself. It can be an expression of inner harmony or creativity.

SINK/SINKING

This is the feeling of losing your control over circumstances or a relationship. It can be a loss of confidence, or possibly feeling overwhelmed by emotions.

SISTER

This is your relationship with, and your feelings concerning, a sister. She may represent qualities in yourself, but they depend on how you feel about her, what age she is in relation to you, and whether you are her brother or sister. So she may depict your feeling side, or an under-expressed part of your personality, rivalry, or feelings of kinship.

SIX
This may depict balance, harmony within a group. (*see* Numbers)

SKATE/SKATING
This is your sense of balance and proportion in life. It can be your skill in keeping balanced in difficult circumstances.

SKIN
This is the way you relate to the world through sensations and contact. It can also depict how you handle criticism and difficulties, as in being "thick-skinned" or "thin-skinned."

SKIRT
This is how you are expressing your sexuality or femininity. The style and colors shown are part of the statement. (*see* Clothes)

SKY
This refers to your mind and the unexpected things that can come from it. It also implies moods, depending on whether it is bright or gray. Things in the sky that are threatening or strange depict distressing things on your mind or ones that cause anxiety. The sky is also huge and can show you the immense potential you have.

SLEEP
To dream of being asleep is

to be unaware of something. It is literally saying there is something of which you are not consciously aware.

SMOKE/SMOKING
Smoke in a dream may suggest danger, or can be intuition about something. It can relate to passions that are about to burst into flames. Smoking a cigarette can represent the power of habit or anxiety in your life. It can also suggest how you feel about smoking. Speech idioms include: go up in smoke, put up a smoke screen, no smoke without fire.

SNAIL
This shows how a snail withdraws quickly into its shell, so this symbol sometimes represents a sensitive situation that makes us withdraw from life. It can suggest vulnerability, or hiding in a protective shell of feelings.

SNAKE
This is your innate life energy. It is also a symbol of inner wisdom, or knowledge of life's secret processes; and of medical healing. The

soul solution

You are an inextricable part of an immense web of life and consciousness. Many of your dreams remind you of this. Remember this when you are in need. If you do not get a response from outside, ask for it from within. Hold a mental image of what you need. You will find that this becomes easier the more you give of yourself to others.

snake can shed its skin, and so symbolizes self-renewal or rebirth. As the life's energy, it can be expressed in many ways. It can also connote attraction and repulsion, sexuality, love, sympathy, emotion, thoughts, higher consciousness, movement, and also the emotions we create that cause illness. This is the snake's poison.

The alchemists put a gold crown on the snake's head symbolizing expanded consciousness arising from the same energy as sexuality. It is often a diadem, gem, or light at its brow symbolizing the possibility of expanded awareness. (*see* Reptile)

SNARE
This represents a seemingly appealing idea or plan, which is basically wrong, or a situation which can end up trapping you.

SNEEZE
This is a spontaneous cleansing of yourself, caused by the inner healing processes rather than conscious intention.

SNOW
This is usually frozen or repressed feelings or emotions. It can sometimes be purity, dormancy, the stilling of the outer life such as in winter, when the seeds and roots rest in the earth or unconscious until the arrival of spring. It can also be the ideas, morals, or thoughts that have frozen your feelings.

SOAP
This is an attempt to come clean, to be free of guilt or something that exists in your con-

science. It can also be something that makes you feel grubby. (*see* Wash)

SOCKS
This is generally to do with how well you present yourself socially, but from afar. Some of the idioms give insight into how socks are used in dreams: pull your socks up; put a sock in it; knock your socks off.

SOFT TOY *see* Toy.

SOLDIER
This symbol suggests some sort of conflict. You may be fighting urges within yourself, or struggling with a decision. There can be a drive because of personal growth to face old hurts, but you are shying away from pain and conflict.

SOLICITOR *see* Lawyer.

SON
This connotes feelings or worries concerning a son. It is the growing part of you. It can be hopes or worries about the future, or your extrovert self, desires connected with self-expression, or parental responsibility.

SOUND/SOUNDS/NOISE
If you hear sounds in your dream, it directly relates to what you feel as you dream the sound. Does the sound you hear produce some pleasure, anxiety, or puzzlement? Whatever it is, consider what that means to you in your normal waking life. Also, you can project your will with sound. So the sound may also be

carrying a force that is going to make something happen.

SOUP

If you have made the soup, it is either a way of giving yourself emotional nourishment, or you are giving of yourself to whoever is going to eat the soup. So the soup, and what happens to it, can stand for the relationship between you and another person. Soup when it is spilled can also suggest a mess, something to be cleared up. (*see* Food)

SOUTH

In some countries, for example, in South America or the southern United States, the south may symbolize different attitudes concerning people of color, or different ways of life. (*see* North)

SPACE

This is opportunity or potential. It is also the amount of freedom you have, depending on the space. Cosmic space usually concerns the vast potential of your mind and what lies behind it, so it is experience beyond thinking.

SPACESHIP

This either suggests being "spacey," i.e., not down to earth, or the way you move beyond the usual boundaries of your thinking and actions. (*see* Rocket)

SPEAK/SPEAKING/SPOKE

This is about communication and the exchange of ideas or feelings. What is it that is being communicated in your dream? If you dream of finding it difficult to speak, this can indicate that you have unexpressed feelings or urges. While awake, let yourself play with the sounds made in your dream to see if you can get any clarification. Making a speech suggests a desire to make yourself understood to others, to see your inner feelings at work in the world, or to be acknowledged.

SPELL

Having a spell put on you, or casting a spell, can indicate something that has caused a powerful association between an event, a situation, and a person, or it can show strong positive or negative emotions. Such emotions can happen while under anesthetic or when you are deeply involved with someone.

SPERM

This suggests a germ of an idea, or the wonderful potential behind life. It is sometimes used in dreams to suggest energy. It can also be an image of the duality of life and the need to commit to an interdependent relationship to unfold inner qualities. (*see* Germs, Seed)

SPHINX

This is the riddle of human existence. Why are we here? Where are we going? It is the individual process or the development of consciousness. It shows a human side emerging from instinctive drives, so it is the human struggle in life. It can also stand for the complete being.

SPIDER

This refers to any emotion or desire that devours the strength or purpose of your life. The spider is also used as a symbol of sexual orgasm, but only if you are terrified, disgusted, or guilty about such feelings. Sometimes, it symbolizes a mother's power, as in the way you are caught in the web of her desires and emotions, and so it can be an inability to break away from the mother. It can also depict you drawing away from fearful things. (*see* Web)

SPIRIT/SPIRITS

To see a spirit, a disembodied personality, in a dream may depict thoughts about death. It can, like a ghost, be about things from the past that haunt you. The spirit in your dream may be a contact with the dead, or those about to be born. Sometimes, the spirit comes to the parents and asks them to form a body for it and a suitable environment as it wishes to born again.

SPRING

The season's appearance is about a new beginning in some area of your life, or some growth. It is a time of coming alive and renewal. Spring water suggests free flowing feelings and rejuvenating energy. It can refer to your source of life and consciousness, especially if the spring is in a cave or underground. (*see* Water)

STAB/STABBED/STABBING

This either refers to aggressive activities, hurtful words, feeling hurt, or strong sexuality. Sometimes we stab someone else in a dream to break connection with what they represent, or to kill off unwelcome feelings. (*see* Weapons)

STAG

This represents the masculine, a male, or it is the male aspect of the personality, or male sexuality.

STAGE

This can refer to your life in general, your stage of development, or what drama is being enacted in your feelings. It can also suggest a desire to be in the limelight, or to be the center of attention. The theme being dramatized is often important to understand, as it reflects concerns in your own life. (*see* Actor)

STAIRCASE/STAIRS

As a baby, stairs presented a huge challenge. To deal with them, you had to develop several major abilities, such as steady balance, confidence, and control of fear. Therefore, stairs represent many feelings to do with achievement, failure, climbing and falling. These feelings also connect with work, relationships, your social standing, or sex. Running up stairs may depict an urge to run away from something happening in your everyday life. Skimming down stairs shows confidence and pleasure.

STAR

This is a hope, a wish, or an ambition. It can be an intuition or a subtle sense of the cosmos and your relationship with it, or subtle influences that shape and direct you. The unconscious portrays human life as being an expression of huge cosmic forces, such as those that occurred from the Big Bang. These subtle but immense forces are often shown as stars in your dreams.

STATION *see* Railway.

STATUE

This symbol connotes emotional coldness, and a person who is perhaps not feeling pain or human empathy.

STEAL/STEALING/STOLEN

This is a feeling that something is being taken from you, or you are taking something, without agreement. Feelings of being unloved may enter into this, as you will feel you are stealing what is not willingly given.

STEEL *see* Iron.

STEPS

This usually refers to the different steps taken in any undertaking. The first step toward marriage is courtship, the next engagement, and so on. (*see* Walking)

STERILIZE

This may express a fear of illness, of germs, or an attempt to cleanse yourself. (*see* Bathing)

STEW

We may be in a stew, in a muddle, or feel confused. A stew can also represent different parts of you being brought together. It can also represent a healthy, sustaining power instead of a confusing one. (*see* Soup, Food)

STING/STUNG

This is something that has hurt you, possibly words or an event. Idioms such as "stinging remarks" also show possible meanings.

STONE

This indicates being unfeeling or having a heart of stone. It can show a frigid person instead of a loving one. To throw stones is to give hardness and coldness, to be unsympathetic, or aggressive to other people. (*see* Rock)

STORK

This represents the soul and is a symbol of birth or babyhood, and perhaps parenthood.

STORM

This indicates difficult emotions, stormy events and relationships.

STOVE *see* Oven.

STRANGLE

This is life or energy being cut off by a fear or repression. Emotions can be held in the neck, so it may be feelings about someone living or dead that you are holding back. (*see* Neck)

STREAM *see* River.

STREET *see* Road.

STRING

This is usually your connections with other people or situations. It can also be your attempts to hold something together, or to form a tie with something or someone.

SUBMARINE

In some dreams it may take the place of the symbol of the whale, and represent powerful feelings and urges emerging from the unconscious. But the submarine is also a way to explore your inner self and wisdom. (*see* Boat)

SUBWAY

This suggests being underground, and usually represents inner or unconscious feelings or tendencies that influence you. This can include

197

childhood feelings or painful memories that are suppressed or hidden, instinctive or intuitive responses, and deep-rooted family or personal attitudes.

SUFFOCATE/SUFFOCATED/ SUFFOCATING

This often reflects the way you relate to your environment, either in a relationship or with work or family. It shows feelings you have no room or opportunity to express. Some types of sleep problems, such as apnea, may also cause this dream.

SUGAR

This represents the enjoyable things in life, or pleasant things in yourself or others. It can be a desire to cover up unpleasant things in your experience or in others.

SUIT *see* Clothes.

SUITCASE *see* Luggage.

SUMMER

This suggests positive feelings, awareness, the middle of your life, and the power of healing and personal warmth.

SUN

This is the symbol of life, energy, and spirit. It represents the whole of your being, or the source of life and consciousness. To sunbathe means to expose yourself to life-giving energies from within. It can mean to release morals, opinions, attitudes, as represented by clothes, and allow your ener-

gies natural expression. It is about all energy and health, happiness and success. Or you can have sunburn, or sunstroke, symbolizing exposure to something that is painful and harmful.

SURF/SURFING

This suggests waves of feeling, inspiration, or experience. It can be meeting the challenges of the swift changes that occur in your life. It can also be about sex and the pleasures or difficulties it gives.

SURGERY

If you are in an operating room, it connects with concerns about your health or well-being. If you are having surgery, you may be feeling somebody is "getting at you" in some way, or you may be experiencing inner changes. If you are due to have surgery, then the dream is probably expressing anxieties.

SWALLOW/SWALLOWED/ SWALLOWING

This is either you taking something in, or if you are swallowing without putting something in your mouth, then you are holding something back—feelings or a healing process.

dream messenger

We have so many roles in life, from employee, cook, parent, and teacher to go-getter and lazybones. The characters in our dreams express all the possibilities we have. Recognizing these roles and using their skills adds great richness to our waking lives.

SWAN

In folklore and mythology, people turn into a swan or God takes the form of a swan. The swan represents the soul, or sometimes the eternal. It may indicate the parts of your inner life that are not understood, or those which are hurt by your environment or others. It can be the loving parts of yourself that are killed or unloved, and which turn into a swan leaving us with a sense of terrible loss. It can therefore be about how when we are deeply hurt emotionally, we actually "leave" the world for a while and shut down.

SWEEP/SWEEPING/SWEPT

This connotes cleaning up your act in some way, perhaps by changing and getting rid of your negative attitudes. Speech idioms suggest other possible meanings: make a clean sweep, sweep someone off their feet, sweep something under the carpet, or sweep the floor with someone.

SWEETS *see* Candy.

SWIMMING

The movement of swimming is an ability to cope with your inner feelings and energies. Water is your feelings, a river, the flow of your emotional energies, and the sea is the whole personality from the outer surface to the depths of the unconscious, so they all interact. Being unable to swim in a dream means you have not learned the skill of keeping afloat in the depth of your own feelings and mental life. To swim easily is to have true confidence in yourself and a trust in life to support all your different activities and efforts. To be at home in the water, is to feel at ease with your sexual urges, ambitions, desires, and instincts. To be threatened by the waves or water, is to be afraid of yourself, of your own feelings, to doubt your ability or strength to face life and all its experiences. You can feel threatened by your innate desires and energies. (*see* Water, Swimming Pool)

SWIMMING POOL

This may indicate the way your life is connected with other people, as when we say, "we are in this together." But it also connects with relaxation and shared social pleasure. Like any pool of water, it can also depict what is going on under the surface of your mind, in your unconscious. (*see* Water)

SWING

The act of rocking is a way of calming down, and is often used by children or traumatized people. It probably has this same significance in dreams. It may also have sexual significance.

SWORD

This may be your ability to discriminate and search for truth, or protective instincts or strength of character, with which you can help and protect others. Also, like any weapon, it may also depict an aggressive attitude or male sexuality.

SYRINGE

This is generally a phallic symbol. But it may represent energy, emotions, and ideas, injected into you, such as schooling, which may be foreign to your real nature. It can also suggest something of only temporary effect. (*see* Injection)

T U V

TABLE

This is your connection or relationship with others. It can be communal or family relationships. It can be the basic down to earth facts of life—a table is a table. Speech idioms are: drink you under the table; on the table; turn the tables; set the table.

TABLET *see* Pill.

TADPOLE

This indicates sperm or pregnancy. It can also be possible feelings arising from prenatal life. (*see* Frog)

TAIL

This may have a phallic meaning. Or it may connote your past or background, or even backbone, in the sense of strength and purpose. It can also be instinctive urges.

TALISMAN

This is some idea, belief or emotion that helps to ward off fear, or the dominating influence of others. It can also be a link or doorway to your own resources of courage, insight, or strength. Occasionally, it represents a healing influence.

TALK/TALKED/TALKING

A difficulty in speaking, or not speaking, shows the possibility of restrained anger or difficult feelings, anxiety, or lack of confidence, or an absence of real contact or communication (*see* Paralyzed). Speaking and not being understood links with the feeling of not being listened to or to frustration. No one talking to you makes you feel isolated or judged (*see* Speak). Most of us talk in our sleep at some point, and it is simply an expression of the dream activity breaking through into speech. But some dreamers carry on long conversations to which their partners respond. This is probably a release of feelings while dreaming.

TANK

If this is an army tank, it suggests the aggressive defensiveness you may use when in conflict with others. If it is a water tank, it is stored emotions, perhaps restrained emotions. It may also at times represent your bladder, or indicate that you are retaining too much water in your body. It is also occasionally the womb, especially if something is swimming about in the tank.

TAPESTRY

This is what you have woven with your actions in life, it is also your own inner life. It is sometimes an indication of your existence in the universal flux of life and death. (*see* Carpet)

TAR

This is something to do with unconscious feelings or a sticky, difficult situation. To dig into tar is to attempt to get below the surface of your mind to find the hidden sources of behavior and feelings.

TARGET

This represents ambitions, hopes, your aims, even your goal in personal growth. Sometimes it is the vagina.

TATTOO

This is an experience that has left an indelible memory or mark. Being bitten by a dog may leave a permanent fear of dogs. Being hurt emotionally by someone may leave a similar effect. A tattoo can also represent how your personal habits or efforts affect you. It may occasionally refer to how you gain identity, or to which group you identify.

TAXI

This is paying for your needs. Or it can be becoming involved with a stranger or someone else to get to where you want to go. The taxi can sometimes represent protection from the sort of threats you feel in everyday life, especially for women. (*see* Car)

TEA

This suggests stimulation. In the same way as alcohol, it represents the change that can affect behavior by something external. It can also represent sociability, encouragement, sympathy, or relaxation. (*see* Coffee)

TEACHER

This is something you are learning or have learned. It can be feelings developed in school that are still active. Perhaps you are dealing with how you related to authority at school.

dream messenger

Lucidity, or being awake while asleep and dreaming, is one of the most profound human possibilities. We may think of space as the great frontier, but there is a galaxy of consciousness to explore in sleep, if only we can wake up.

TEDDY BEAR

This is a childish way of expressing a need for security or comfort. Like any toy, it can represent the way an outer object can help to create your own feelings of security or companionship. (*see* Doll, Toy)

TEENAGER

In general, the teenager relates to that period of life and the feelings you felt or experienced while you were an adolescent. The teenage dream can be about uncertainty or inexperience in relationships, along with powerful sexual/romantic attraction or feelings, and maturing sexually. Dreams containing a teenager may also deal with concerns about sexual issues, a lack of confidence and experience, and the experimentation of that time. The action and drama of the dream will define which of these is represented.

If it is a female teenager, it is generally about your feeling or emotional side rather than your thinking or assertive side. If you are a female teenager dreaming of a female teenager and it is a known friend, it probably represents the attitudes and qualities, or lack of them, seen in the friend. If it is an imagined female, it usually depicts you, perhaps in a way you may not usually see yourself. This is usually because the dream about a teenager is playing out issues of importance in your life. A dead teenager suggests hurt feelings of love or wanting to be loved, damaged self-esteem, or feelings of value in the world. This often relates to a difficult time in your teens when you killed some facet of your personality or love.

TEETH

Teeth can represent your bite, your effectiveness or your power in life. They may represent biting remarks or hurtful words. They are your ability to "chew" over a problem, or to get a taste of, or try to experience, what you are considering. If you dream of your teeth falling out, the cause may be a sense of losing someone you love or who is close. This leaves a gap in your life such as you feel when a tooth comes out. Missing teeth also suggest getting older, or feelings or fears about aging.

TELEPHONE

This can be communication or contact with yourself or others. If you do not answer, it may suggest you are unwilling to listen to your inner feelings or intuitive advice, or be in relationships with others. If there is no one on the other end, it suggests feeling alone and perhaps unwanted. An emergency call is probably a desperate attempt to be heard, or a cry for emotional help in a difficult situation.

TELESCOPE

This suggests trying to understand something more clearly, or getting a closer look at things that were not clear before. It may also show

you making something big out of a small experience, such as making a mountain out of a molehill.

TELEVISION/TV

This suggests what you feel, understand or intuitively know about what is going on in other people's lives or the world. It is being aware of the drama that is taking place in your own life that you may have overlooked. It is also the strategy you use to blank out the world and relax.

TEMPTATION

This is the conflict between different aspects of yourself, perhaps sexual urges and social fears, or personal boundaries.

TEN

This may depict teamwork, or being part of a group action. This also represents a new beginning on a higher level. It is a fresh start, almost as if from scratch, but all the past experience contributes to this new phase. (*see* Numbers)

TENNIS *see* Games.

TENT

This is letting go of civilized aids or ways of life, so it is getting away from your usual situation. It can also signify holidays or youthful exploration.

TERROR

This is an inability to face or cope with the emotions, fears, ideas, or urges represented in the dream. It is important to find out where you felt that sort of terror in the past as this releases its hold on you. This is not easy, because many memories have never been verbalized, or occurred either before you spoke or when you were under anesthetic. But they can be brought to the surface through steady dream exploration.

TEST/TESTS/TESTING

This is an attempt to deal with the difficult questions or problems that life poses. It is a fear of inadequacy or of being tested. It is about comparing yourself with others, or with the opinion of others. It can be about doubts concerning your fitness and capability in life, marriage, or parenthood, or stress in connection with a competitive job or situation. It may be responses still active from school experiences. Testing equipment may indicate an aspect of your body, or perhaps a skill you have. It may also refer to your sexual capability. Medical tests normally relate to concerns about your health, or can suggest getting pleasure from being examined.

TESTICLES

These relate to the power of masculine sexuality and the drive or aggression that it arouses. The idiom that is regularly used—"got the balls"—suggesting a daring attitude and courage, sums this up.

THEATER *see* Stage.

THERMOMETER

This is a gauge of your emotional warmth or coldness, or it can also be a measure of your health, or it may be anxiety about it. (*see* Barometer, Cold, Heat)

THERMOS/FLASK

This is keeping alive a feeling, hope, or inspiration. This can apply to warm or cold feelings.

THIRST *see* Drink.

THORN

This relates to painful experiences, from which it is difficult to move on.

THREAD

This is a line of thought or action, delicate or fine connections, or directions that can be easily lost or broken unless care is taken. Or it can mean a fine or tiny idea or energy you easily lose, in the same way as when life hangs by a thread. It may link with the word threadbare.

THREE

This frequently represents the family: mother, father, and child. But it can be any unity of the positive and negative to create a new condition. (*see* Numbers)

THROAT

This is an ability to speak or express your own needs and opinions. It is also a vulnerable area. (*see* Neck)

THUNDER

This is a warning of stormy emotions, particularly anger.

TICKET/FARE

To get the ticket is to get the idea, method, or capability. A ticket represents the ability to pass through barriers or difficulties in life, as the price has been paid in experience or self-giving. It can also mean a sense of validity and ease, or possibly a lack of it.

TIDAL WAVE/TSUNAMI

This relates to a great release of energy or emotions. This may be felt as a great threat, but is simply energy and can be directed. It just needs experience to ride such high energy.

TIDE

This is opportunity or power of events. It is the ebb and flow of enthusiasm, desires, cravings, ambition or energy. (*see* Moon, Sea)

TIE/TIED/TYING

This is creating bonds, either in the form of unifying, binding, or restricting. It is also trying to mend something or keep things together. (*see* String)

TIGER/TIGRESS

This is power, anger, sexual power, inner anxiety, or terrifying urges. It can be a fear of another person's anger or forcefulness. Sometimes, it is the power of a mother's protectiveness, or it can be a woman's anger or sexual craving.

dream fact

David Watson, a professor of psychology at the University of Indiana, says that people who are creative, imaginative, and prone to fantasy are more likely to have vivid dreams and to remember them. The possible reason for this is that they allow more stimuli to arise into consciousness.

TIN

When seen as a metal, it suggests softness as well as durability. As a can it links with protection and the storage of memories, or nourishing feelings and experiences.

TIRE

This represents the wear and tear of dealing with everyday life. It is the attitudes and strengths that carry you over the smooth and rough patches of life. If the tire is punctured, it may indicate a health problem or setback.

TOAD

This suggests uncomfortable feelings. It is also the deeply biological processes of your body, of reproduction and transformation, the tadpole to toad process from conception to birth. (*see* Frog, Tadpole)

TOILET

Many people find their only privacy in the toilet, so it can depict your need for, or feelings about, privacy. The toilet is also where you release tension or get rid of things your body no longer needs. So it can indicate letting of old feelings. (*see* Feces, Urine)

TOMCAT

Male sexuality, aggressiveness, and promiscuity. (*see* Cat)

TONGUE

This is your inner feelings, your ability to communicate, or an expression of anger or dislike. It can also suggest the male sex organ. Speech idioms include: cat got your tongue, bite your tongue, slip of the tongue, tongue in cheek.

TOOLS

This is self-expression, your capabilities, practicality, and skills. It is the attitudes that enable you to make changes in your life, and your skill to do so.

TORCH *see* Searchlight.

TORNADO

This is threatening influences pushing you toward things of which you may be afraid. It is pressure in some form. It can be a tremendous mental or emotional energy release that feels as if it may overwhelm you. (*see* Wind, Air)

TORPEDO

This is your unconscious desire to injure others, or it can be injury by others, or hitting below the belt. It is also a sexual symbol.

TORTOISE

This indicates the outer hardness or shell, in which we may hide when others try to contact us deeply. The animal symbolizes slow but patient efforts, sensitivity and shyness.

TOTEM

This is your unconscious awareness of the heritage from ancestors.

TOUCH/TOUCHED/TOUCHING

This indicates the degree of relationship with another person or an aspect of you. It is the connection with an influence, and the experience of something other than you.

TOWER

This is either your attitudes that keep you separate and aloof from people, a means of protecting yourself from human contact or conflict, or it is a way of standing above events and getting a wider view of them.

TOWN *see* City or Town.

TOY

This is childhood habits, desires or attitudes that you have not yet outgrown or changed. You may want the sort of non-threatening relationship you had with your parents, or just be seeking love and affection. When we are children, our toys can be extremely important. So a cuddly or soft toy may mean to us the only non-threatening relationship we have, and so depicts security, love, and the ability to control instead of be controlled. It can therefore represent the ability to create, with the aid of an external object, an internal source of love and assurance. As an adult it may suggest a desire for a non-threatening emotional relationship. It can also be a means of venting anger or pain. (*see* Doll)

TRAIN *see* Railway.

TRAMP

This is unacceptable parts of yourself and others, which can be held back and so depicted as a ragged, unsociable person. If an attempt is made to find ways to express or accept these repressed parts of yourself, then the beggar or tramp changes in subsequent dreams and develops positive and useful characteristics. It can also depict all the excuses we make about not living our best.

TRANSPARENT

This is being able to see what is going on inside yourself, in other people, or in a situation. (*see* Glass)

TRAP/TRAPPED/TRAPPING

We are all trapped in old ideas or habits that may have been applicable at one time, but which are now detrimental, such as hurts and responses that still linger. These traps are often depicted by prisons, snares, barriers, ropes, threatening people, or animals. Finding your way through them is the great adventure of life. Out of this arises your inner strength, allowing you to wake up to whom you really are, letting you emerge into your real life and identity. (*see* Snare)

TRASH/TRASH CAN *see* Garbage.

TRAVEL

This is your movement through life, your aging process, your search for meaning and new experiences. It can also suggest a way of keeping away from extended, lasting, and therefore confrontational relationships.

TREADMILL

This can be a feeling that life is nothing but work and effort. It can also suggest that you are trapped by duty and the regular demands made on you.

TREE/TREES

The tree is one of the great dream symbols, representing your whole physical, psychological, and social growth as a person. The roots depict your connection with the earth through food, air, and water, as well as your psychological roots in family and culture. The trunk shows your body and what you have developed in your life: the main thrust of your expression. The branches are the different avenues you have explored and developed: your children, your relationships and ideas. The seeds or flowers are your own fruition: the expression of what is deeply your own unique creativity. They are also your reproduction as a parent with children or ideas in the lives of others. Dead wood represents parts of you that no longer carry life and energy, perhaps ideas or opinions you no longer hold. A tree that is struck with lightning represents sudden change, even death. (*see* Cross, Wood)

TRESPASSING

This can be forcing your attentions on someone, or vice versa. It can be doing something that you know is invasive or disliked.

TRUCK *see* Lorry.

TRUNK *see* Car, Chest.

TUBE *see* Subway.

TUNNEL

If the tunnel is dark, it usually signifies entering into experiences you do not understand and are not fully aware of. It is usually past experiences that are felt but not verbalized or made conscious yet. It can also be entering into your unconscious. It can also be reliving the experience of birth.

TURQUOISE *see* Jewels.

TWELVE

This number represents completion. For example, the twelve months of the year encompass the four seasons. It also can depict the twelve traditional aspects of human personality shown by the signs of the Zodiac. For some people it can also represent teamwork. (*see* Numbers)

TWO

This usually refers to a partnership, either in a sexual relationship, or as a parent or child, or in business. It also connects with conflict or opposites, or any sort of duality. (*see* Numbers)

UFO *see* Flying Saucer.

ULCER *see* Boil.

UMBILICAL

This represents ties based on dependence rather than love or mutual interests. It can also refer to a strong tie to your mother, or to life in the womb.

UNCLE

This depends on how well you know your uncle and what part he has played in your life. In general, the uncle may represent your father. But he also could be an example of the areas in which the males of your family can achieve or fail. The uncle also stands for influences from the family, or your family background or heritage. (*see* Family)

UNDER/UNDERNEATH

This can imply a wide range of meanings, depending on the dream's context. When you are under a roof or a tree, it can suggest protection. It can imply being ruled or dominated by someone, or feeling they are superior, if you are in some way underneath them, as suggested by the idiom "under the thumb." It can point to your own superior feelings if something or someone is underneath you in some way. The idiom "under a cloud" also shows how we use this word to describe being depressed or feeling down.

UNDERGROUND *see* Subway.

UNDRESS

This is revealing your true feelings. It is about casting off restraining or inhibiting attitudes, fears, or morals. It can be a desire to display or express yourself more openly. (*see* Naked)

UNEARTH

This is about discovering things you have forgotten or not been aware of previously. This can be your feelings about a past love or unconscious thoughts. (*see* Digging)

UNIFORM

This is about conformity and orthodoxy. It is also authority, power, and an expression of a universal activity. A priest has the power of the church behind him; a policeman has the power of the law. So the uniform may imply these influences acting on you. The uniform may also depict your identification with a social role, such as that of a nurse or teacher. In this case it may be about how much you need that role for your own sense of confidence, or maybe how you are changing in the role.

UP/UPWARD/UPPER

In many dreams this points directly to the strategies you use to deal with emotions or situations that undermine confidence or positive feelings. For example, you may divert your attention from something that depresses you by switching the television on, visiting a friend, drinking alcohol, or smoking. Wherever possible, it is worth meeting the feelings you are trying to escape from in the dream. Do this by imagining yourself in the dream again and turning to face whatever it is you are escaping. Notice how you react, and what feelings or memories arise. (*see* Ascend)

URINE

To urinate is to release tensions, whether they are sexual, emotional, professional, or educational. Urine can also symbolize sexual feelings, or experiences in the womb.

UTERUS

This usually links directly with the ability to bear a child. It is to give birth in some way, either to a child or to a creative project. (*see* Vagina)

VACATION

This refers to being relaxed, or to experiencing a change in your feelings. It can also suggest a change from your usual way of life. It can be an opportunity to express yourself differently, or to meet some new experiences, or it can be an attempt to be happy.

VACCINATION

This may be illustrating the type of feelings or thoughts that you use, or can use, to deal with any negative influences in your life. (*see* Injection, Syringe)

VAGINA

This represents not only sexual feelings and desires, but is a symbol of complete womanhood and femininity. The shape of the vagina and womb represents the human qualities of sympathy, receptivity, loving acceptance, or a desire to absorb. The womb is a symbol of fertility. It is the willing sacrifice of personal resources, life, energies, and ideas, so that the new life, new love, new impulse can take form. The new idea or creation uses the old parts of you, but reshapes them, adding new features or qualities. The vagina and womb shape the growth of the new impulse or form. The female or male qualities must not be confused with personality. The conscious personality is a very flexible and shape-shifting thing. It can be male or female in quality no matter what one's gender. But in dreams, the female is the receptive, creative aspect of this shape-shifting personality.

VALLEY

This suggests a descent into material values, gloominess, outer activity, practical issues, and sometimes into problems and fears. It can also represent the female vagina. *Cwm* in Welsh is the word for a valley between the hills but also refers to the vagina. Of course the valley can also mean everyday life with all its variety and richness.

VAMPIRE

This refers to an idea or fear that is draining energy, ambition, or resolution. This can be a negative relationship that you are not dealing with well, so that you feel it is draining your energy or sense of well-being. It can be difficult feelings about sex or a sexual relationship, or feelings about not being independent, indicating that you feel psychologically linked to someone, such as a parent.

VASE *see* Cup.

VAULT

This may represent memories or influences from your past. It can also be something valuable or deeply important, which you have locked away or buried. If the vault is connected with burial, then it depicts feelings you have about death or the dead.

VD

This is a feeling of being unclean in connection with sexual activity.

VEGETABLE

This is your basic down-to-earth needs. It may also suggest your dietary needs. (*see* Food)

VENEER

This represents your outer self, something shallow, or something that hides your desires or longings. It relates to reactions, which are quite different, and of a rougher, or coarser quality.

VERMIN

This is the fears or anxieties you have, your sense of horror or repulsion about something, or some aspect of society or human behavior. It can be irritations or thoughts that are persistently "bugging" you. It can also be frightening or disturbing instincts or urges that you are regularly feeling.

VERTIGO

This imagery suggests anxieties or a loss of confidence. It may also indicate that you are on the verge of something that you usually do not allow yourself to experience. So you sense a vastness that makes you feel very uncomfortable or anxious.

VICTIM/VICTIMIZED

This suggests that you have a passive relationship with others, not acknowledging or expressing your own wants or needs. It may also be that you are victimizing someone else who is not strong enough to stand against your desires or will. You may be using past hurts to remain passive and to bemoan your fate. This is a form of blaming that puts the responsibility onto other people.

VINE

This indicates your growth as a person, and your potential to bear fruit in some way. In some dreams it may also show some general family connections.

VIOLIN

This symbol relates to your heartfelt feelings and your innermost longings. It can also be about pathos or subtle feelings. (*see* Music, Musical Instrument)

VOLCANO *see* Eruption.

VOMIT *see* Sick.

VOYAGE *see* Travel, Boat.

VULTURE
This is about feelings to do with waiting for someone to die, or a situation of living off the unfortunate experiences of others.

true dream story

Susan dreamed that she was in a large unknown building with lots of corridors. She goes through a door that leads to an identical corridor, but realizes that she is lost. Knowing who we are and what our satisfying direction is in life is not easy. The possibilities, which in the dream are symbolized by all the corridors, are countless. It helps if you ask for a dream showing what your roots are, and what your best direction is.

WAITRESS

This may mean that you feel you are providing for others' needs. In which case ask yourself if your own needs are being met. If you are being waited on, it may deal with feelings about being supported or helped, or feeling that your needs are satisfied. This can also be word play for waiting for something or someone.

WALK/WALKING

This usually depicts personal effort, or making your own way at your own pace. The conditions or surroundings where you are walking suggest what you feel about your progress and your personal situation. The direction in which you are walking, shows the aim of your activities and hopes. The future is represented by where you are going. If you are walking backward, it suggests a wrong attitude.

WALLET

This suggests your abilities to deal with external events easily. It can be about confidence and sometimes a sense of identity or value. So loss of a wallet indicates feelings of being less capable or powerful. (*see* Money)

WALLPAPER

This often represents a veneer, or sometimes superficial characteristics that act as a concealment or to hide the real person beneath the covering.

WANT/WANTED/WANTING

Whenever the words "want" or "wanting" appear in your dreams, it suggests urges or desires you may not be acknowledging well in your conscious life. Sometimes, the urge may be misdirected, such as loving someone who cannot love you in return. But the urge is still there to be loved, and some other source of love needs to be found. When it is a "don't want" in the dream, change it to a positive: "I didn't want to go with my mother" can become "I wanted to do my own thing." This gives an open channel for expression, rather than suppression.

WAR *see* Battle.

WARDROBE *see* Closet.

WAREHOUSE

This suggests memories or aspects of yourself put into storage, such as potential or ambition while you are bringing up children.

WARMTH

This is physical well-being and perhaps rejuvenation and relaxation. It is also affection and closeness in a relationship. (*see* Heat)

WARP/WARPED

This represents your inner feelings or energies that are misdirected by outer beliefs or fears.

It is getting the wrong idea or it can also be a misunderstanding.

WASH/WASHED/WASHING

This is clearing out feelings such as despair or self-doubt, or it can be fears about health, or possibly your neurotic phobias. Sometimes, this is shown as a healing of past hurts or tensions, even a warming of cold emotions. Washing your hair shows you changing your attitude or the way you present yourself to others, or altering your viewpoint or the way you think about something. Washing the vagina or penis is the clearing out of negative sexual feelings or dealing with the results of pent-up sexuality. Washing your hands shows you getting rid of feelings about something that you have done or in which you were involved. (*see* Baptism, Soap, Water)

WASP

This is irritability, hate, spitefulness, anger, or vengeance. It can be painful or hurtful remarks or emotions.

WATER

This usually denotes your flowing feelings or ability to respond to people. It can therefore be your emotions, desires, or moods, depending on how the water appears in your dream. If it is muddy, it means your feelings are influenced by outer circumstances, worries, material problems, or values. If it is clear and sparkling, it symbolizes faith, fearlessness, pure feelings, hope, and joy.

Water takes the form of any vessel that contains it. So it represents your ability to be influenced either by fears, hope, understanding or ignorance, love or duty, and so on. This is important as it means your anxieties direct the torrent or energy called emotion. As emotions can heal or kill this is something that needs attention. (*see* Baptism, River, Sea)

WEAPONS

This suggests fears or desires connected with hurting or being hurt. The weapon often hides a deeply felt childhood pain or fear that has not been dealt with, so it may come out as anger or rage. Some weapons, such as guns or knives, can also represent male sexuality or any fears you may have about it.

WEATHER

This is a symbol of moods and emotions. Idioms include: having a sunny disposition; stormy weather; clouds can have a silver lining; a person can have a flood of tears; or we say dry up, brighten up, or stop looking so gloomy. Sunshine usually represents happiness, life-giving energies, growth, and being positive. Cloudiness links to despair, fear, depression, and gloomy attitudes. Rain can be a release of emotion in a pleasant, relaxing manner, or a flood of emotion that overcomes you. Storms are anger, violence, or a dramatic release of emotions. (*see* Rain, Storm, Sun)

WEB

This is something you may inadvertently get caught up in and find it difficult to extricate yourself from. It may suggest a sticky end to a relationship or project. The dream web can also depict the intricate and powerful connections we have with other people and with life. (*see* Spider, Maze)

WELL

This is drawing on your own inner depths and the resources that lie behind your personal self. This may include deeply perceptive intuition or healing. It can also refer to the vagina. (*see* Water)

WEREWOLF

This is your own, or somebody else's, rapacious desires, animal lusts, urges, or hates. (*see* Vampire)

WHALE

This represents the enormous forces existing in the unconscious that are intelligent and upon which our life depends. It is the power to dive under the surface of the mind to become aware of this world that is normally hidden from view. (*see* Fish)

WHEAT *see* Corn.

WHEEL

This indicates changes or luck, as with the wheel of fortune. It is also the ability to get things moving or rolling. Speech idioms include: a big wheel; at the wheel; the wheels fall off; fifth wheel; set of wheels; shoulder to the wheel. (*see* Circle)

WHIP

This suggests domination by someone or it can also be the desire to hurt people or be hurt. Depending on the context, it may also link with sexuality that contains guilt or pain.

soul solution

Love can reach beyond the limitations we usually place upon ourselves. A mother, dreaming that her son was in trouble, awoke and prayed for his safety. Her son, asleep in a hotel room, heard his mother's voice calling him in a dream. As he awoke, he realized that the hotel was on fire and managed to escape to safety.

WHITE

This can depict feeling cleansed, or awareness, or, if it is used with clothes or a wedding dress, purity. But in some dreams, it links with threat and fear that can arise from many official buildings, such as hospitals, that use the color white. A white animal suggests wisdom and intuitive understanding.

WIDOW

This may depict unconscious desires to be alone. In a man's dream, it may point to desires for an experienced, available woman. In a married woman's dream, it can show anxieties about being alone, or a way of dealing with the husband's death. Because women tend to live longer than men, they often dream of a husband's death to get used to the expected loss.

WIFE

This is how you feel about your relationship with your wife. Your feelings for her may be dramatized in the dream. It may stand for your emotional, irrational nature, or intuition. If you are not married, then it may show you practicing this role to test your feelings. You may even experiment with different scenarios. If you are already a married woman, it may be showing you what you feel about your current role as a wife.

WIG

This is disguising your real image. It can be worries about your appearance or a need to remain unidentified. (*see* Hair)

WIND

This suggests changeability, the ever shifting mental processes or unseen influences in your life. It can be ideas or other influences that move or pressure you. (*see* Air)

WINDOW

This is your outlook on life, your awareness of other people and outer events. (*see* Glass)

WINE

This is vitality. It is an influence that changes the way you feel, or it can be an artificial means of coping with stress. It can be the social methods used for a person to become part of the group. (*see* Alcohol, Tea)

WINTER

This is the end of a season of growth or activity. It indicates rest, inner processes that have not shown themselves in consciousness, or death or inactivity. It is the falling away of outer movements to concentrate on inner consciousness. It can also depict a hard time in life or business, perhaps a period of cold, in the sense of nothing growing in your life, or little feelings. (*see* Cold, Ice)

WIRELESS *see* Radio.

WISE ANIMAL

We often forget that human beings lived and survived for millions of years before they attained self-awareness or even speech. The shrewd survival lessons learned are not lost, but remain in us as unconscious resources that can be triggered by some events or situations. These traits of frequently depicted by a wise of white haired animal. The wisdom may often be about social relationship, something the old part of us knows so much about in an instinctive way. See: Animal

WITCH

This is what you feel about your mother in a negative way. It is the inner forces of your unconscious that are being misdirected. It can be the desire to influence others via their unconscious fears, weaknesses or superstitions. If the witch is wise and kindly, she represents a positive mother symbol, inner wisdom, mother nature, intuition, or your inner consciousness. (*see* Mother)

WOLF

This symbol usually represents fears about your own urges or anger, or just plain childhood fear. Fear is a natural or instinctive reaction, and one of the ways we may deal with it is anger, or by withdrawing, or calling on our fight-or-flight reaction. If you face your wolf, you may gain the power it has and redirect all its emotional energy to you. But the wolf can suggest existing alone, as with the lone wolf. It also indicates an image of caring parenthood and love.

WOMAN

The woman can be a mother figure, a lover, child or tyrant, depending on the dream figure and the drama of the dream. If you are a woman, the dream woman usually depicts some facet of your personality or potential. To define this, use the technique of standing in the role of the dream character. If you are a man, the woman generally illustrates an aspect of how you feel about and relate to women. She will also illustrate the less expressed part of you. (*see* Girl)

WOMB

This indicates childbirth, pregnancy, female receptiveness and the ability to nurture life. While returning to the womb can represent an infantile event, it really symbolizes the experience at that time. This is a state of mind that is merged with all consciousness, yet undefined, lacking self-awareness. (*see* Uterus)

WOOD

In general, wood represents ideas, opinions, or habits that are a fixed part of your nature. Just as the tree is originally green and supple but becomes hard and fixed as solid wood, so our opinions and attitudes, as they develop, are first pliable, and then often become rigid. Unless these habits and ideas allow for further growth, the life principle that ever seeks further development is either repressed, or leaves the old wood to rot. So, an old dying tree trunk represents parts of you that are no longer capable of adapting to incoming ideas and experiences. Cutting up wood, and building new things with it, is to use old ideas in new ways.

However, a wood, or collection of trees, has quite a different significance. In folklore and myth, the symbol is used a great deal. Dante, at the beginning of *The Divine Comedy*, says he is lost in a wood. Here it represents not only what has grown in your life and is established, but also what is natural and unconscious. So the wood can represent relaxation, or an inner journey. (*see* Tree)

WOOL

This may represent the soft, indulgent things of life, gentle thoughts, and pleasure, as is shown by wool-gathering.

WORK/WORKED/WORKING

This nearly always connects with your work activities, ambitions, or actual work environment and situation. If you are actually working it shows your attempts to change a situation or create something.

WORLD

Sometimes this depicts the "world" or viewpoints that you have created out of your attitudes and responses to events and people, so it is dealing with your personal interactions with them. The end of the world in a dream can mean that one way of life is coming to a close. Or it may point to worries about death. Dreaming of other worlds suggests different ways of approaching life.

WORM

This relates to being low, possible decay, or earthiness.

WORSHIP

This is opening yourself to the influence of what you worship, or to the influence of the ideas or feelings involved in the act of worshipping. It can also be a type of experience that transcends your usual self. In this case it can be a realization of your being.

WRECK

This is damage you have experienced to some aspect of your self-image, or even your physical body. If it is an old wreck, such as a shipwreck, it can point to the memories and feelings you are feeling surrounding an old relationship or situation.

WRITING

This is expressing your inner self. It can be clarifying feelings, materializing or recording them so that you make your inner feelings more defined or less vague. It can also be about how you communicate.

X-RAYS

These are invisible influences in your life. It can be a penetrating insight, or a fear of being seen through, or looking at your inner self. It can also be a fear of developing an illness or inner faults.

dream messenger

Great insights and wisdom can arise from meeting the Wise Old Woman or Wise Old Man in your dreams. Gandalf in *The Lord of the Rings* is an archetypal Wise Old Man. These figures represent a synthesis of all you have experienced.

XYLOPHONE

This suggests something playing on your feelings or sympathies.

YACHT *see* Boat.

YEAST

These are the tiny ideas or inner forces that can ferment in your being and eventually change your whole life.

YELLOW

This is sometimes linked with cowardice, but also, since it is a warm color, with hopeful feelings. (*see* Color)

YOGA/YOGI

This probably relates to some sort of inner disciplines of mind or body you have been practicing, or which has influenced you. Practicing yoga or dreaming of a male or female yogi can also suggest new and personal introspective insights, contact with your wholeness, or possibly withdrawal from the world for some reason.

ZERO

This is perhaps feelings or sensations of loss. It can also connote the emptiness we often fear, but it is also the balm of sleep and the quietness that underlies all the noises of physical life. (*see* Numbers)

ZIPPER

This may link with your general appearance. For example, you may be saying, "Is my zipper fastened?" Sometimes it can be connections with others or relate to secrecy, such as in the expression: "Keep it zipped!"

Bibliography

Books

Dream Analysis

Corriere and Hart, *Dreaming and Waking*, Culver City: Peace Press, 1980.

Delaney, Dr. Gayle, *Sexual Dreams*, New York: Ballantine Books, 1994.

Jung, Carl, *Man and His Symbols*, London: Picador, 1978.

Stevens, W. O., *The Mystery of Dreams*, London: Allen & Unwin, 1950.

Sugrue, T., *There is a River–The Story of Edgar Cayce*, Virginia: ARE Press, 2003.

Van de Castle, PhD., R., *In Our Dreaming Mind*, Virginia: ARE Press, 2003.

The Collective Unconscious

Bucke, R. M., *Cosmic Consciousness–A Study in the Evolution of the Human Mind*, Bedford, M.A.: Applewood Press, 2001.

Capra, F., *The Tao of Physics*, London: Flamingo, 1992.

Vega, S., *Collision With The Infinite*, Moreton-on-Marsh: Windrush Press, 1996.

Watson, S., *Supernature*, Manchester: Coronet, 1974.

Zukav, G., *The Dancing Wu Li Masters*, New York: Perennial, 2001.

Websites

Author Tony Crisp's website is to be found at:

www.dreamhawk.com

Other useful websites include:

www.sleeps.com

www.susanhendricks.com

SOLVING A SPECIFIC PROBLEM
The answer to the math progression puzzle on page 32 is: One, Two, Three, Four, Five. The forward sequence runs "SSENT"; Six, Seven, Eight, Nine, Ten.

Index of Dream Themes and Objects